ITIL®
Foundation
ITIL 4 Edition

AXELOS
GLOBAL BEST PRACTICE

part of Williams Lea Tag

Published by TSO (The Stationery Office), part of Williams Lea,
and available from:

Online
www.tsoshop.co.uk

Mail, Telephone, Fax & E-mail
TSO
PO Box 29, Norwich, NR3 1GN
Telephone orders/General enquiries: 0333 202 5070
Fax orders: 0333 202 5080
E-mail: customer.services@tso.co.uk
Textphone 0333 202 5077

TSO@Blackwell and other Accredited Agents

AXELOS
Full details on how to contact AXELOS can be found at:
https://www.axelos.com
For further information on qualifications and training accreditation, please visit:
https://www.axelos.com/certifications
https://www.axelos.com/archived-pages/becoming-an-axelos-partner/training-organization-and-trainer-accreditation
For all other enquiries, please email: ask@axelos.com

First edition 2019
Second impression 2019

ISBN 9780113316076

Printed in the United Kingdom for The Stationery Office
Material is FSC certified and produced using ECF pulp, sourced from fully sustainable forests.

P002959377   c10   02/19

Contents

Welcome to ITIL 4

At this new stage in the development of the IT industry, AXELOS is delighted to present ITIL 4, the latest step in the evolution of IT **best practice**. By building on our experience and bringing fresh and forward-looking thinking to the marketplace, ITIL 4 equips your business to deal with the challenges currently faced by the industry.

The adoption of **ITIL** as the most widely used guidance in the world on IT service management (ITSM) will continue with ITIL 4. It ensures continuity with existing ways of working (where service management is already successful) by integrating modern and emerging practices with established and proven know-how. ITIL 4 also provides guidance on these new methods to help individuals and organizations to see their benefits and move towards using them with confidence, focus, and minimal disruption.

ITIL 4's holistic approach raises the profile of service management in organizations and industries, setting it within a more strategic context. Its focus tends to be on end-to-end product and service management, from demand to value.

ITIL 4 is the result of a great amount of global research and development work across the IT and service management industries; this work has involved active practitioners, trainers, consultants, vendors, technicians, and business customers. The architect team has collaborated with the wider stakeholders and users of ITIL to ensure that the content meets the modern requirements of continuity, innovation, flexibility, and value.

ITIL training provides individuals with a structured approach for developing their competencies in the current and future workplace. The accompanying guidance also helps organizations to take advantage of the new and upcoming technologies, succeed in making their digital transformations, and create value as needed for themselves and their customers.

ITIL Foundation is the beginning of your ITIL 4 journey. It will open your mind to the wider, more advanced guidance provided in the other ITIL publications and training that will support your growth and development.

Welcome to the new generation of IT best practice!

Mark Basham
CEO
AXELOS Global Best Practice

About this publication

ITIL Foundation is the first publication of ITIL 4, the latest evolution of the most widely adopted guidance for ITSM. Its audience ranges from IT and business students taking their first steps in service management to seasoned professionals familiar with earlier versions of ITIL and other sources of industry best practice.

ITIL 4 Foundation will:

- provide readers with an understanding of the ITIL 4 service management framework and how it has evolved to adopt modern technologies and ways of working
- explain the concepts of the service management framework to support candidates studying for the ITIL 4 Foundation exam
- act as a reference guide that practitioners can use in their work, further studies, and professional development.

We hope you will find it useful.

About the ITIL story

The guidance provided in this publication can be adopted and adapted for all types of organization and service. To show how the concepts of ITIL can be practically applied to an organization's activities, *ITIL Foundation* follows the exploits of a fictional company on its ITIL journey.

This company, Axle Car Hire, is undergoing a transformation to modernize its services and improve its customer satisfaction and retention levels, and is using ITIL to do this. In each chapter of the text, the employees of Axle will describe how the company is improving its services, and explain how they are using ITIL best practice to do this.

ITIL storyline sections appear throughout the text, separated by a distinct border.

Axle Car Hire

Axle Car Hire is a global company, with its headquarters based in Seattle. Axle was formed 10 years ago, and currently employs approximately 400 staff across Europe, the US, and Asia-Pacific.

Initially, the company experienced strong growth and consistently high customer satisfaction ratings. For the first six years, repeat business accounted for around 30 per cent of all bookings. Shareholders could expect handsome quarterly dividends. However, over the past four years, the company has experienced a downturn. Customer satisfaction ratings have consistently declined and repeat bookings are rare. Competitors are offering new and innovative options to traditional vehicle hire. Car-pooling, ride-share, and driverless cars are big draws. Customers have also come to expect online and app interfaces as standard for the company's services.

In this evolving market, Axle Car Hire faces an uncertain future. The board is keen to improve customer satisfaction levels. They want to attract and retain customers, and improve the company's bottom line. They've appointed a new CIO, Henri. Henri was chosen for his experience in digitalized services and his track record in successful, large-scale IT transformations. He understands the impact of digital **service offering**s, not only for customer satisfaction levels, but also for employee retention rates.

Henri's strong background in ITIL and ITSM means that he values ITIL certification, and his hiring policy reflects this. Having worked with **Design Thinking**, **DevOps**, and **Agile** methodologies, he believes sustainable business requires a blended approach to ITSM.

Henri is keen to see how his team can redefine the car-hire experience and ensure that Axle Car Hire is the first choice for new and existing customers.

Meet the Axle employees

Here are four key employees of Axle Car Hire:

 Henri Is the new CIO of Axle Car Hire. He is a successful business executive who's prepared to shake things up. He believes in an integrated approach to ITSM.

 Su Is the Axle Car Hire product manager for travel experience, and has worked for Axle for the past five years. Su is smart, meticulous, and passionate about the environment.

 Radhika Is the Axle Car Hire IT business analyst, and it is her job to understand the user requirements of Axle Car Hire staff and customers. She is inquisitive and energetic, and strives to maintain a positive relationship with all her customers, both internal and external. Radhika works mostly on discovery and planning activities, rather than in IT operations. She asks a lot of questions and is great at spotting patterns and trends.

 Marco Is the Axle Car Hire IT delivery manager. He is process-driven and continually references the ITIL framework to help him manage positive service relationships. However, Marco has had little exposure to a blended or collaborative approach to service management.

CHAPTER 1

INTRODUCTION

1 Introduction

1.1 IT service management in the modern world

According to the World Trade Organization,[1] services comprise the largest and most dynamic component of both developed and developing economies. Services are the main way that **organization**s create **value** for themselves and their **customers**. Almost all services today are IT-enabled, which means there is tremendous benefit for organizations in creating, expanding, and improving their IT service management **capability**.

Technology is advancing faster today than ever before. Developments such as **cloud computing**, infrastructure as a service (IaaS), machine learning, and blockchain have opened fresh opportunities for value creation, and led to IT becoming an important business **driver** and source of competitive advantage. In turn, this positions IT service management as a key strategic capability.

To ensure that they remain relevant and successful, many organizations are embarking on major transformational **programme**s to exploit these opportunities. While these transformations are often referred to as 'digital', they are about more than technology. They are an evolution in the way organizations work, so that they can flourish in the face of significant and ongoing **change**. Organizations must balance the need for stability and predictability with the rising need for operational agility and increased velocity. Information and technology are becoming more thoroughly integrated with other organizational capabilities, silos are breaking down, and cross-functional teams are being utilized more widely. **Service management** is changing to address and support this organizational shift and ensure opportunities from new technologies, and new ways of working, are maximized.

Service management is evolving, and so is ITIL, the most widely adopted guidance on IT service management (ITSM) in the world.

1.2 About ITIL 4

ITIL has led the ITSM industry with guidance, training, and certification programmes for more than 30 years. ITIL 4 brings ITIL up to date by re-shaping much of the established ITSM **practice**s in the wider context of **customer experience**, **value stream**s, and **digital transformation**, as well as embracing new ways of working, such as **Lean**, Agile, and DevOps.

ITIL 4 provides the guidance organizations need to address new service management challenges and utilize the potential of modern technology. It is designed to ensure a flexible, coordinated and integrated system for the effective **governance** and management of IT-enabled services.

---

1   https://www.wto.org/english/tratop_e/serv_e/serv_e.htm

1.3 The structure and benefits of the ITIL 4 framework

The key components of the ITIL 4 framework are the ITIL **service value system (SVS)** and the four dimensions model.

1.3.1 The ITIL SVS

The ITIL SVS represents how the various components and activities of the organization work together to facilitate value creation through IT-enabled **service**s. These can be combined in a flexible way, which requires integration and coordination to keep the organization consistent. The ITIL SVS facilitates this integration and coordination and provides a strong, unified, value-focused direction for the organization. The structure of the ITIL SVS is shown in Figure 1.1, and is repeated in Chapter 4, where it is described in more detail.

The core components of the ITIL SVS are:

- the **ITIL service value chain**
- the ITIL practices
- the **ITIL guiding principles**
- governance
- continual improvement.

The ITIL service value chain provides an operating **model** for the creation, delivery, and continual improvement of services. It is a flexible model that defines six key activities that can be combined in many ways, forming multiple value streams. The service value chain is flexible enough to be adapted to multiple approaches, including DevOps and centralized IT, to address the need for multimodal service management. The adaptability of the value chain enables organizations to react to changing **demand**s from their **stakeholder**s in the most effective and efficient ways.

The flexibility of the service value chain is further enhanced by the ITIL practices. Each ITIL practice supports multiple service value chain activities, providing a comprehensive and versatile toolset for ITSM practitioners.

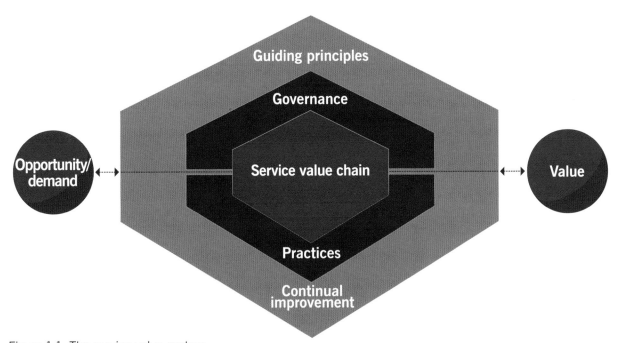

Figure 1.1 The service value system

The ITIL guiding principles can be used to guide an organization's decisions and actions and ensure a shared understanding and common approach to service management across the organization. The ITIL guiding principles create the foundation for an organization's **culture** and behaviour from strategic decision-making to day-to-day operations.

The ITIL SVS also includes governance activities that enable organizations to continually align their operations with the strategic direction set by the governing body.

Every component of the ITIL SVS is supported by continual improvement. ITIL provides organizations with a simple and practical improvement model to maintain their resilience and agility in a constantly changing **environment**.

1.3.2 The four dimensions model

To ensure a holistic approach to service management, ITIL 4 outlines **four dimensions of service management**, from which each component of the SVS should be considered. The four dimensions are:

- **organizations and people**
- **information and technology**
- **partners and suppliers**
- **value streams and processes**.

By giving each of the four dimensions an appropriate amount of focus, an organization ensures its SVS remains balanced and effective. The four dimensions are described in Chapter 3.

The ITIL story: The CIO's vision for Axle

Henri: *These days, the pace of industry change is rapid, with the term 'Fourth Industrial Revolution' now widely used. Companies such as Axle are competing with disruptors that include driverless cars and car share.*

Service expectations have changed since Axle was created 10 years ago. Customers want immediate access to services via apps and online services. Axle's booking app is out of date, and our technology isn't keeping pace with changes in our service offerings.

My vision for Axle is that we become the most recognized car-hire brand in the world. We'll continue to offer outstanding customer service while maintaining competitive car-hire rates. After all, Axle is now about more than just hiring a vehicle. We must focus on our customers' whole travel experience.

CHAPTER 2

KEY CONCEPTS OF SERVICE MANAGEMENT

2 Key concepts of service management

A shared understanding of the key concepts and terminology of ITIL by organizations and individuals is critical to the effective use of this guidance to address real-world service management challenges. To that end, this chapter explains some of the most important concepts of service management, including:

- the nature of value and value co-creation
- organizations, **service provider**s, service consumers, and other stakeholders
- **product**s and services
- **service relationship**s
- value: **outcomes**, **cost**s, and **risk**s.

These concepts apply to all organizations and services, regardless of their nature and underpinning technology. But the first thing that must be outlined is the most fundamental question of all: What is 'service management'?

 Definition: Service management

A set of specialized organizational capabilities for enabling value for customers in the form of services.

Developing the specialized organizational capabilities mentioned in the definition requires an understanding of:

- the nature of value
- the nature and scope of the stakeholders involved
- how value creation is enabled through services.

The ITIL story: Axle's services

 Su: *At Axle, our service is travel experience. We provide this service to our customers to create value both for them and for Axle. Service management helps us to realize this value.*

The ITIL story: Axle's customers

Here are three of Axle Car Hire's frequent customers, whom you will meet as the story unfolds:

 Ichika Is a university student on holiday with no fixed plans. She hopes to visit music festivals as part of her travel experience. Apart from that, her travel is flexible. She is tech-savvy and quickly adapts to new applications and solutions. She is interested in trying new and exciting digital services.

 Faruq Is recently retired and typically holidays alone. He is thoughtful and enjoys learning about and adopting new technology. Faruq often makes his travel plans on the go, as his needs can change, based on personal or health considerations.

 Amelia Is the facilities manager at an organic food distribution company called Food for Fuel. Their head office is in central London, but many Food for Fuel consumers are in regional areas. This means access by public transport is typically infrequent, unreliable, and expensive. Consequently, Food for Fuel provides its sales staff with vehicles to enable them to conveniently and reliably visit existing and potential customers.

2.1 Value and value co-creation

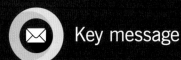

Key message

The purpose of an organization is to create value for stakeholders.

The term 'value' is used regularly in service management, and it is a key focus of ITIL 4; it must therefore be clearly defined.

Definition: Value

The perceived benefits, usefulness, and importance of something.

Inherent in this definition is the understanding that value is subject to the perception of the stakeholders, whether they be the customers or consumers of a service, or part of the service provider organization(s). Value can be subjective.

2.1.1 Value co-creation

There was a time when organizations self-identifying as 'service providers' saw their role as delivering value to their customers in much the same way that a package is delivered to a building by a delivery company. This view treated the relationship between the service provider and the service consumer as mono-directional and distant. The provider delivers the service and the consumer receives value; the consumer plays no role in the creation of value for themselves. This fails to take into consideration the highly complex and interdependent service relationships that exist in reality.

Increasingly, organizations recognize that value is co-created through an active collaboration between providers and consumers, as well as other organizations that are part of the relevant service relationships. Providers should no longer attempt to work in isolation to define what will be of value to their customers and **user**s, but actively seek to establish mutually beneficial, interactive relationships with their consumers, empowering them

The ITIL story: Value

 Marco: *We're planning to release a generous new offering, giving an extra day of car hire with every booking.*

 Henri: *However, we must remember that value means different things for different people. Axle has a broad range of customers, and each of them has their own requirements for car hire. We need to make sure that any changes to our services are actually providing some type of value to our customers.*

 Ichika: *To me, 'value' means freedom of movement. I want my travel to be easy, hassle-free, and flexible. I opt in to mailing lists and subscriptions when it suits me. I take frequent short trips and rarely visit the same location twice. An extra day of car hire won't always suit my plans.*

 Faruq: *I don't travel often, so I don't have my own car. The value of a car-hire service for me is the on-demand availability of a car that suits my needs. I spend less money on car hire each year than it would cost me to maintain and run my own car.*

Value means it meets my budget. Being retired means I'm flexible, with very few commitments or deadlines. When I'm on holiday, I only plan a few days ahead. An extra day of car hire offers real value to me.

 Amelia: *The value of car hire for my organization, Food for Fuel, is two-fold. First, we need the ability to reach our customers. Second, we're keen to lower our costs and risks by hiring cars instead of running our own fleet.*

As a regular customer who books car hire on behalf of my sales reps and staff, I value a consistent and reliable standard of service. Travel and car hire at Food for Fuel is pre-planned and typically only requires daily hire. There's not much value in an extra day of car hire for my organization.

 Henri: *We also have to think about how value is created for Axle. The most obvious value we receive when we hire out our cars is revenue. For our service consumers, value includes easy access to a vehicle when they need it, without the overall expense of car ownership. In both cases, we need a combination of the two for the value to be realized. In that way, we co-create value through our service relationships.*

to be creative collaborators in the service value chain. Stakeholders across the service value chain contribute to the definition of requirements, the design of service solutions and even to the service creation and/or provisioning itself (see section 4.5).

Value will be explored in greater depth later in this chapter. Before that, however, it is important to outline the various stakeholders who are involved in value co-creation and the language used in ITIL to describe them.

2.2 Organizations, service providers, service consumers, and other stakeholders

In service management there are many different kinds of stakeholder, each of which must be understood in the context of the creation of value in the form of services. First, the term 'organization' needs to be defined.

Definition: Organization

A person or a group of people that has its own functions with responsibilities, authorities, and relationships to achieve its objectives.

Organizations vary in size and complexity, and in their relation to legal entities, from a single person or a team to a complex network of legal entities united by common objectives, relationships, and authorities.

As societies and economies evolve, the relationships between and within organizations become more complex. Each organization depends on others in its operation and development. Organizations may hold different roles, depending on the perspective under discussion. For example, an organization that coordinates adventure vacations can fill the role of a service provider to a travel agent when it sells a vacation, while simultaneously filling the role of service consumer when it purchases airport transfers to add to their vacation packages.

2.2.1 Service providers

Key message

When provisioning services, an organization takes on the role of the service provider. The provider can be external to the consumer's organization, or they can both be part of the same organization.

In the most traditional views of ITSM, the provider organization is seen as the IT department of a company, and the other departments or other functional units in the company are regarded as the consumers. This is, however, only one very simple provider-consumer model. A provider could be selling services on the open market to other businesses, to individual consumers, or it could be part of a service alliance, collaborating to provide services to consumer organizations. The key is that the organization in the provider role has a clear understanding of who its consumers are in a given situation and who the other stakeholders are in the associated service relationships.

The ITIL story: Service providers

Henri: *Axle Car Hire acts as a service provider. We provide cars for hire. At the same time, other organizations, such as mechanics and the companies that we buy our cars from, act as service providers for Axle.*

2.2.2 Service consumers

Key message

When receiving services, an organization takes on the role of the service consumer.

Service consumer is a generic role that is used to simplify the definition and description of the structure of service relationships. In practice, there are more specific roles involved in **service consumption**, such as customers, users, and **sponsor**s. These roles can be separate or combined.

Definitions

● **Customer** A person who defines the requirements for a service and takes responsibility for the outcomes of service consumption.
● **User** A person who uses services.
● **Sponsor** A person who authorizes budget for service consumption.

For example, if a company wishes to purchase mobile phone services for its employees from a wireless carrier (the service provider), the various consumer roles may be distributed as follows:

● The chief information officer (CIO) and key communications team members fill the role of customer when they analyse the mobile communications requirements of the company's employees, negotiate the contract with the wireless carrier and monitor the carrier's **performance** against the contracted requirements.
● The chief financial officer (CFO) fills the role of the sponsor when they review the proposed service arrangement and approve the cost of the contract as negotiated.
● The employees (including the CIO, CFO, and communications team members) fill the role of users when they order, receive, and use the mobile phone services as per the agreed contract.

In another example, an individual private consumer of the same wireless carrier (a person using the mobile network) simultaneously acts as a user, customer, and sponsor.

The ITIL story: Axle's service consumers

 Su: *Our most obvious service consumers are the people and organizations who hire our cars, visit our offices, and use our website and booking app. For example, Ichika and Faruq are service consumers, and so is Food for Fuel. They are also our customers.*

 Radhika: *Users are the people who make use of our services. Our car-hire users are the drivers and passengers in our vehicles.*

 Marco: *Sponsors are the people who authorize budgets. For Axle Car Hire, our sponsors include Amelia from Food for Fuel, who approves the travel budget even if she doesn't travel herself.*

 Henri: *Individual service consumers such as Ichika and Faruq approve their own budgets, define their requirements for car hire, and drive the cars. Therefore, Ichika and Faruq act as sponsors, customers, and users. Sometimes, though, they may share the trip with fellow drivers (friends or family members). In this case, their contracts will include other users.*

It is important to identify these roles in service relationships to ensure effective communication and stakeholder management. Each of these roles may have different, and sometimes even conflicting, expectations from services, and different definitions of value.

2.2.3 Other stakeholders

A key focus of service management, and of ITIL, is the way that organizations co-create value with their consumers through service relationships. Beyond the consumer and provider roles, there are usually many other stakeholders that are important to value creation. Examples include individual employees of the provider organization, partners and **supplier**s, investors and shareholders, government organizations such as regulators, and social groups. For the success, and even the continued existence of an organization, it is important that relationships with all key stakeholders are understood and managed. If stakeholders are unhappy with what the organization does or how it does it, the provider's relationships with its consumers can be in jeopardy.

Products and services create value for stakeholders in a number of ways. Some are quite direct such as the generation of revenue, while others are more indirect such as employee experience. Table 2.1 provides examples of value for several different types of stakeholder.

Detailed recommendations on the management of value for different stakeholders can be found in other ITIL 4 publications and supplementary materials.

Table 2.1 Examples of value for different types of stakeholder

Stakeholder	Example of value for stakeholder
Service consumers	Benefits achieved; costs and risks optimized
Service provider	Funding from the consumer; business development; image improvement
Service provider employees	Financial and non-financial incentives; career and professional development; sense of purpose
Society and community	Employment; taxes; organizations' contribution to the development of the community
Charity organizations	Financial and non-financial contributions from other organizations
Shareholders	Financial benefits, such as dividends; sense of assurance and stability

2.3 Products and services

The central component of service management is, of course, the service. The nature of services will now be considered, and an outline given of the relationship between a service and a product.

2.3.1 Configuring resources for value creation

Key message

The services that an organization provides are based on one or more of its products. Organizations own or have access to a variety of **resource**s, including people, information and technology, value streams and processes, and partners and suppliers. Products are **configuration**s of these resources, created by the organization, that will potentially be valuable for its customers.

Definitions

- **Services** A means of enabling value co-creation by facilitating outcomes that customers want to achieve, without the customer having to manage specific costs and risks.
- **Product** A configuration of an organization's resources designed to offer value for a consumer.

Each product that an organization offers is created with a number of target consumer groups in mind, and the products will be tailored to appeal to, and meet the needs of, these groups. A product is not exclusive to one consumer group, and can be used to address the needs of several different groups. For example, a software service can be offered as a 'lite' version, for individual users, or as a more comprehensive corporate version.

Products are typically complex and are not fully visible to the consumer. The portion of a product that the consumer actually sees does not always represent all of the components that comprise the product and support its delivery. Organizations define which product components their consumers see, and tailor them to suit their target consumer groups.

2.3.2 Service offerings

Key message

Service providers present their services to consumers in the form of service offerings, which describe one or more services based on one or more products.

Definition: Service offering

A formal description of one or more services, designed to address the needs of a target consumer group. A service offering may include **goods**, access to resources, and **service action**s.

Service offerings may include:

● goods to be supplied to a consumer (for example, a mobile phone). Goods are supposed to be transferred from the provider to the consumer, with the consumer taking the responsibility for their future use

● access to resources granted or licensed to a consumer under agreed terms and conditions (for example, to the mobile network, or to the network storage). The resources remain under the provider's control and can be accessed by the consumer only during the agreed service consumption period

● service actions performed to address a consumer's needs (for example, user support). These actions are performed by the service provider according to the agreement with the consumer.

Examples of different types of service offering are shown in Table 2.2.

Services are offered to target consumer groups, and those groups may be either internal or external to the service provider organization. Different offerings can be created based on the same product, which allows it to be used

Table 2.2 Components of a service offering

Component	Description	Examples
Goods	Supplied to the consumer	A mobile phone
	Ownership is transferred to the consumer	A physical server
	Consumer takes responsibility for future use	
Access to resources	Ownership is not transferred to the consumer	Access to the mobile network, or to network storage
	Access is granted or licensed to the consumer under agreed terms and conditions	
	The consumer can only access the resources during the agreed consumption period and according to other agreed service terms	
Service actions	Performed by the service provider to address a consumer's needs	User support
	Performed according to an agreement with the consumer	Replacement of a piece of equipment

The ITIL story: Axle's service offerings

Su: *Axle's service offerings include car hire and the various options we provide to address different travel needs. These offerings include discounted insurance, a loyalty programme, and complimentary travel products which include bottled water, tissues, badge holders for parking permits, and baby seats.*

Our consumers are a diverse group and expect different travel experiences. For example, our corporate consumers don't usually need baby seats or weekend rates. At the same time, some individual customers aren't interested in free airport car collection if they're only travelling locally.

All our service offerings include access to our website and booking app.

in multiple ways to address the needs of different consumer groups. For example, a software service can be offered as a limited free version, or as a comprehensive paid-for version, based on one product of the service provider.

2.4 Service relationships

To create value, an organization must do more than simply provide a service. It must also cooperate with the consumers in service relationships.

Key message

Service relationships are established between two or more organizations to co-create value. In a service relationship, organizations will take on the roles of service providers or service consumers. The two roles are not mutually exclusive, and organizations typically both provide and consume a number of services at any given time.

2.4.1 The service relationship model

When services are delivered by the provider, they create new resources for service consumers, or modify their existing ones. For example:

● a training service improves the skills of the consumer's employees
● a broadband service allows the consumer's computers to communicate
● a car-hire service enables the consumer's staff to visit clients
● a software development service creates a new application for the service consumer.

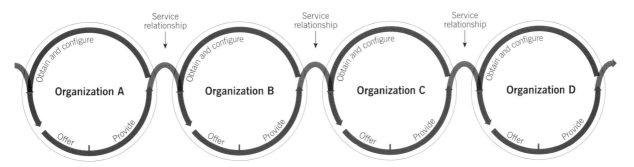

Figure 2.1 The service relationship model

The service consumer can use its new or modified resources to create its own products to address the needs of another target consumer group, thus becoming a service provider. These interactions are shown in Figure 2.1.

 Definitions

- **Service relationship** A cooperation between a service provider and service consumer. Service relationships include **service provision**, service consumption, and **service relationship management**.

- **Service provision** Activities performed by an organization to provide services. Service provision includes:
  - management of the provider's resources, configured to deliver the service
  - ensuring access to these resources for users
  - fulfilment of the agreed service actions
  - service level management and continual improvement.

  Service provision may also include the supplying of goods.

- **Service consumption** Activities performed by an organization to consume services. Service consumption includes:
  - management of the consumer's resources needed to use the service
  - service actions performed by users, including utilizing the provider's resources, and requesting service actions to be fulfilled.

  Service consumption may also include the receiving (acquiring) of goods.

- **Service relationship management** Joint activities performed by a service provider and a service consumer to ensure continual value co-creation based on agreed and available service offerings.

The ITIL story: Axle's service relationships

Henri: *Axle has service relationships with many service providers and consumers, both internal and external. Some services provided to Axle create new resources for the business, such as car manufacturers selling cars to us. Other services, such as the work done for us by our internal car cleaning team, and mechanics outside of Axle, change our existing resources by ensuring that our cars are clean and functional.*

Axle can use these resources in other relationships to provide its own services, in the form of car hire, to consumers, i.e. our customers.

These are just a few examples of the service relationships that Axle has. The organization as a whole has many more.

2.5 Value: outcomes, costs, and risks

This section will focus on how an organization in the role of service provider should evaluate what its services should do and how its services should be provided to meet the needs of consumers.

Key message

Achieving desired outcomes requires resources (and therefore costs) and is often associated with risks. Service providers help their consumers to achieve outcomes, and in doing so, take on some of the associated risks and costs (see the definition of service in section 2.3.1). On the other hand, service relationships can introduce new risks and costs, and in some cases, can negatively affect some of the intended outcomes, while supporting others.

Service relationships are perceived as valuable only when they have more positive effects than negative, as depicted in Figure 2.2. Outcomes, and how they influence and are influenced by the other elements, will now be discussed.

2.5.1 Outcomes

Acting as a service provider, an organization produces **output**s that help its consumers to achieve certain outcomes.

Definitions

● **Output** A tangible or intangible deliverable of an activity.
● **Outcome** A result for a stakeholder enabled by one or more outputs.

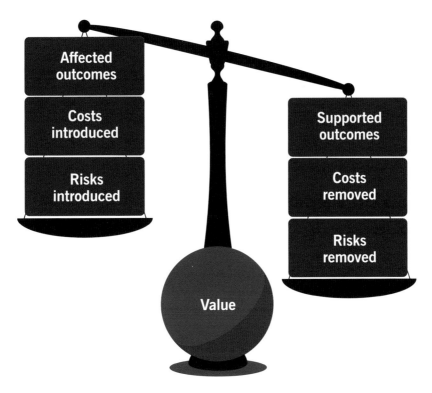

Figure 2.2 Achieving value: outcomes, costs, and risks

It is important to be clear about the difference between outputs and outcomes. For example, one output of a wedding photography service may be an album in which selected photos are artfully arranged. The outcome of the service, however, is the preservation of memories and the ability of the couple and their family and friends to easily recall those memories by looking at the album.

Depending on the relationship between the provider and the consumer, it can be difficult for the provider to fully understand the outcomes that the consumer wants to achieve. In some cases they will work together to define the desired outcomes. For example, **business relationship manager**s (BRMs) in internal IT or HR departments may regularly talk with customers and discuss their needs and expectations. In other cases, the consumers articulate their expectations quite clearly, and the provider expects them to do so, such as when standardized services are offered to a wide consumer group. This is how mobile operators, broadband service providers, and transport companies usually operate. Finally, some service providers predict or even create demand for certain outcomes, forming a target group for their services. This may happen with innovative services addressing needs that consumers were not even aware of before. Examples of this include social networks or smart home solutions.

The ITIL story: Outputs and outcomes

 Henri: *At Axle, our key output is a car that is clean, roadworthy, and well maintained.*

 Su: *For our service consumers, outcomes include travel that is convenient and affordable, and meets a range of needs. This includes self-drive holidays, client site visits, and travel to see family and friends.*

2.5.2 Costs

Definition: Cost

The amount of money spent on a specific activity or resource.

From the service consumer's perspective, there are two types of cost involved in service relationships:

● costs removed from the consumer by the service (a part of the value proposition). This may include costs of staff, technology, and other resources, which the consumer does not need to provide

● costs imposed on the consumer by the service (the costs of service consumption). The total cost of consuming a service includes the price charged by the service provider (if applicable), plus other costs such as staff training, costs of network utilization, procurement, etc. Some consumers describe this as what they have to 'invest' to consume the service.

Both types of cost are considered when the consumer assesses the value which they expect the service to create. To ensure that the correct decisions are made about the service relationship, it is important that both types of cost are fully understood.

From the provider's perspective, a full and correct understanding of the cost of service provision is essential. Providers need to ensure that services are delivered within budget constraints and meet the financial expectations of the organization (see section 5.1.11).

2.5.3 Risks

Definition: Risk

A possible **event** that could cause harm or loss, or make it more difficult to achieve objectives. Can also be defined as uncertainty of outcome, and can be used in the context of measuring the probability of positive outcomes as well as negative outcomes.

As with costs, there are two types of risk that are of concern to service consumers:

● risks removed from a consumer by the service (part of the value proposition). These may include **failure** of the consumer's server hardware or lack of staff availability. In some cases, a service may only reduce a consumer's risks, but the consumer may determine that this reduction is sufficient to support the value proposition

● risks imposed on a consumer by the service (risks of service consumption). An example of this would be a service provider ceasing to trade, or experiencing a security breach.

It is the duty of the provider to manage the detailed level of risk on behalf of the consumer (see section 5.1.10). This should be handled based on a balance of what matters most to the consumer and to the provider. The consumer contributes to the reduction of risk through:

● actively participating in the definition of the requirements of the service and the clarification of its required outcomes

● clearly communicating the **critical success factor**s (CSFs) and constraints that apply to the service

● ensuring the provider has access to the necessary resources of the consumer throughout the service relationship.

2.5.4 Utility and warranty

To evaluate whether a service or service offering will facilitate the outcomes desired by the consumers and therefore create value for them, the overall **utility** and **warranty** of the service should be assessed.

 Definitions

● **Utility** The functionality offered by a product or service to meet a particular need. Utility can be summarized as 'what the service does' and can be used to determine whether a service is 'fit for purpose'. To have utility, a service must either support the performance of the consumer or remove constraints from the consumer. Many services do both.

● **Warranty** Assurance that a product or service will meet agreed requirements. Warranty can be summarized as 'how the service performs' and can be used to determine whether a service is 'fit for use'. Warranty often relates to **service level**s aligned with the needs of service consumers. This may be based on a formal agreement, or it may be a marketing message or brand image. Warranty typically addresses such areas as the **availability** of the service, its capacity, levels of security and continuity. A service may be said to provide acceptable assurance, or 'warranty', if all defined and agreed conditions are met.

The assessment of a service must take into consideration the impact of costs and risks on utility and warranty to generate a complete picture of the viability of a service.

Both utility and warranty are essential for a service to facilitate its desired outcomes and therefore help create value. For example, a recreational theme park may offer many exciting rides designed to deliver thrilling experiences for park visitors (utility), but if a significant number of the rides are frequently unavailable due to mechanical difficulties, the park is not fulfilling the warranty (it is not fit for use) and the consumers will not receive their expected value. Likewise, if the rides are always up and running during advertised hours, but they do not have features that provide the levels of excitement expected by visitors, the utility is not fulfilled, even though the warranty is sufficient. Again, consumers would not receive the expected value.

The ITIL story: A new supplier (Craig's Cleaning)

Su: *Axle's recent customer satisfaction surveys consistently revealed low ratings for car cleanliness. This hampered our customers' travel experience and was a contributing factor for low repeat bookings.*

Henri: *Axle Car Hire made the decision to outsource the cleaning of all vehicles to a service provider. Previously, cleaning of our vehicle fleet was performed by an internal department. The cost and effort to maintain equipment, update rosters, and manage an inflexible workforce were unsustainable.*

*It is important to understand that the risk of **outsourcing** any task or service is that an organization loses skills and capabilities. However, car cleaning is a service requiring specialized equipment as well as a flexible and motivated workforce. Continual investment in this service is something that is not beneficial for Axle.*

At face value, outsourcing may appear to cost an organization more than using internal resources. Initially this may be true; however, over time and correctly managed, outsourcing services should be beneficial to both the organization and supplier. The benefit for Axle is that we can concentrate on our core business. After all, we're not a cleaning company.

Marco: *There are always pros and cons to outsourcing. Let's have a look at the outcomes, costs, and risks that are introduced and removed.*

Pros	Cons
Users will be happy with our cars' cleanliness	Axle will lose an opportunity to offer car cleaning as a service
Axle will no longer need to maintain its own cleaning facilities	
	Axle will need to pay the cleaning company
The risk of cars being damaged during cleaning will be removed from Axle. This risk will now be with the supplier and their insurance company	Axle will have a heavy dependency on the external cleaning company, and their staff will have wide access to our premises

Su: *By partnering with a specialist cleaning organization, Axle can focus its resources on providing a better service for our users. It will also help to optimize our costs, increasing value for the organization.*

Craig is the owner of Craig's Cleaning. Craig is methodical, reliable, and well respected by his staff. With his team, Craig is keen to contribute to the Axle vision of offering a high-standard travel experience.

Craig: *Axle Car Hire decided to outsource its car cleaning service, and Craig's Cleaning was chosen to take this on. My organization is now responsible for the cleanliness of the entire Axle vehicle fleet.*

Henri: *The service Craig's Cleaning is providing is only one component of the Axle customer experience. Clean cars are one output of our overall service, and they contribute directly to the customers' travel experience. This helps Axle's clients to achieve their outcomes.*

Su: *Craig's Cleaning is doing a great job! The cars have never been cleaner, and our customer satisfaction ratings for car cleanliness are steadily on the increase.*

Axle and Craig's Cleaning have worked on a cleaning schedule together, with focus on car cleaning turnaround times during peak hours. Axle is responsible for providing Craig and his team with timely notice of any changes that can impact this schedule. For example, Axle may need to expand its cleaning requirements in the light of new service offerings, such as the one Marco is developing.

 Marco: *Axle has a goal to become a greener company and help the environment. We would like Craig's Cleaning to support us in this goal and aim for the same sustainable growth as us.*

2.6 Summary

This chapter has covered the key concepts in service management, in particular the nature of value and value co-creation, organizations, products, and services. It has explored the often complex relationships between service providers and consumers, and the various stakeholders involved. The chapter has also covered the key components of consumer value: benefits, costs, and risks, and how important it is to understand the needs of the customer when designing and delivering services. These concepts will be built upon over the next few chapters, and guidance provided on applying them in practical and flexible ways.

CHAPTER 3

THE FOUR DIMENSIONS OF SERVICE MANAGEMENT

3 The four dimensions of service management

The previous chapter outlined the concepts that are key to service management. The objective of an organization is to create value for its stakeholders, and this is achieved through the provision and consumption of services. The ways in which the various components and activities of an organization work together to create this value is described by the ITIL SVS. However, before this is explored further, the four dimensions of service management must be introduced. These dimensions are relevant to, and impact upon, all elements of the SVS.

To achieve their desired outcomes and work as effectively as possible, organizations should consider all aspects of their behaviour. In practice, however, organizations often become too focused on one area of their initiatives and neglect the others. For example, process improvements may be planned without proper consideration for the people, partners, and technology involved, or technology solutions can be implemented without due care for the **process**es or people they are supposed to support. There are multiple aspects to service management, and none of these are sufficient to produce the required outcomes when considered in isolation.

 Key message

To support a holistic approach to service management, ITIL defines four dimensions that collectively are critical to the effective and efficient facilitation of value for customers and other stakeholders in the form of products and services. These are:

● organizations and people
● information and technology
● partners and suppliers
● value streams and processes.

These four dimensions represent perspectives which are relevant to the whole SVS, including the entirety of the service value chain and all ITIL practices. The four dimensions are constrained or influenced by several external factors that are often beyond the **control** of the SVS.

The four dimensions, and the relationships between them, are represented in Figure 3.1.

Failing to address all four dimensions properly may result in services becoming undeliverable, or not meeting expectations of quality or **efficiency**. For example, failing to consider the value streams and processes dimension holistically can lead to wasteful work, duplication of efforts, or worse, work that conflicts with what is being done elsewhere in the organization. Equally, ignoring the partners and suppliers dimension could mean that outsourced services are misaligned with the needs of the organization. The four dimensions do not have sharp boundaries and may overlap. They will sometimes interact in unpredictable ways, depending on the level of complexity and uncertainty in which an organization operates.

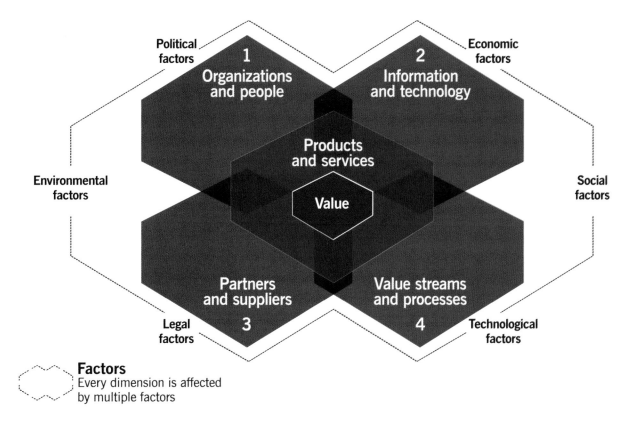

Factors
Every dimension is affected
by multiple factors

Figure 3.1 The four dimensions of service management

It is important to note that the four dimensions of service management apply to all services being managed, as well as to the SVS in general. It is therefore essential that these perspectives should be considered for every service, and that each one should be addressed when managing and improving the SVS at all levels.

An overview of the four dimensions is provided below, and more detailed guidance on addressing the dimensions in practice can be found in other ITIL 4 publications.

The ITIL story: The four dimensions of service management

Henri: *As an IT team, we are responsible for the information and technology at Axle Car Hire. However, effective IT management is much more than just managing technology. We must also consider the wider organization and people involved in Axle's car-hire service, our relationships with partners and suppliers, and the value streams, processes, and technologies that we use.*

3.1 Organizations and people

The first dimension of service management is organizations and people.

The effectiveness of an organization cannot be assured by a formally established structure or system of authority alone. The organization also needs a culture that supports its objectives, and the right level of capacity and competency among its workforce. It is vital that the leaders of the organization champion and advocate values

Key message

The complexity of organizations is growing, and it is important to ensure that the way an organization is structured and managed, as well as its roles, responsibilities, and systems of authority and communication, is well defined and supports its overall strategy and operating model.

which motivate people to work in desirable ways. Ultimately, however, it is the way in which an organization carries out its work that creates shared values and attitudes, which over time are considered the organization's culture.

As an example, it is useful to promote a culture of trust and transparency in an organization that encourages its members to raise and escalate issues and facilitates corrective actions before any issues have an impact on customers. Adopting the ITIL guiding principles can be a good starting point for establishing a healthy organizational culture (see section 4.3).

People (whether customers, employees of suppliers, employees of the service provider, or any other stakeholder in the service relationship) are a key element in this dimension. Attention should be paid not only to the skills and competencies of teams or individual members, but also to management and leadership styles, and to communication and collaboration skills. As practices evolve, people also need to update their skills and competencies. It is becoming increasingly important for people to understand the interfaces between their specializations and roles and those of others in the organization, to ensure proper levels of collaboration and coordination. For example, in some areas of IT (such as software development or user support), there is a growing acknowledgement that everyone should have a broad general knowledge of the other areas of the organization, combined with a deep specialization in certain fields.

Every person in the organization should have a clear understanding of their contribution towards creating value for the organization, its customers, and other stakeholders. Promoting a focus on value creation is an effective method of breaking down organizational silos.

The organizations and people dimension of a service covers roles and responsibilities, formal organizational structures, culture, and required staffing and competencies, all of which are related to the creation, delivery, and improvement of a service.

The ITIL story: Axle's organization and people

 Henri: *The organizations and people dimension of Axle's car-hire services includes my IT team and other teams within the organization, such as procurement, HR, and facilities.*

3.2 Information and technology

The second dimension of service management is information and technology. As with the other three dimensions, information and technology applies both to service management and to the services being managed.

Detailed guidance on the role of information and technology in service management can be found in other ITIL publications.

Key message

When applied to the SVS, the information and technology dimension includes the information and knowledge necessary for the management of services, as well as the technologies required. It also incorporates the relationships between different components of the SVS, such as the inputs and outputs of activities and practices.

The technologies that support service management include, but are not limited to, workflow **management system**s, knowledge bases, inventory systems, communication systems, and analytical tools. Service management increasingly benefits from developments in technology. Artificial intelligence, machine learning, and other cognitive computing solutions are used at all levels, from strategic planning and portfolio optimization to system **monitoring** and user support. The use of mobile platforms, cloud solutions, remote collaboration tools, automated testing, and deployment solutions has become common practice among service providers.

In the context of a specific **IT service**, this dimension includes the information created, managed, and used in the course of service provision and consumption, and the technologies that support and enable that service. The specific information and technologies depend on the nature of the services being provided and usually cover all levels of IT architecture, including applications, databases, communication systems, and their integrations. In many areas, IT services use the latest technology developments, such as blockchain, artificial intelligence, and cognitive computing. These services provide a business differentiation potential to early adopters, especially in highly competitive industries. Other technology solutions, such as cloud computing or mobile apps, have become common practice across many industries globally.

In relation to the information component of this dimension, organizations should consider the following questions:

● What information is managed by the services?
● What supporting information and knowledge are needed to deliver and manage the services?
● How will the information and knowledge assets be protected, managed, archived, and disposed of?

For many services, information management is the primary means of enabling customer value. For example, an HR service facilitates value creation for its customers by enabling the organization to access and maintain accurate information about its employees, their employment, and their benefits, without exposure of private information to unauthorized parties. A network management service facilitates value creation for its users by maintaining and providing accurate information about an organization's active network connections and utilization, allowing it to adjust its network bandwidth capacity. Information is generally the key output of the majority of IT services which are consumed by business customers.

Another key consideration in this dimension is how information is exchanged between different services and service components. The information architecture of the various services needs to be well understood and continually optimized, taking into account such criteria as the availability, **reliability**, accessibility, timeliness, accuracy, and relevance of the information provided to users and exchanged between services.

The challenges of information management, such as those presented by security and regulatory **compliance** requirements, are also a focus of this dimension. For example, an organization may be subject to the European Union's General Data Protection Regulation (GDPR), which influences its information management policies and practices. Other industries or countries may have regulations that impose constraints on the collection and management of data of multinational corporations. For example, in the US the Health Insurance Portability and Accountability Act of 1996 provides data privacy and security provisions for safeguarding medical information.

Most services nowadays are based on IT, and are heavily dependent on it. When considering a technology for use in the planning, design, transition, or **operation** of a product or service, questions an organization may ask include:

● Is this technology compatible with the current architecture of the organization and its customers? Do the different technology products used by the organization and its stakeholders work together? How are emerging technologies (such as machine learning, artificial intelligence, and **Internet of Things**) likely to disrupt the service or the organization?

● Does this technology raise any regulatory or other compliance issues with the organization's policies and information security controls, or those of its customers?

● Is this a technology that will continue to be viable in the foreseeable future? Is the organization willing to accept the risk of using aging technology, or of embracing emerging or unproven technology?

● Does this technology align with the strategy of the service provider, or its service consumers?

● Does the organization have the right skills across its staff and suppliers to support and maintain the technology?

● Does this technology have sufficient automation capabilities to ensure it can be efficiently developed, deployed, and operated?

● Does this technology offer additional capabilities that might be leveraged for other products or services?

● Does this technology introduce new risks or constraints to the organization (for example, locking it into a specific vendor)?

The culture of an organization may have a significant impact on the technologies it chooses to use. Some organizations may have more of an interest in being at the cutting edge of technological advances than others. Equally the culture of some organizations may be more traditional. One company may be keen to take advantage of artificial intelligence, while another may barely be ready for advanced data analysis tools.

The nature of the business will also affect the technology it makes use of. For example, a company that does significant business with government clients may have restrictions on the use of some technologies, or have significantly higher security concerns that must be addressed. Other industries, such as finance or life sciences, are also subject to restrictions around their use of technology. For example, they usually cannot use open source and public services when dealing with sensitive data.

The ITIL story: Axle's information and technology

Henri: *The information and technology dimension of Axle Car Hire represents the information created and managed by teams. It also includes the technologies that support and enable our services. Applications and databases such as our booking app and financial system are part of the information and technology dimension as well.*

 ## Definition: Cloud computing

A model for enabling on-demand network access to a shared pool of configurable computing resources that can be rapidly provided with minimal management effort or provider interaction.

ITSM in the modern world: cloud computing

ITSM has been focusing on value for users and customers for years, and this focus is usually technology-agnostic: what matters is not the technology, but the opportunities it creates for the customers. Although for the most part this is a perfectly acceptable approach, organizations cannot ignore new architectural solutions and the evolution of technology in general. Cloud computing has become an architectural shift in IT, introducing new opportunities and risks, and organizations have had to react to it in ways that are most beneficial for themselves, their customers, and other stakeholders.

Key characteristics of cloud computing include:

● on-demand availability (often self-service)
● network access (often internet access)
● resource pooling (often among multiple organizations)
● rapid elasticity (often automatic)
● measured service (often from service consumer's perspective).

In the context of ITSM, cloud computing changes **service architecture** and the distribution of responsibilities between service consumers, service providers, and their partners. It especially applies to in-house service providers, i.e. the organization's internal IT departments. In a typical situation, adoption of the cloud computing model:

● replaces some infrastructure, previously managed by the service provider, with a partner's cloud service
● decreases or removes the need for infrastructure management expertise and the resources of the service provider
● shifts the focus of service monitoring and control from the in-house infrastructure to a partner's services
● changes the cost structure of the service provider, removing specific capital expenditures and introducing new operating expenditures and the need to manage them appropriately
● introduces higher requirements for network availability and security
● introduces new security and compliance risks and requirements, applicable to both the service provider and its partner providing the cloud service
● provides users with opportunities to scale service consumption using self-service via simple standard requests, or even without any requests.

All these affect multiple service providers' practices, including, but not limited to:

● service level management
● **measurement and reporting**
● information security management
● service continuity management
● supplier management
● **incident management**
● problem management
● service request management
● service configuration management.

Another important effect of cloud computing, resulting from the computing resources' elasticity, is that the cloud infrastructure may enable significantly faster **deployment** of new and changed services, thus supporting high-velocity service delivery. The ability to configure and deploy computing resources with the same speed as new applications is an important prerequisite for the success of DevOps and similar initiatives. This supports modern organizations in their need for faster time to market and digitalization of their services.

Considering the influence of cloud computing on organizations, it is important to make decisions about the use of this model at the strategic level of the organization, involving all levels of stakeholders, from governance to operations.

3.3 Partners and suppliers

The third dimension of service management is partners and suppliers. Every organization and every service depend to some extent on services provided by other organizations.

 Key message

The partners and suppliers dimension encompasses an organization's relationships with other organizations that are involved in the design, development, deployment, delivery, support, and/or continual improvement of services. It also incorporates contracts and other agreements between the organization and its partners or suppliers.

Relationships between organizations may involve various levels of integration and formality. This ranges from formal contracts with clear separation of responsibilities, to flexible **partnership**s where parties share common goals and risks, and collaborate to achieve desired outcomes. Some relationship examples are shown in Table 3.1. Note that the forms of cooperation described are not fixed but exist as a spectrum. An organization acting as a service provider will have a position on this spectrum, which will vary depending on its strategy and objectives for customer relationships. Likewise, when an organization acts as a service consumer, the role it takes on will

Table 3.1 Relationships between organizations

Form of cooperation	Outputs	Responsibility for the outputs	Responsibility for achievement of the outcomes	Level of formality	Examples
Goods supply	Goods supplied	Supplier	Customer	Formal supply contract/invoices	Procurement of computers and phones
Service delivery	Services delivered	Provider	Customer	Formal agreements and flexible cases	Cloud computing (infrastructure of platform as a service)
Service partnership	Value co-created	Shared between provider and customer	Shared between provider and customer	Shared goals, generic agreements, flexible case-based arrangements	Employee onboarding (shared between HR, facilities and IT)

depend on its strategy and objectives for **sourcing** and supplier management. When it comes to using partners and suppliers, an organization's strategy should be based on its goals, culture, and business environment. For example, some organizations may believe that they will be best served by focusing their attention on developing certain core competencies, using partners and suppliers to provide other needs. Other organizations may choose to rely as much as possible on their own resources, using partners and suppliers as little as possible. There are, of course, many variations between these two opposite approaches.

One method an organization may use to address the partners and suppliers dimension is service integration and management. This involves the use of a specially established integrator to ensure that service relationships are properly coordinated. Service integration and management may be kept within the organization, but can also be delegated to a trusted partner.

Factors that may influence an organization's strategy when using suppliers include:

- **Strategic focus** Some organizations may prefer to focus on their core competency and to outsource non-core supporting functions to third parties; others may prefer to stay as self-sufficient as possible, retaining full control over all important functions.

- **Corporate culture** Some organizations have a historical preference for one approach over another. Long-standing cultural bias is difficult to change without compelling reasons.

- **Resource scarcity** If a required resource or skillset is in short supply, it may be difficult for the service provider to acquire what is needed without engaging a supplier.

- **Cost concerns** A decision may be influenced by whether the service provider believes that it is more economical to source a particular requirement from a supplier.

- **Subject matter expertise** The service provider may believe that it is less risky to use a supplier that already has expertise in a required area, rather than trying to develop and maintain the subject matter expertise in house.

- **External constraints** Government regulation or **policy**, industry codes of conduct, and social, political or legal constraints may impact an organization's supplier strategy.

- **Demand patterns** Customer activity or demand for services may be seasonal or demonstrate high degrees of variability. These patterns may impact the extent to which organizations use external service providers to cope with variable demand.

The last decade has seen an explosion in companies that offer technical resources (infrastructure) or capabilities (platforms, software) 'as a service'. These companies bundle goods and services into a single product offering that can be consumed as a utility, and is typically accounted for as operating expenditure. This frees companies from investing in costly infrastructure and software assets that need to be accounted for as capital expenditure.

The ITIL story: Axle's partners and suppliers

Henri: *The partners and suppliers dimension for Axle includes suppliers such as Go Go Gas and Craig's Cleaning, as well as internet service providers and developers.*

3.4 Value streams and processes

The fourth dimension of service management is value streams and processes. Like the other dimensions, this dimension is applicable to both the SVS in general, and to specific products and services. In both contexts it defines the activities, workflows, controls, and **procedure**s needed to achieve agreed objectives.

Key message

Applied to the organization and its SVS, the value streams and processes dimension is concerned with how the various parts of the organization work in an integrated and coordinated way to enable value creation through products and services. The dimension focuses on what activities the organization undertakes and how they are organized, as well as how the organization ensures that it is enabling value creation for all stakeholders efficiently and effectively.

ITIL gives organizations acting as service providers an operating model that covers all the key activities required to manage products and services effectively. This is referred to as the ITIL service value chain (see section 4.5).

The service value chain operating model is generic and in practice it can follow different patterns. These patterns within the value chain operation are called value streams.

3.4.1 Value streams for service management

Key message

A value stream is a series of steps that an organization uses to create and deliver products and services to a service consumer. A value stream is a combination of the organization's value chain activities (see section 4.5 for more details on value chain activities and Appendix A for examples of value streams).

Definition: Value stream

A series of steps an organization undertakes to create and deliver products and services to consumers.

Identifying and understanding the various value streams an organization has is critical to improving its overall performance. Structuring the organization's activities in the form of value streams allows it to have a clear picture of what it delivers and how, and to make continual improvements to its services.

Organizations should examine how they perform work and map all the value streams they can identify. This will enable them to analyse their current state and identify any barriers to workflow and non-value-adding activities, i.e. waste. Wasteful activities should be eliminated to increase productivity.

Opportunities to increase value-adding activities can be found across the service value chain. These may be new activities or modifications to existing ones, which can make the organization more productive. Value stream optimization may include process automation or adoption of emerging technologies and ways of working to gain efficiencies or enhance user experience.

Value streams should be defined by organizations for each of their products and services. Depending on the organization's strategy, value streams can be redefined to react to changing demand and other circumstances, or remain stable for a significant amount of time. In any case, they should be continually improved to ensure that the organization achieves its objectives in an optimal way. Value stream mapping is described in more detail in other ITIL 4 publications.

3.4.2 Processes

 Key message

A process is a set of activities that transform inputs to outputs. Processes describe what is done to accomplish an objective, and well-defined processes can improve productivity within and across organizations. They are usually detailed in procedures, which outline who is involved in the process, and **work instruction**s, which explain how they are carried out.

 Definition: Process

A set of interrelated or interacting activities that transform inputs into outputs. A process takes one or more defined inputs and turns them into defined outputs. Processes define the sequence of actions and their dependencies.

When applied to products and services, this dimension helps to answer the following questions, critical to service design, delivery, and improvement:

● What is the generic delivery model for the service, and how does the service work?
● What are the value streams involved in delivering the agreed outputs of the service?
● Who, or what, performs the required service actions?

Specific answers to these questions will vary depending on the nature and architecture of the service.

The ITIL story: Axle's value streams and processes

 Radhika: *The value streams and processes dimension represents the series of activities that are carried out within Axle. Value streams help Axle to identify wasteful activity and remove obstacles that hinder the organization's productivity.*

3.5 External factors

Service providers do not operate in isolation. They are affected by many external factors, and work in dynamic and complex environments that can exhibit high degrees of volatility and uncertainty and impose constraints on how the service provider can work. To analyse these external factors, frameworks such as the PESTLE (or PESTEL) model are used. PESTLE is an acronym for the political, economic, social, technological, legal, and environmental factors that constrain or influence how a service provider operates.

Collectively, these factors influence how organizations configure their resources and address the four dimensions of service management. For example:

● Government and societal attitudes towards environmentally friendly products and services may result in the organization investing more in tools and technologies that meet external expectations. An organization may choose to partner with other organizations (or source services from external providers) who can demonstrate environmentally friendly credentials. For example, some companies publish product environmental reports that describe their products' performance against their policies around climate change, safer materials, and other resources.

● Economic and societal factors may influence organizations to create several versions of the same product to address various consumer groups that show different buying patterns. One example is music and video streaming services, many of which have a free tier (with advertising), a premium tier (without advertising), and in some cases a 'family plan' that allows multiple individual profiles under one paid-for account.

● Data protection laws or regulations (like GDPR) have changed how companies must collect, process, access, and store customer data, as well as how they work with external partners and suppliers.

3.6 Summary

The four dimensions represent a holistic approach to service management, and organizations should ensure that there is a balance of focus between each dimension. The impact of external factors on the four dimensions should also be considered. All four dimensions and the external factors that affect them should be addressed as they evolve, considering emerging trends and opportunities. It is essential that an organization's SVS is considered from all four dimensions, as the failure to adequately address or account for one dimension, or an external factor, can lead to sub-optimal products and services.

The ITIL story: Balancing the four dimensions

Marco: *To make Axle's services as effective as possible, we use the best combination of our people, our teams, our value streams, and our ways of working. We now engage a blended approach to service management, incorporating DevOps, Design Thinking, and Agile into product development. We also use new technologies such as robotics, AI, and machine learning, striving to be efficient and Lean, and to automate wherever possible.*

CHAPTER 4

THE ITIL SERVICE VALUE SYSTEM

4 The ITIL service value system

4.1 Service value system overview

For service management to function properly, it needs to work as a system. The ITIL SVS describes the inputs to this system (opportunity and demand), the elements of this system (organizational governance, service management, continual improvement, and the organization's capabilities and resources), and the outputs (achievement of organizational objectives and value for the organization, its customers, and other stakeholders).

 Key message

The ITIL SVS describes how all the components and activities of the organization work together as a system to enable value creation. Each organization's SVS has interfaces with other organizations, forming an ecosystem that can in turn facilitate value for those organizations, their customers, and other stakeholders.

The key inputs to the SVS are opportunity and demand. Opportunities represent options or possibilities to add value for stakeholders or otherwise improve the organization. Demand is the need or desire for products and services among internal and external consumers. The outcome of the SVS is value, that is, the perceived benefits, usefulness, and importance of something. The ITIL SVS can enable the creation of many different types of value for a wide group of stakeholders.

The ITIL SVS includes the following components:

- **Guiding principles** Recommendations that can guide an organization in all circumstances, regardless of changes in its goals, strategies, type of work, or management structure.
- **Governance** The means by which an organization is directed and controlled.
- **Service value chain** A set of interconnected activities that an organization performs to deliver a valuable product or service to its consumers and to facilitate value realization.
- **Practices** Sets of organizational resources designed for performing work or accomplishing an objective.
- **Continual improvement** A recurring organizational activity performed at all levels to ensure that an organization's performance continually meets stakeholders' expectations. ITIL 4 supports continual improvement with the ITIL continual improvement model.

The purpose of the SVS is to ensure that the organization continually co-creates value with all stakeholders through the use and management of products and services. The structure of the SVS is shown in Figure 4.1. The left side of the figure shows opportunity and demand feeding into the SVS from both internal and external sources. The right side shows value created for the organization, its customers, and other stakeholders.

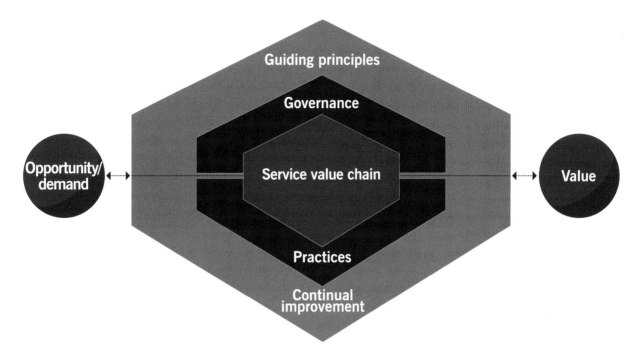

Figure 4.1 The ITIL service value system

The ITIL SVS describes how all the components and activities of the organization work together as a system to enable value creation. These components and activities, together with the organization's resources, can be configured and reconfigured in multiple combinations in a flexible way as circumstances change, but this requires the integration and coordination of activities, practices, teams, authorities and responsibilities, and all parties to be truly effective.

One of the biggest challenges an organization can face when trying to work effectively and efficiently with a shared **vision**, or to become more Agile and resilient, is the presence of organizational silos. Organizational silos can form in many ways and for many different reasons. Silos can be resistant to change and can prevent easy access to the information and specialized expertise that exists across the organization, which can in turn reduce efficiency and increase both cost and risk. Silos also make it more difficult for communication or collaboration to occur across different groups.

A siloed organization cannot act quickly to take advantage of opportunities or to optimize the use of resources across the organization. It is often unable to make effective decisions about changes, due to limited visibility and many hidden agendas. Practices can also become silos. Many organizations have implemented practices such as organizational change management or incident management without clear interfaces with other practices. All practices should have multiple interfaces with one another. The exchange of information between practices should be triggered at key points in the workflow, and is essential to the proper functioning of the organization.

The architecture of the ITIL SVS specifically enables flexibility and discourages siloed working. The service value chain activities and the practices in the SVS do not form a fixed, rigid structure. Rather, they can be combined in multiple value streams to address the needs of the organization in a variety of scenarios. This publication provides examples of service value streams, but none of them are definite or prescriptive. Organizations should be able to define and redefine their value streams in a flexible, yet safe and efficient manner. This requires continual improvement activity to be carried out at all levels of the organization; the ITIL continual improvement model helps to structure this activity. Finally, the continual improvement and overall operation of an organization are shaped by the ITIL guiding principles. The guiding principles create a foundation for a shared culture across the organization, thus supporting collaboration and cooperation within and between the teams, and removing the need for constraints and controls previously provided by silos.

With these components, the ITIL SVS supports many work approaches, such as Agile, DevOps and Lean (see Glossary), as well as traditional process and project management, with a flexible value-oriented operating model.

An organization can take any number of forms, including, but not limited to, sole trader, company, corporation, firm, enterprise, authority, partnership, charity or institution, or any part or combination thereof, whether incorporated or not, and be either public or private. This means that the scope of the SVS can be a whole organization or a smaller subset of that organization. To achieve the maximum value from the SVS and to properly address the issue of organizational silos, it is preferable to include the whole organization in the scope rather than a subset.

The rest of this chapter will explore each element of the SVS.

Organizational agility and organizational resilience

For an organization to be successful, it must achieve organizational agility to support internal changes, and **organizational resilience** to withstand and even thrive in changing external circumstances. The organization must also be considered as part of a larger ecosystem of organizations, all delivering, coordinating, and consuming products and services.

Organizational agility is the ability of an organization to move and adapt quickly, flexibly, and decisively to support internal changes. These might include changes to the scope of the organization, mergers and acquisitions, changing organizational practices, or technologies requiring different skills or organizational structure and changes to relationships with partners and suppliers.

Organizational resilience is the ability of an organization to anticipate, prepare for, respond to, and adapt to both incremental changes and sudden disruptions from an external perspective. External influences could be political, economic, social, technological, legal or environmental. Resilience cannot be achieved without a common understanding of the organization's priorities and objectives, which sets the direction and promotes alignment even as external circumstances change.

The ITIL SVS provides the means to achieve organizational agility and resilience and to facilitate the adoption of a strong unified direction, focused on value and understood by everyone in the organization. It also enables continual improvement throughout the organization.

4.2 Opportunity, demand, and value

 Key message

Opportunity and demand trigger activities within the ITIL SVS, and these activities lead to the creation of value. Opportunity and demand are always entering into the system, but the organization does not automatically accept all opportunities or satisfy all demand.

Opportunity represents options or possibilities to add value for stakeholders or otherwise improve the organization. There may not be demand for these opportunities yet, but they can still trigger work within the system. Organizations should prioritize new or changed services with opportunities for improvement to ensure their resources are correctly allocated.

Demand represents the need or desire for products and services from internal and **external customer**s. A definition of value, and what constitutes value for different stakeholders, can be found in Chapter 2.

4.3 The ITIL guiding principles

Key message

A guiding principle is a recommendation that guides an organization in all circumstances, regardless of changes in its goals, strategies, type of work, or management structure. A guiding principle is universal and enduring.

Table 4.1 Overview of the guiding principles

Guiding principle	Description
Focus on value	Everything that the organization does needs to map, directly or indirectly, to value for the stakeholders.
	The focus on value principle encompasses many perspectives, including the experience of customers and users.
Start where you are	Do not start from scratch and build something new without considering what is already available to be leveraged. There is likely to be a great deal in the current services, processes, programmes, **project**s, and people that can be used to create the desired outcome.
	The current state should be investigated and observed directly to make sure it is fully understood.
Progress iteratively with feedback	Do not attempt to do everything at once. Even huge initiatives must be accomplished iteratively. By organizing work into smaller, manageable sections that can be executed and completed in a timely manner, it is easier to maintain a sharper focus on each effort.
	Using feedback before, throughout, and after each iteration will ensure that actions are focused and appropriate, even if circumstances change.
Collaborate and promote visibility	Working together across boundaries produces results that have greater buy-in, more relevance to objectives, and increased likelihood of long-term success.
	Achieving objectives requires information, understanding, and trust. Work and consequences should be made visible, hidden agendas avoided, and information shared to the greatest degree possible.
Think and work holistically	No service, or element used to provide a service, stands alone. The outcomes achieved by the service provider and service consumer will suffer unless the organization works on the service as a whole, not just on its parts.
	Results are delivered to internal and external customers through the effective and efficient management and dynamic integration of information, technology, organization, people, practices, partners, and agreements, which should all be coordinated to provide a defined value.
Keep it simple and practical	If a process, service, action or **metric** fails to provide value or produce a useful outcome, eliminate it. In a process or procedure, use the minimum number of steps necessary to accomplish the objective(s). Always use outcome-based thinking to produce practical solutions that deliver results.
Optimize and automate	Resources of all types, particularly HR, should be used to their best effect. Eliminate anything that is truly wasteful and use technology to achieve whatever it is capable of. Human intervention should only happen where it really contributes value.

The guiding principles defined here embody the core messages of ITIL and of service management in general, supporting successful actions and good decisions of all types and at all levels. They can be used to guide organizations in their work as they adopt a service management approach and adapt ITIL guidance to their own specific needs and circumstances. The guiding principles encourage and support organizations in continual improvement at all levels.

These principles are also reflected in many other frameworks, methods, **standard**s, philosophies, and/or bodies of knowledge, such as Lean, Agile, DevOps, and COBIT. This allows organizations to effectively integrate the use of multiple methods into an overall approach to service management.

The guiding principles are applicable to practically any initiative and to all relationships with stakeholder groups. For example, the first principle, focus on value, can (and should) be applied not only to service consumers, but to all relevant stakeholders and their respective definitions of value.

Table 4.1 provides a high-level introduction to the guiding principles. Additional details for each principle are presented later in this chapter.

ITIL, Agile, and DevOps

Agile methods, when applied to software development, focus on the delivery of incremental changes to software products while responding to the changing (or evolving) needs of users. They foster a culture of continual learning, flexibility, and willingness to try new approaches and adapt to rapidly changing needs. Agile ways of working include techniques such as timeboxing work, self-organizing and cross-functional teams, and ongoing collaboration and communication with customers and users.

Agile software development teams often focus on the rapid delivery of product increments at the expense of a more holistic view that considers the operability, reliability, and **maintainability** of these products in a **live environment**. Similarly, continual learning and improvement initiatives can focus on bettering the articulation and prioritization of user needs, or streamlining the procedures to develop, test, and deploy working software. While these initiatives can provide valuable outcomes, they also run the risk of being out of sync with other initiatives at a service level.

Just as Agile techniques provide service organizations with a flow of product and software increments, ITIL can also provide software development organizations with a wider perspective and language with which to engage other service teams. Adopting Agile without ITIL can lead to higher costs over time, such as the costs of adopting different technologies and architectures, and costs to release, operate, and maintain software increments. Similarly, implementing ITIL without Agile techniques can risk losing focus on value for customers and users, creating slow-moving and highly centralized bureaucracies.

When Agile and ITIL are adopted together, software development and service management can progress at a similar cadence, share a common terminology, and ensure that the organization continues to co-create value with all its stakeholders. Some of the ways in which ITIL and Agile can work together include:

● streamlining practices such as change control

● establishing procedures to incorporate and prioritize the management of unplanned interruptions (**incident**s), and to investigate the causes of failure

● separating interactions, if necessary, between 'systems of record' (e.g. the **configuration management database**) needed to manage services from 'systems of engagement' (e.g. collaboration tools) used by software development teams.

DevOps methods build on Agile software development and service management techniques by emphasizing close collaboration between the roles of software development and technical operations. Using high degrees of automation to free up the time of skilled professionals so that they can focus on value-adding activities, DevOps is able to shine a light on aspects such as operability, reliability, and maintainability of software products that can assist in the management of services. Cultural aspects that DevOps practitioners advocate can, and should, be extended across the value stream and all service value chain activities so that product and service teams are aligned with the same goals and use the same methods.

It is often said that DevOps combines software development techniques (Agile), good governance and a holistic approach to value co-creation (ITIL), and an obsession with learning about and improving the way in which value is generated (Lean). As such, the adoption of DevOps methods presents further opportunities to improve the way in which software products are developed and managed, such as:

- creating fast **feedback loop**s from delivery and support to software development and technology operations
- streamlining value chain activities and value streams so that demand for work can be quickly converted to value for multiple stakeholders
- differentiating deployment management from release management
- advocating a 'systems view' that emphasizes close collaboration between enterprise governance, service teams, software development, and technology operations.

4.3.1 Focus on value

Key message

All activities conducted by the organization should link back, directly or indirectly, to value for itself, its customers, and other stakeholders.

This section is mostly focused on the creation of value for service consumers. However, a service also contributes to value for the organization and other stakeholders. This value may come in various forms, such as revenue, customer loyalty, lower cost, or growth opportunities. The following recommendations can be adapted to address various stakeholder groups and the value that is created for them by the organization.

4.3.1.1 Who is the service consumer?

When focusing on value, the first step is to know who is being served. In each situation the service provider must, therefore, determine who the service consumer is and who the key stakeholders are (for example, customers, users, or sponsors; see section 2.2 for more details). In doing this, the service provider should consider who will receive value from what is being delivered or improved.

The ITIL story: Axle's new technology

Axle is considering introducing several pieces of new technology into their cars. In the following sections the Axle team looks at what new technology could be introduced and uses the ITIL guiding principles to help decide on the best course of action.

Su: *One aspect of our service we are considering is the collection and return of vehicles. This process remains very manual. Some of our regional depots continue to use paper-based forms to register customers. Customers don't want to waste time completing forms for identification when this information has already been provided during the online booking process.*

To improve the customer identification process, Axle could use biometric technology to identify our customers.

Marco: *Biometric technology uses scanned graphical data for personal identification. It's fast and reliable, and widely used in other industries. For example, the airline industry is using it for security screening, check-in, and even for aircraft boarding. We could use fingerprint or facial recognition scans to quickly identify our customers, and automate the car collection and return process.*

Radhika: *We need to be mindful of regulations such as GDPR and the possible risks to data security this technology could bring.*

Marco: *Axle also wants to trial automated identification of damage to returned vehicles, including scratches, dents, and broken lights. Potentially the technology could even identify fuel levels. This would automate the calculation of any fuel charges incurred by our customers, which is also a manual process.*

Su: *Our customers want simplicity and speed while maintaining comfort and safety on the road. Biometric technology and car scanning would be a source of opportunity to meet evolving customer demands.*

Marco: *Our services already rely on technology, and the intelligence of smartphones and personal devices to meet customer needs and expectations. The adoption of biometric technology is a natural progression. Anyone who can access their phone with a thumbprint or facial recognition will be comfortable and confident using the same technology to collect or return a car.*

Henri: *We can't make the mistake of trying to implement every innovation at once, even if they all sound like the ideal solution for Axle Car Hire. We need a framework in place to make sure value is realized, and to govern our decisions. It's also important that none of our existing customers are disadvantaged, even as we venture into new surroundings. For example, not all our customers are tech-savvy. This is especially true for our elderly customers, who represent a large percentage of our customer base for leisure travel. We also need to balance innovation with existing operational demands.*

4.3.1.2 The consumer's perspectives of value

Next the service provider must understand what is truly of value to the service consumer. The service provider needs to know:

- why the consumer uses the services
- what the services help them to do
- how the services help them achieve their goals
- the role of cost/financial consequences for the service consumer
- the risks involved for the service consumer.

Value can come in many forms, such as increased productivity, reduced negative impact, reduced costs, the ability to pursue new markets, or a better competitive position. Value for the service consumer:

- is defined by their own needs
- is achieved through the support of intended outcomes and optimization of the service consumer's costs and risks
- changes over time and in different circumstances.

4.3.1.3 The customer experience

An important element of value is the experience that service consumers have when they interact with the service and the service provider. This is frequently called customer experience (CX) or user experience (UX) depending on the adopted definitions, and it must be actively managed.

CX can be defined as the entirety of the interactions a customer has with an organization and its products. This experience can determine how the customer feels about the organization and its products and services.

CX is both objective and subjective. For example, when a customer orders a product and receives what they ordered at the promised price and in the promised delivery time, the success of this aspect of their experience is objectively measurable. On the other hand, if they don't like the style or layout of the website they are ordering from, this is subjective. Another customer might really enjoy the design.

4.3.1.4 Applying the principle

To apply this principle successfully, consider this advice:

- **Know how service consumers use each service** Understand their expected outcomes, how each service contributes to these, and how the service consumers perceive the service provider. Collect feedback on value on an ongoing basis, not just at the beginning of the service relationship.

- **Encourage a focus on value among all staff** Teach staff to be aware of who their customers are and to understand CX.

- **Focus on value during normal operational activity as well as during improvement initiatives** The organization as a whole contributes to the value that the customer perceives, and so everybody within the organization must maximize the value they create. The creation of value should not be left only to the people working on exciting projects and new things.

- **Include focus on value in every step of any improvement initiative** Everybody involved in an improvement initiative needs to understand what outcomes the initiative is trying to facilitate, how its value will be measured, and how they should be contributing to the co-creation of that value.

The ITIL story: Focus on value

 Radhika: *When Axle expanded to the Asia-Pacific region, we undertook research focused on customers travelling outside their native countries. The results found that American and European customers travelling to these areas had concerns around unfamiliar road rules and safety.*

 Marco: *Axle is introducing a certified, third-party driver assistance system called Axle Aware. The system checks external surroundings and internal conditions in the car. It includes cameras to monitor the area around the car, and an artificial intelligence program with local road rules. It can even let the driver know when fatigue is starting to set in.*

The system will alert the driver to approaching dangers and potential road rule breaches. For example, in Australia, local road rules dictate that drivers are required to give a minimum of 1 metre when passing cyclists at a speed of 60 km/h or less, or 1.5 metres when the speed is more than 60 km/h.

 Su: *Many visiting tourists will be mostly focused on driving on the correct side of the road and won't know about this rule, but the Axle Aware system does!*

 Marco: *Studies have shown that systems such as this significantly decrease accident rates and serious injuries.*

 Su: *This means that the value to our consumers is a safer travel experience. It will be cheaper too, as they will have fewer penalties for breaking rules they are not familiar with!*

 **Henri:** *The value for Axle Car Hire is improved customer satisfaction, reduced repair costs and lower insurance premiums.*

 Marco: *This type of innovation will also provide additional value for some of our partners and suppliers.*

 Radhika: *For example, we've updated our contract with our fleet maintenance partner. Maintenance will now include Axle Aware. The value to our maintenance partner is the additional revenue.*

4.3.2 Start where you are

 ## Key message

In the process of eliminating old, unsuccessful methods or services and creating something better, there can be great temptation to remove what has been done in the past and build something completely new. This is rarely necessary, or a wise decision. This approach can be extremely wasteful, not only in terms of time, but also in terms of the loss of existing services, processes, people, and tools that could have significant value in the improvement effort. Do not start over without first considering what is already available to be leveraged.

The ITIL story: Axle's booking app

Marco: *The Axle booking app was first developed two years ago. The app is no longer meeting business requirements. It can't cater for the advances in technology we're using now, such as the biometric system and the driver assistance system.*

For example, we need our app to have the capability to scan and validate our customers' fingerprints and facial images. The current coding simply can't support that. We need a new app!

4.3.2.1 Assess where you are

Services and methods already in place should be measured and/or observed directly to properly understand their current state and what can be re-used from them. Decisions on how to proceed should be based on information that is as accurate as possible. Within organizations there is frequently a discrepancy between reports and reality. This is due to the difficulty of accurately measuring certain data, or the unintentional bias or distortion of data that is produced through reports. Getting data from the source helps to avoid assumptions which, if proven to be unfounded, can be disastrous to timelines, budgets, and the quality of results.

Those observing an activity should not be afraid to ask what may seem to be stupid questions. It can sometimes be beneficial for a person with little or no prior knowledge of the service to be part of the observation, as they have no preconceptions of the service, and may spot things that those more closely involved with it would miss.

The ITIL story: Assessing the current state

Henri: *Everyone likes the idea of a new app, and IT is keen to start gathering user requirements so that we can start development. However, before we develop an entirely new app, let's assess the current state of the app we have to see if there's any functionality we can re-use.*

The current process for booking a car meets basic requirements, and doesn't need to change. We just need additional functionality. For example, the process for recording, storing, and calculating points for our loyalty programme won't change.

We should also consider the limits of the technology that our customers use. If we want to introduce biometric data recognition, users will need to have modern devices. I am not sure they all do, so we should investigate constraints and opportunities here.

Marco: *Our current booking app is working well. Incident data indicates that customers make very few **call**s to the service desk. This indicates that the current functionality is fit for use and meets customer requirements.*

Henri: *However, our focus groups indicate that customers avoid using the app because it's slow and difficult to use. Previously, upgrades focused on technology, not the requirements of our customers. We didn't have the flexibility to easily configure functionality to match new and changing service offerings. So the reliability and usability of the booking app can't be assessed solely using the data from incidents logged.*

We need to confirm these findings with other research.

4.3.2.2 The role of measurement

The use of measurement is important to this principle. It should, however, support but not replace what is observed, as over-reliance on data analytics and reporting can unintentionally introduce biases and risks in decision-making. Organizations should consider a variety of techniques to develop knowledge of the environments in which they work. Although it is true that some things can only be understood through measuring their effect (for example, natural phenomena such as the wind), direct observation should always be the preferred option. Too often existing data is used with no consideration of direct personal investigation.

It should be noted that the act of measuring can sometimes affect the results, making them inaccurate. For example, if a **service desk** knows it is being monitored on length of time spent on the phone, it might focus too much on minimizing customer engagement (thus leading to good reports), rather than actually helping users resolve issues to their satisfaction. People are very creative in finding ways to meet the metrics they are measured against. Therefore, metrics need to be meaningful and directly relate to the desired outcome.

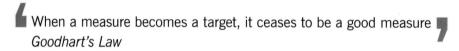

When a measure becomes a target, it ceases to be a good measure
Goodhart's Law

4.3.2.3 Applying the principle

Having a proper understanding of the current state of services and methods is important to selecting which elements to re-use, alter, or build upon. To apply this principle successfully, consider this advice:

● Look at what exists as objectively as possible, using the customer or the desired outcome as the starting point. Are the elements of the current state fit for purpose and fit for use? There are likely to be many elements of the current services, practices, projects, and skills that can be used to create the desired future state, provided the people making this judgement are objective.

● When examples of successful practices or services are found in the current state, determine if and how these can be replicated or expanded upon to achieve the desired state. In many, if not most, cases, leveraging what already exists will reduce the amount of work needed to transition from the current state to the desired state. There should be a focus on learning and improvement, not just replication and expansion.

● Apply your risk management skills. There are risks associated with re-using existing practices and processes, such as the continuation of old behaviours that are damaging to the service. There are also risks associated with putting something new in place, such as new procedures not being performed correctly. These should be considered as part of the decision-making process, and the risks of making or not making a change evaluated to decide on the best course of action.

● Recognize that sometimes nothing from the current state can be re-used. Regardless of how desirable it may be to re-use, repurpose and recycle, or even upcycle, there will be times when the only way to achieve the desired result is to start over entirely. It should be noted, however, that these situations are very rare.

4.3.3 Progress iteratively with feedback

Key message

Resist the temptation to do everything at once. Even huge initiatives must be accomplished iteratively. By organizing work into smaller, manageable sections that can be executed and completed in a timely manner, the focus on each effort will be sharper and easier to maintain.

Improvement iterations can be sequential or simultaneous, based on the requirements of the improvement and what resources are available. Each individual iteration should be both manageable and managed, ensuring that tangible results are returned in a timely manner and built upon to create further improvement.

A major improvement initiative or programme may be organized into several significant improvement initiatives, and each of these may, in turn, comprise smaller improvement efforts. The overall initiative or programme, as well as its component iterations, must be continually re-evaluated and potentially revised to reflect any changes in circumstances and ensure that the focus on value has not been lost. This re-evaluation should make use of a wide range of feedback channels and methods to ensure that the **status** of the initiative and its progress are properly understood.

4.3.3.1 The role of feedback

Whether working to improve a service, group of services, practice, process, technical environment, or other service management element, no improvement iteration occurs in a vacuum. While the iteration is being undertaken, circumstances can change and new priorities can arise, and the need for the iteration may be altered or even eliminated. Seeking and using feedback before, throughout, and after each iteration will ensure that actions are focused and appropriate, even in changing circumstances.

A feedback loop is a term commonly used to refer to a situation where part of the output of an activity is used for new input. In a well-functioning organization, feedback is actively collected and processed along the value chain. Well-constructed feedback mechanisms facilitate understanding of:

● end user and customer perception of the value created
● the efficiency and **effectiveness** of value chain activities
● the effectiveness of service governance as well as management controls
● the interfaces between the organization and its partner and supplier network
● the demand for products and services.

Once received, feedback can be analysed to identify improvement opportunities, risks, and issues.

4.3.3.2 Iteration and feedback together

Working in a timeboxed, iterative manner with feedback loops embedded into the process allows for:

● greater flexibility

● faster responses to customer and business needs

● the ability to discover and respond to failure earlier

● an overall improvement in quality.

Having appropriate feedback loops between the participants of an activity gives them a better understanding of where their work comes from, where their outputs go, and how their actions and outputs affect the outcomes, which in turn enables them to make better decisions.

The ITIL story: Progress iteratively

 Marco: *It's now been three months since Axle released the first iteration of its new app. We began by making it available solely to trusted VIP customers. We worked with their feedback to refine the booking process.*

 Radhika: *We learned that the app needed to be flexible so we could make changes easily based on rapidly evolving customer requirements. For example, our business customers wanted the app to automatically record distance travelled. Working with our product team, we were easily able to add this functionality.*

 Su: *The app is now easily configurable, allowing Axle to quickly add new functions and features based on customer feedback.*

4.3.3.3 Applying the principle

To apply this principle successfully, consider this advice:

● **Comprehend the whole, but do something** Sometimes the greatest enemy to progressing iteratively is the desire to understand and account for everything. This can lead to what is sometimes called 'analysis paralysis', in which so much time is spent analysing the situation that nothing ever gets done about it. Understanding the big picture is important, but so is making progress.

● **The ecosystem is constantly changing, so feedback is essential** Change is happening constantly, so it is very important to seek and use feedback at all times and at all levels.

● **Fast does not mean incomplete** Just because an iteration is small enough to be done quickly does not mean that it should not include all the elements necessary for success. Any iteration should be produced in line with the concept of the **minimum viable product**. A minimum viable product is a version of the final product which allows the maximum amount of validated learning with the least effort.

4.3.4 Collaborate and promote visibility

 Key message

When initiatives involve the right people in the correct roles, efforts benefit from better buy-in, more relevance (because better information is available for decision-making) and increased likelihood of long-term success.

Creative solutions, enthusiastic contributions, and important perspectives can be obtained from unexpected sources, so inclusion is generally a better policy than exclusion. Cooperation and collaboration are better than isolated work, which is frequently referred to as 'silo activity'. Silos can occur through the behaviour of individuals and teams, but also through structural causes. This typically happens where functions or business units in an organization are impeded or unable to collaborate, because their processes, systems, documentation, and communications are designed to fulfil the needs of only a specific part of the organization. Applying the guiding principle of think and work holistically (see section 4.3.5) can help organizations to break down barriers between silos of work.

Recognition of the need for genuine collaboration has been one of the driving factors in the evolution of what is now known as DevOps. Without effective collaboration, neither Agile, Lean, nor any other ITSM framework or method will work.

Working together in a way that leads to real accomplishment requires information, understanding, and trust. Work and its results should be made visible, hidden agendas should be avoided, and information should be shared to the greatest degree possible. The more people are aware of what is happening and why, the more they will be willing to help.

When improvement activity occurs in relative silence, or with only a small group being aware of the details, assumptions and rumours can prevail. Resistance to change will often arise as staff members speculate about what is changing and how it might impact them.

4.3.4.1 Whom to collaborate with

Identifying and managing all the stakeholder groups that an organization deals with is important, as the people and perspectives necessary for successful collaboration can be sourced within these stakeholder groups. As the name suggests, a stakeholder is anyone who has a stake in the activities of the organization, including the organization itself, its customers and/or users, and many others. The scope of stakeholders can be extensive.

The first and most obvious stakeholder group is the customers. The main goal of a service provider is to facilitate outcomes that its customers are interested in, so the customers have a large stake in the service provider's ability to manage services effectively. Some organizations, however, do a poor job of interacting with customers. A service provider may feel that it is too difficult to get input or feedback from the customer, and that the resulting delays are a waste of time. Equally, customers may feel that, after they have defined their requirements, the service provider can be left to deliver the service with no further contact needed. When it comes to the improvement of a service provider's practices, the customer may not see any need to be involved at all. In the end, however, the right level of collaboration with customers will lead to better outcomes for the organization, its customers, and other stakeholders.

Other examples of stakeholder collaboration include:

- developers working with other internal teams to ensure that what is being developed can be operated efficiently and effectively. Developers should collaborate with technical and non-technical operational teams to make sure that they are ready, willing, and able to transition the new or changed service into operation, perhaps even participating in testing. Developers can also work with operations teams to investigate defects (**problems**) and to develop **workaround**s or permanent fixes to resolve these defects
- suppliers collaborating with the organization to define its requirements and brainstorm solutions to customer problems
- relationship managers collaborating with service consumers to achieve a comprehensive understanding of service consumer needs and priorities
- customers collaborating with each other to create a shared understanding of their business issues
- internal and external suppliers collaborating with each other to review shared processes and identify opportunities for optimization and potential automation.

4.3.4.2 Communication for improvement

The contribution to improvement of each stakeholder group at each level should be understood; it is also important to define the most effective methods to engage with them. For example, the contribution to improvement from customers of a public cloud service may be through a survey or checklist of options for different functionalities. For an **internal customer** group, the contribution to improvement may come from feedback solicited via a workshop or a collaboration tool on the organization's intranet.

Some contributors may need to be involved at a very detailed level, while others can simply be involved as reviewers or approvers. Depending on the service and the relationship between the service provider and the service consumer, the expectations about the level and type of collaboration can vary significantly.

4.3.4.3 Increasing urgency through visibility

When stakeholders (whether internal or external) have poor visibility of the workload and progression of work, there is a risk of creating the impression that the work is not a priority. If an initiative is communicated to a team, department, or another organization and then is never, or rarely, mentioned again, the perception will be that the change is not important. Equally, when staff members attempt to prioritize improvement work versus other tasks that have daily urgency, improvement work may seem to be a low-priority activity unless its importance has been made transparent and it is supported by the organization's management.

Insufficient visibility of work leads to poor decision-making, which in turn impacts the organization's ability to improve internal capabilities. It will then become difficult to drive improvements as it will not be clear which ones are likely to have the greatest positive impact on results. To avoid this, the organization needs to perform such critical analysis activities as:

- understanding the flow of work in progress
- identifying bottlenecks, as well as excess capacity
- uncovering waste.

It is important to involve and address the needs of stakeholders at all levels. Leaders at various levels should also provide appropriate information relating to the improvement work in their own communications to others. Together, these actions will serve to reinforce what is being done, why it is being done, and how it relates to the stated vision, mission, goals, and objectives of the organization. Determining the type, method, and frequency of such messaging is one of the central activities related to communication.

The ITIL story: Working collaboratively

 Henri: *As well as being iterative, our work on the new Axle booking app is also collaborative. We include many of our teams, such as developers, testers, and support staff, and of course, our customers and users. This approach enables us to improve our services in a more responsive and targeted manner, based on feedback.*

4.3.4.4 Applying the principle

To apply this principle successfully, consider this advice:

● **Collaboration does not mean consensus** It is not necessary, or even always wise, to get consensus from everyone involved in an initiative before proceeding. Some organizations are so concerned with getting consensus that they try to make everyone happy and end up either doing nothing or producing something that does not properly suit anyone's needs.

● **Communicate in a way the audience can hear** In an attempt to bring different stakeholders into the loop, many organizations use very traditional methods of communication, or they use the same method for all communication. Selecting the right method and message for each audience is critical for success.

● **Decisions can only be made on visible data** Making decisions in the absence of data is risky. Decisions should be made about what data is needed, and therefore what work needs to be made visible. There may be a cost to collecting data, and the organization must balance that cost against the benefit and intended usage of the data.

4.3.5 Think and work holistically

 Key message

No service, practice, process, department, or supplier stands alone. The outputs that the organization delivers to itself, its customers, and other stakeholders will suffer unless it works in an integrated way to handle its activities as a whole, rather than as separate parts. All the organization's activities should be focused on the delivery of value.

Services are delivered to internal and external service consumers through the coordination and integration of the four dimensions of service management (see Chapter 3).

Taking a holistic approach to service management includes establishing an understanding of how all the parts of an organization work together in an integrated way. It requires end-to-end visibility of how demand is captured and translated into outcomes. In a complex system, the alteration of one element can impact others and, where possible, these impacts need to be identified, analysed and planned for.

> ## The ITIL story: Think and work holistically
>
> **Su:** *Currently, Axle is working on many initiatives. We have a schedule of iterative releases of our new booking app, as well as our Axle Aware advanced driver assistance system, and the new biometric scanning for collection and return of vehicles.*
>
> **Henri:** *With so much activity, we need to understand the impacts both upstream and downstream. For example, a decision to expand our booking app with a new functionality would need to consider any resource constraints for our support teams.*

4.3.5.1 Applying the principle

To apply this principle successfully, consider this advice:

● **Recognize the complexity of the systems** Different levels of complexity require different heuristics for decision-making. Applying methods and rules designed for a simple system can be ineffective or even harmful in a complex system, where relationships between components are complicated and change more frequently.

● **Collaboration is key to thinking and working holistically** If the right mechanisms are put in place for all relevant stakeholders to collaborate in a timely manner, it will be possible to address any issue holistically without being unduly delayed.

● **Where possible, look for patterns in the needs of and interactions between system elements** Draw on knowledge in each area to identify what is essential for success, and which relationships between elements influence the outcomes. With this information, needs can be anticipated, standards can be set, and a holistic view point can be achieved.

● **Automation can facilitate working holistically** Where the opportunity and sufficient resources are available, automation can support end-to-end visibility for the organization and provide an efficient means of integrated management.

4.3.6 Keep it simple and practical

 Key message

Always use the minimum number of steps to accomplish an objective. Outcome-based thinking should be used to produce practical solutions that deliver valuable outcomes. If a process, service, action, or metric fails to provide value or produce a useful outcome, then eliminate it. Although this principle may seem obvious, it is frequently ignored, resulting in overly complex methods of work that rarely maximize outcomes or minimize cost.

Trying to provide a solution for every exception will often lead to over-complication. When creating a process or a service, designers need to think about exceptions, but they cannot cover them all. Instead, rules should be designed that can be used to handle exceptions generally.

The ITIL story: Keep it simple and practical

Su: *Axle's marketing department has indicated they would like to launch a new end-of-year promotion. The promotion would include a free upgrade to a luxury vehicle during February and the chance to win an overseas holiday.*

To enter, customers will submit an article titled 'My Best Driving Holiday Adventure'. The marketing team will then collect and analyse the customer data and create an app that targets their travel preferences.

Henri: *Our developers are already busy with an implementation schedule for biometric services. We need speed to market for this functionality. We must prioritize our work based on the expected value.*

4.3.6.1 Judging what to keep

When analysing a practice, process, service, metric, or other improvement target, always ask whether it contributes to value creation.

When designing or improving service management, it is better to start with an uncomplicated approach and then carefully add controls, activities, or metrics when it is seen that they are truly needed.

Critical to keeping service management simple and practical is understanding exactly how something contributes to value creation. For example, a step in a process may be perceived by the operational staff involved as a waste of time. However, from a corporate perspective, the same step may be important for regulatory compliance and therefore valuable in an indirect, but nevertheless important, way. It is necessary to establish and communicate a holistic view of the organization's work so that individual teams or groups can think holistically about how their work is being influenced by, and in turn influences, others.

The ITIL story: Judging what to keep

Marco: *Our original booking app captured a lot of data, such as how long it took a customer to complete each form in the booking app. But we discovered that the data provided little value for decision-making. The true value lay in how long the overall booking process took. We refined the booking app fields and improved its overall speed by removing this data capture function.*

4.3.6.2 Conflicting objectives

When designing, managing, or operating practices, be mindful of conflicting objectives. For example, the management of an organization may want to collect a large amount of data to make decisions, whereas the people who must do the record-keeping may want a simpler process that does not require as much data entry. Through the application of this and the other guiding principles, the organization should agree on a balance between its competing objectives. In this example, this could mean that services should only generate data that will truly provide value to the decision-making process, and record-keeping should be simplified and automated where possible to maximize value and reduce non-value-adding work.

4.3.6.3 Applying the principle

To apply this principle successfully, consider this advice:

- **Ensure value** Every activity should contribute to the creation of value.
- **Simplicity is the ultimate sophistication** It may seem harder to simplify, but it is often more effective.
- **Do fewer things, but do them better** Minimizing activities to include only those with value for one or more stakeholders will allow more focus on the quality of those actions.
- **Respect the time of the people involved** A process that is too complicated and bureaucratic is a poor use of the time of the people involved.
- **Easier to understand, more likely to adopt** To embed a practice, make sure it is easy to follow.
- **Simplicity is the best route to achieving quick wins** Whether in a project, or when improving daily operations activities, **quick win**s allow organizations to demonstrate progress and manage stakeholder expectations. Working in an iterative way with feedback will quickly deliver incremental value at regular intervals.

4.3.7 Optimize and automate

 Key message

Organizations must maximize the value of the work carried out by their human and technical resources. The four dimensions model (outlined in Chapter 3) provides a holistic view of the various constraints, resource types, and other areas that should be considered when designing, managing, or operating an organization. Technology can help organizations to scale up and take on frequent and repetitive tasks, allowing human resources to be used for more complex decision-making. However, technology should not always be relied upon without the capability of human intervention, as automation for automation's sake can increase costs and reduce organizational robustness and resilience.

Optimization means to make something as effective and useful as it needs to be. Before an activity can be effectively automated, it should be optimized to whatever degree is possible and reasonable. It is essential that limits are set on the optimization of services and practices, as they exist within a set of constraints which may include financial limitations, compliance requirements, time constraints, and resource availability.

4.3.7.1 The road to optimization

There are many ways in which practices and services can be optimized. The concepts and practices described in ITIL, particularly the practices of continual improvement, and measurement and reporting (see sections 5.1.2 and 5.1.5), are essential to this effort. The specific practices an organization uses to improve and optimize performance may draw upon guidance from ITIL, Lean, DevOps, **Kanban**, and other sources. Regardless of the specific techniques, the path to optimization follows these high-level steps:

- **Understand and agree the context in which the proposed optimization exists** This includes agreeing the overall vision and objectives of the organization.
- **Assess the current state of the proposed optimization** This will help to understand where it can be improved and which improvement opportunities are likely to produce the biggest positive impact.

- **Agree what the future state and priorities of the organization should be, focusing on simplification and value** This typically also includes standardization of practices and services, which will make it easier to automate or optimize further at a later point.
- **Ensure the optimization has the appropriate level of stakeholder engagement and commitment**
- **Execute the improvements in an iterative way** Use metrics and other feedback to check progress, stay on track, and adjust the approach to the optimization as needed.
- **Continually monitor the impact of optimization** This will help to identify opportunities to improve methods of working.

4.3.7.2 Using automation

Automation typically refers to the use of technology to perform a step or series of steps correctly and consistently with limited or no human intervention. For example, in organizations adopting **continuous deployment**, it refers to the automatic and continuous release of code from development through to **live**, and often automatic testing occurring in each environment. In its simplest form, however, automation could also mean the standardization and streamlining of manual tasks, such as defining the rules of part of a process to allow decisions to be made 'automatically'. Efficiency can be greatly increased by reducing the need for human involvement to stop and evaluate each part of a process.

Opportunities for automation can be found across the entire organization. Looking for opportunities to automate standard and repeating tasks can help save the organization costs, reduce human error, and improve employee experience.

The ITIL story: Optimize and automate

Marco: *Axle has started to trial the new biometric technology, and the tests are going well. We're keen to implement this technology in all our depots.*

Radhika: *Before Axle introduced biometrics, there were many manual, paper-based processes. Axle staff used paper checklists to carry out vehicle damage checks. Their notes then had to be entered in a database, which was only available on desktop computers. It was not real time or accessible across other systems.*

Su: *This work was usually put aside until the end of the day, and details were often lost. We had to improve the process of data capture before automating.*

Radhika: *We can automate almost anything. But let's get the business rules and processes right first.*

4.3.7.3 Applying the principle

To apply this principle successfully, consider this advice:

- **Simplify and/or optimize before automating** Attempting to automate something that is complex or sub-optimal is unlikely to achieve the desired outcome. Take time to map out the standard and repeating processes as far as possible, and streamline where you can (optimize). From there you can start to automate.

- **Define your metrics** The intended and actual result of the optimization should be evaluated using an appropriate set of metrics. Use the same metrics to define the **baseline** and measure the achievements. Make sure that the metrics are outcome-based and focused on value.

- **Use the other guiding principles when applying this one** When optimizing and automating, it is smart to follow the other principles as well:

  - **Progress iteratively with feedback** Iterative optimization and automation will make progress visible and increase stakeholder buy-in for future iterations.

  - **Keep it simple and practical** It is possible for something to be simple, but not optimized, so use these two principles together when selecting improvements.

  - **Focus on value** Selecting what to optimize and automate and how to do so should be based on what will create the best value for the organization.

  - **Start where you are** The technology already available in the organization may have features and functionalities that are currently untapped or under-utilized. Make use of what is already there to implement opportunities for optimization and automation quickly and economically.

4.3.8 Principle interaction

As well as being aware of the ITIL guiding principles, it is also important to recognize that they interact with and depend upon each other. For example, if an organization is committed to progressing iteratively with feedback, it should also think and work holistically to ensure that each iteration of an improvement includes all the elements necessary to deliver real results. Similarly, making use of appropriate feedback is key to collaboration, and focusing on what will truly be valuable to the customer makes it easier to keep things simple and practical.

Organizations should not use just one or two of the principles, but should consider the relevance of each of them and how they apply together. Not all principles will be critical in every situation, but they should all be reviewed on each occasion to determine how appropriate they are.

4.4 Governance

4.4.1 Governing bodies and governance

Key message

Every organization is directed by a governing body, i.e. a person or group of people who are accountable at the highest level for the performance and compliance of the organization. All sizes and types of organization perform governance activities; the governing body may be a board of directors or executive managers who take on a separate governance role when they are performing governance activities. The governing body is accountable for the organization's compliance with policies and any external regulations.

Organizational governance is a system by which an organization is directed and controlled. Governance is realized through the following activities:

● **Evaluate** The evaluation of the organization, its strategy, portfolios, and relationships with other parties. The governing body evaluates the organization on a regular basis as stakeholders' needs and external circumstances evolve.

● **Direct** The governing body assigns responsibility for, and directs the preparation and implementation of, organizational strategy and policies. Strategies set the direction and prioritization for organizational activity, future investment, etc. Policies establish the requirements for behaviour across the organization and, where relevant, suppliers, partners, and other stakeholders.

● **Monitor** The governing body monitors the performance of the organization and its practices, products, and services. The purpose of this is to ensure that performance is in accordance with policies and direction.

Organizational governance evaluates, directs, and monitors all the organization's activities, including those of service management.

4.4.2 Governance in the SVS

The role and position of governance in the ITIL SVS depends on how the SVS is applied in an organization. The SVS is a universal model that can be applied to an organization as a whole, or to one or more of its units or products. In the latter case, some organizations delegate authority to perform governance activities at different levels. The governing body of the organization should retain oversight of this to ensure alignment with the objectives and priorities of the organization.

In ITIL 4, the guiding principles and continual improvement apply to all components of the SVS, including governance. In an organization, the governing body can adopt the ITIL guiding principles and adapt them, or define its own specific set of principles and communicate them across the organization. The governing body should also have visibility of the outcomes of continual improvement activities and the measurement of value for the organization and its stakeholders.

Regardless of the scope of the SVS and the positioning of the components, it is crucial to make sure that:

● the service value chain and the organization's practices work in line with the direction given by the governing body

● the governing body of the organization, either directly or through delegation of authority, maintains oversight of the SVS

● both the governing body and management at all levels maintain alignment through a clear set of shared principles and objectives

● the governance and management at all levels are continually improved to meet expectations of the stakeholders.

4.5 Service value chain

The central element of the SVS is the service value chain, an operating model which outlines the key activities required to respond to demand and facilitate value realization through the creation and management of products and services.

As shown in Figure 4.2, the ITIL service value chain includes six value chain activities which lead to the creation of products and services and, in turn, value.

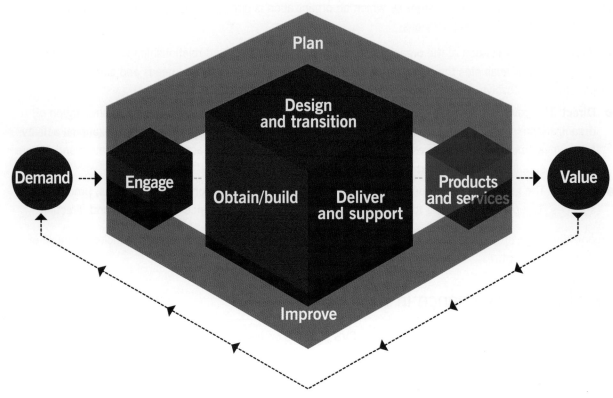

Figure 4.2 The ITIL service value chain

Key message

The six value chain activities are:

● **plan**

● **improve**

● **engage**

● **design and transition**

● **obtain/build**

● **deliver and support**.

These activities represent the steps an organization takes in the creation of value. Each activity transforms inputs into outputs. These inputs can be demand from outside the value chain or outputs of other activities. All the activities are interconnected, with each activity receiving and providing triggers for further action.

To convert inputs into outputs, the value chain activities use different combinations of ITIL practices (sets of resources for performing certain types of work), drawing on internal or **third-party** resources, processes, skills, and competencies as required. For example, the engage activity might draw on supplier management, service desk management, relationship management, and service request management to respond to new demands for products and services, or information from various stakeholders (see Chapter 5 for more information on practices).

Regardless of which practices are deployed, there are some common rules when using the service value chain:

● All incoming and outgoing interactions with parties external to the value chain are performed via *engage*
● All new resources are obtained through *obtain/build*
● Planning at all levels is performed via *plan*
● Improvements at all levels are initiated and managed via *improve*.

To carry out a certain task or respond to a particular situation, organizations create service value streams. These are specific combinations of activities and practices, and each one is designed for a particular scenario. Once designed, value streams should be subject to continual improvement.

A value stream might, for example, be created for a situation where a user of a service needs an incident to be resolved. The value stream will be designed specifically to resolve this issue, and will provide a complete guide to the activities, practices, and roles involved. A more detailed outline of this and other examples of value streams can be found in Appendix A.

Example of a service value chain, its practices, and value streams

A mobile application development company has a value chain, enabling the full cycle of application development and management, from business analysis to development, release, and support. The company has developed a number of practices, supported with specialized resources and techniques:

● business analysis
● development
● testing
● release and deployment
● support.

Although the high-level steps are universal, different products and clients need different streams of work. For example:

● The development of a new application for a new client starts with initial engagement (pre-sale), then proceeds to business analysis, prototyping, the drawing up of agreements, development, testing, and eventually to release and support.

● Changing an existing application to meet new requirements of existing clients does not include pre-sale and involves business analysis, development, testing, and support in a different way.

● Fixing an **error** in a live application may be initiated in support, proceed with rolling back to a previous stable version (**release**), then moves to development, testing, and release of a fix.

● Experiments with new or existing applications to expand the target audience may start with innovation planning and prototyping, then proceed to development, and eventually to a **pilot** release for a limited group of users to test their perception of the changes made.

These are examples of value streams: they combine practices and value chain activities in various ways to improve products and services and increase potential value for the consumers and the organization.

ITSM in the modern world: Agile ITSM

For an organization to be successful, it must be able to adapt to changing circumstances while remaining functional and effective. This might include changes to the products and services it provides and consumes, as well as changes to its structure and practices. In the modern world, where IT is essential for all organizations, IT and IT management are expected to be Agile.

For many IT professionals, agility refers to software development and is associated with the Agile Manifesto, proclaimed in 2001. The manifesto promoted new approaches to software development, and valued customer experience, collaboration, and rapid changes over detailed planning and documentation, controls, and requirements. Agile software development methods have been adopted by many companies and software teams since then, and in many cases have proven to be effective.

Agile software development usually includes:

- continually evolving requirements, collected through feedback analysis and direct observation
- breaking development work into small increments and iterations
- establishing product-based cross-functional teams
- visually presenting (Kanban) and regularly discussing (daily stand-ups) work progress
- presenting a working (at least, the minimum viable) software to the stakeholders at the end of each iteration.

If applied successfully, Agile software development enables fast responses to the evolving needs of service consumers. However, in many organizations, Agile software development has not provided the expected benefits, often due to lack of Agile methods in the other phases of the service **lifecycle**. This fragmented agility makes little sense for the organization, as the overall performance of the value chain is defined by that of the slowest part. A holistic approach to the service value chain should be adopted to make sure that the service provider is Agile throughout the service lifecycle. This means that agility should become a quality of all service management dimensions and all service value chain activities.

One of the greatest obstacles to service value chain agility used to be the rigidity of infrastructure solutions. It could take months to deploy the necessary infrastructure for a new software program, which made all development agility invisible and irrelevant for the service consumer. This problem has, to a great extent, been solved as technology has evolved. Virtualization, fast broadband and mobile connections, and cloud computing have allowed organizations to treat their **IT infrastructure** as a service or as a code, thus providing infrastructure changes with a velocity that was previously only possible for software. Once the technical problem was resolved, Agile methods could be applied to infrastructure configuration and deployment. This stimulated integration between software and infrastructure teams, and consequently between development and operations.

Many principles of Agile development can and should be applied to service operations and support. Operational changes and **service request**s can be handled in small iterations by dedicated product or service-focused teams, with constant feedback and high visibility. Daily operational activities can and should be visible and prioritized together with other tasks. All service management activities can and should continually provide, collect, and process feedback.

Agility is not a software development feature; it is an important quality of organizations in their entirety. Agile activities require Agile funding and adjusted financial and compliance controls, Agile resourcing, Agile contracting, Agile procurement, etc. If being Agile is adopted as a key principle, an organization should be able to survive and prosper in a constantly changing environment. Applied in a fragmented way, Agile methods can become a costly and wasteful complication.

The ITIL story: Value chains and value streams

 Henri: *At Axle Car Hire, the value chain is the way that our company operates. It has multiple value streams. Each value stream adopts and adapts the activities of the value chain for carrying out particular tasks. For example, there is one value stream for innovation, and another for providing standard services to existing customers.*

The value stream for providing standard services to existing customers represents the activities that are carried out when a customer hires a car. This starts with engagement, when a customer contacts Axle, and then proceeds to delivery, when they receive a car (although engagement can still happen at this stage).

Some value chain activities may be ongoing throughout a particular value stream, or may not be involved at all. In this stream, planning activity is continuous, but design and procurement activities will typically not be involved. The stream ends with more engagement activities, when cars are returned by customers, feedback is given, and orders are closed.

 Marco: *Value chain activities do not have to happen in a particular order. Axle's innovation value stream is triggered by opportunity, and then goes to planning, designing, building or obtaining, transitioning, and finally to delivering. This stream often includes procurement activities. For example, we procure software and hardware for our biometric solutions.*

 Henri: *We manage value streams for different objectives, combining the value chain activities and supporting them with practices. Every value stream should be effective and efficient, and subject to continual improvement.*

The following sections outline the value chain activities and define the purpose, inputs, and outputs for each. As each value stream is made up of a different combination of activities and practices, the inputs and outputs listed will not always apply, as they are specific to particular value streams. For example, the 'strategic, tactical, and operational plans' output of the plan value chain activity is formed as a result of strategic, tactical, and operational planning respectively. Each of these levels is likely to involve different resources, have a different planning cycle, and be triggered by different events. The lists of inputs and outputs given are not prescriptive, and they can and should be adjusted when organizations design their value streams.

4.5.1 Plan

 ## Key message

The purpose of the plan value chain activity is to ensure a shared understanding of the vision, current status, and improvement direction for all four dimensions and all products and services across the organization.

The key inputs to this activity are:

- policies, requirements, and constraints provided by the organization's governing body
- consolidated demands and opportunities provided by *engage*
- value chain performance information, improvement status reports, and improvement initiatives from *improve*
- knowledge and information about new and changed products and services from *design and transition*, and *obtain/build*
- knowledge and information about third-party service components from *engage*.

The key outputs of this activity are:

- strategic, tactical, and operational plans
- portfolio decisions for *design and transition*
- architectures and policies for *design and transition*
- improvement opportunities for *improve*
- a product and **service portfolio** for *engage*
- contract and agreement requirements for *engage*.

4.5.2 Improve

Key message

The purpose of the improve value chain activity is to ensure continual improvement of products, services, and practices across all value chain activities and the four dimensions of service management.

The key inputs to this value chain activity are:

- product and service performance information provided by *deliver and support*
- stakeholders' feedback provided by *engage*
- performance information and improvement opportunities provided by all value chain activities
- knowledge and information about new and changed products and services from *design and transition*, and *obtain/build*
- knowledge and information about third-party service components from *engage*.

The key outputs of this value chain activity are:

- improvement initiatives for all value chain activities
- value chain performance information for *plan* and the governing body
- improvement status reports for all value chain activities
- contract and agreement requirements for *engage*
- service performance information for *design and transition*.

4.5.3 Engage

Key message

The purpose of the engage value chain activity is to provide a good understanding of stakeholder needs, transparency, and continual engagement and good relationships with all stakeholders.

The key inputs to this value chain activity are:

- a product and service portfolio provided by *plan*
- high-level demand for services and products provided by internal and external customers
- detailed requirements for services and products provided by customers
- requests and feedback from customers
- incidents, service requests, and feedback from users
- information on the completion of user support tasks from *deliver and support*
- marketing opportunities from current and potential customers and users
- cooperation opportunities and feedback provided by partners and suppliers
- contract and agreement requirements from all value chain activities
- knowledge and information about new and changed products and services from *design and transition*, and *obtain/build*
- knowledge and information about third-party service components from suppliers and partners
- product and service performance information from *deliver and support*
- improvement initiatives from *improve*
- improvement status reports from *improve*.

The key outputs of this value chain activity are:

- consolidated demands and opportunities for *plan*
- product and service requirements for *design and transition*
- user support tasks for *deliver and support*
- improvement opportunities and stakeholders' feedback for *improve*
- change or project initiation requests for *obtain/build*
- contracts and agreements with external and internal suppliers and partners for *design and transition*, and *obtain/build*
- knowledge and information about third-party service components for all value chain activities
- service performance reports for customers.

4.5.4 Design and transition

 Key message

The purpose of the design and transition value chain activity is to ensure that products and services continually meet stakeholder expectations for quality, costs, and time to market.

The key inputs to this activity are:

● portfolio decisions provided by *plan*

● architectures and policies provided by *plan*

● product and service requirements provided by *engage*

● improvement initiatives provided by *improve*

● improvement status reports from *improve*

● service performance information provided by *deliver and support*, and *improve*

● service components from *obtain/build*

● knowledge and information about third-party service components from *engage*

● knowledge and information about new and changed products and services from *obtain/build*

● contracts and agreements with external and internal suppliers and partners provided by engage.

The key outputs of this activity are:

● requirements and **specification**s for *obtain/build*

● contract and agreement requirements for *engage*

● new and changed products and services for *deliver and support*

● knowledge and information about new and changed products and services to all value chain activities

● performance information and improvement opportunities for *improve*.

4.5.5 Obtain/build

 Key message

The purpose of the obtain/build value chain activity is to ensure that service components are available when and where they are needed, and meet agreed specifications.

The key inputs to this activity are:

● architectures and policies provided by *plan*

● contracts and agreements with external and internal suppliers and partners provided by *engage*

- goods and services provided by external and internal suppliers and partners
- requirements and specifications provided by de*sign and transition*
- improvement initiatives provided by *improve*
- improvement status reports from *improve*
- change or project initiation requests provided by *engage*
- change requests provided by *deliver and support*
- knowledge and information about new and changed products and services from *design and transition*
- knowledge and information about third-party service components from *engage*.

The key outputs of this activity are:

- service components for *deliver and support*
- service components for *design and transitio*n
- knowledge and information about new and changed service components to all value chain activities
- contract and agreement requirements for *engage*
- performance information and improvement opportunities for *improve*.

4.5.6 Deliver and support

 Key message

The purpose of the deliver and support value chain activity is to ensure that services are delivered and supported according to agreed specifications and stakeholders' expectations.

The key inputs to this activity are:

- new and changed products and services provided by *design and transition*
- service components provided by *obtain/build*
- improvement initiatives provided by *improv*e
- improvement status reports from *improve*
- user support tasks provided by *engage*
- knowledge and information about new and changed service components and services from *design and transition*, and *obtain/build*
- knowledge and information about third-party service components from *engage*.

The key outputs of this activity are:

- services delivered to customers and users
- information on the completion of user support tasks for *engage*
- product and service performance information for *engage* and *improve*
- improvement opportunities for *improve*
- contract and agreement requirements for *engage*

- change requests for *obtain/build*
- service performance information for *design and transition*.

Further details on the service value chain activities can be found in other ITIL 4 publications and supplementary materials.

4.6 Continual improvement

Continual improvement takes place in all areas of the organization and at all levels, from strategic to operational. To maximize the effectiveness of services, each person who contributes to the provision of a service should keep continual improvement in mind, and should always be looking for opportunities to improve.

The continual improvement model applies to the SVS in its entirety, as well as to all of the organization's products, services, service components, and relationships. To support continual improvement at all levels, the ITIL SVS includes:

- the ITIL continual improvement model, which provides organizations with a structured approach to implementing improvements
- the improve service value chain activity, which embeds continual improvement into the value chain
- the **continual improvement practice**, supporting organizations in their day-to-day improvement efforts.

The ITIL continual improvement model can be used as a high-level guide to support improvement initiatives. Use of the model increases the likelihood that ITSM initiatives will be successful, puts a strong focus on customer value, and ensures that improvement efforts can be linked back to the organization's vision. The model supports an iterative approach to improvement, dividing work into manageable pieces with separate goals that can be achieved incrementally.

Figure 4.3 provides a high-level overview of the ITIL continual improvement model.

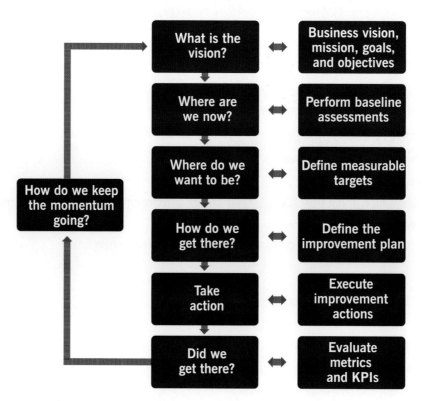

Figure 4.3 The continual improvement model

The ITIL story: Improving Axle

Henri would like Axle to become a greener company and introduce more environmentally friendly practices into its work. Over the following sections the Axle team uses the steps of the continual improvement model to implement changes to the organization.

 Henri: *At Axle we strive for continual improvement at all levels. One of our objectives is to be a greener business and incorporate sustainable principles into every business decision. My team is committed to this initiative. As part of our service relationship model, our partners and suppliers are also involved in this.*

It is important to remember that the scope and details of each step of the model will vary significantly based on the subject and the type of improvement. It should be recognized that this model can serve as a workflow, but it can also be used simply as a high-level reminder of a sound thought process to ensure improvements are properly managed. The flow seeks to ensure that improvements are linked to the organization's goals and are properly prioritized, and that improvement actions produce sustainable results.

Logic and common sense should always prevail when using the continual improvement model. The steps of this model do not need to be carried out in a linear fashion, and it may be necessary to re-evaluate and return to a previous step at some point. Critical judgement should always be applied when using this model.

4.6.1 Steps of the continual improvement model

This section provides more detail on each step of the continual improvement model. An organization can adjust these steps to its culture and goals. The model is simple and flexible, and can just as easily be used in an Agile culture as in a more traditional waterfall culture.

4.6.1.1 Step 1: What is the vision?

 Key message

Each improvement initiative should support the organization's goals and objectives. The first step of the continual improvement model is to define the vision of the initiative. This provides context for all subsequent decisions and links individual actions to the organization's vision for the future.

This step focuses on two key areas:

- The organization's vision and objectives need to be translated for the specific business unit, department, team, and/or individual, so that the context, objectives, and boundaries for any improvement initiative are understood.
- A high-level vision for the planned improvement needs to be created.

The work within this step should ensure that:

● the high-level direction has been understood

● the planned improvement initiative is described and understood in that context

● the stakeholders and their roles have been understood

● the expected value to be realized is understood and agreed

● the role of the person or team responsible for carrying out the improvement is clear in relation to achieving the organization's vision.

If this step is skipped, improvements might only be optimized for the people or teams involved rather than the whole organization, or non-value-adding activities might become the sole focus of improvements.

The ITIL story: What is the vision?

 Henri: *Axle's vision is for the business to become one of the top three green car-hire companies globally. A continual improvement initiative called Axle Green was created for this purpose.*

 Craig: *As a supplier of cleaning services to Axle, I'll support them in this improvement initiative.*

4.6.1.2 Step 2: Where are we now?

 ## Key message

The success of an improvement initiative depends on a clear and accurate understanding of the starting point and the impact of the initiative. An improvement can be thought of as a journey from Point A to Point B, and this step clearly defines what Point A looks like. A journey cannot be mapped out if the starting point is not known.

A key element in this step is a current state assessment. This is an assessment of existing services, including the users' perception of value received, people's competencies and skills, the processes and procedures involved, and/or the capabilities of the available technological solutions. The organization's culture, i.e. the prevailing values and attitudes across all stakeholder groups, also needs to be understood to decide what level of organizational change management is required.

Current state assessments should be done through objective measurement whenever possible. This will allow for an accurate understanding of the issues associated with the current state and, once the initiative is implemented, enable proper measurement of the level of improvement achieved by comparison with the initial state. If a good measurement system is in place, the information to fulfil this step may already have been provided when the proposed improvement was initially documented.

If this step is skipped, the current state will not be understood and there will not be an objective baseline measurement. It will therefore be difficult to track and measure the effectiveness of the improvement activities, as the new state cannot be compared with a previous state at a later point.

The ITIL story: Where are we now?

Su: *We need to understand the baseline. How do we know if we've improved, if we don't know where we started? Currently, only 5 per cent of the vehicles in our fleet are electric.*

Craig: *Only 20 per cent of my cleaning products are biodegradable.*

4.6.1.3 Step 3: Where do we want to be?

Key message

Just as the previous step (Step 2) describes Point A on the improvement journey, Step 3 outlines what Point B, the target state for the next step of the journey, should look like. A journey cannot be mapped out if the destination is not clear.

Based on the results of the first two steps, a gap analysis can be performed, which evaluates the scope and nature of the distance to be travelled from the starting point to the achievement of the initiative's vision. It is important to note that the initial vision of the initiative is aspirational and may never be achieved in full. Improvement is the goal, not perfection. This step should define one or more prioritized actions along the way to completing the vision for the improvement, based on what is known at the starting point. Improvement opportunities can be identified and prioritized based on the gap analysis, and improvement objectives can be set, along with critical success factors (CSFs) and **key performance indicator**s (KPIs).

The agreed objectives, CSFs, and KPIs need to follow what is known as the SMART principle. They should be specific, measurable, achievable, relevant, and time-bound. It is much easier to define the route of the improvement journey if the exact destination is known. It is important to note that the target state represents progress towards the vision, not the achievement of the entire vision.

If this step is skipped, the target state will remain unclear. It will be difficult to prepare a satisfactory explanation of what key stakeholders stand to gain from the improvement initiative, which may result in low support or even pushback.

The ITIL story: Where do we want to be?

Su: *Within five years, we want 50 per cent of our fleet to consist of electric vehicles. The other half should comply with the strictest ecological requirements for petrol and diesel cars.*

Craig: *One of my targets is that 90 per cent of my cleaning products will be biodegradable within the next two years.*

Radhika: *This is a great initiative. In our IT team, we want to use biodegradable cups. We would also like Axle to use environmentally friendly light bulbs in all our offices.*

4.6.1.4 Step 4: How do we get there?

Now that the start and end points of the improvement journey have been defined, a specific route can be agreed. Based on the understanding of the vision of the improvement and the current and target states, and combining that knowledge with subject matter expertise, a plan for addressing the challenges of the initiative can be created.

Key message

The plan for Step 4 can be a straightforward and direct route to completing a single simple improvement, or it may be more involved. The most effective approach to executing the improvement may not be clear, and it will sometimes be necessary to design experiments that will test which options have the most potential.

Even if the path to follow is clear, it may be most effective to carry out the work in a series of iterations, each of which will move the improvement forward part of the way. With each iteration, there is an opportunity to check progress, re-evaluate the approach, and change direction if appropriate.

If this step is skipped, the execution of the improvement is likely to flounder and fail to achieve what is required of it. Failed improvements erode confidence and can make it difficult to get support for future improvements.

The ITIL story: How do we get there?

Craig: *My plan is to replace our current stocks of cleaning products with biodegradable options as we run out. Meanwhile, we'll test new products to find the optimal balance of price and quality.*

Su: *Sometimes knowing how you get there is easy, but replacing half of our fleet with electric cars is a bigger challenge. We don't want excess cars in our car lots if they're not being used. We must also consider specifics and infrastructure in different countries, as well as local regulations.*

Radhika: *We're encouraging the use of ceramic cups over plastic ones. We're discontinuing the purchase of plastic cups, and we are buying ceramic cups for all our offices.*

4.6.1.5 Step 5: Take action

Key message

In Step 5 the plan for the improvement is acted upon. This could involve a traditional waterfall-style approach, but it could be more appropriate to follow an Agile approach by experimenting, iterating, changing directions, or even going back to previous steps.

Some improvements take place as part of a big initiative that makes a lot of change, whereas other improvements are small but significant. In some cases, a larger change is effected through the implementation of multiple smaller improvement iterations. Even if the path to complete the improvement seemed clear when it was planned, it is important to remain open to change throughout the approach. Achieving the desired results is the objective, not rigid adherence to one view of how to proceed.

During the improvement, there needs to be continual focus on measuring progress towards the vision and managing risks, as well as ensuring visibility and overall awareness of the initiative. ITIL practices such as organizational change management (section 5.1.6), measurement and reporting (section 5.1.5), risk management (section 5.1.10) and, of course, continual improvement (section 5.1.2) are important factors in achieving success in this step.

Once this step is completed, the work will be at the end point of the journey, resulting in a new current state.

The ITIL story: Take action

 Craig: *We have started to replace our stocks of cleaning products with biodegradable options. We've found some great new products to use, and even managed to save money by using cheaper alternatives that don't compromise on quality.*

 Su: *We have started to phase out some of our older petrol and diesel cars and replace them with new electric models. We have carried out a thorough check of the petrol and diesel cars we are keeping to ensure they meet ecological requirements, and will take action to fix this where they do not.*

 Radhika: *We have brought the new biodegradable cups and environmentally friendly light bulbs into our offices and started to remove the plastic cups.*

4.6.1.6 Step 6: Did we get there?

This step involves checking the destination of the journey to be sure that the desired point has been reached.

 ## Key message

Too often, once an improvement plan is set in motion, it is assumed that the expected benefits have been achieved, and that attention can be redirected to the next initiative. In reality, the path to improvement is filled with various obstacles, so success must be validated.

For each iteration of the improvement initiative, both the progress (have the original objectives been achieved?) and the value (are those objectives still relevant?) need to be checked and confirmed. If the desired result has not been achieved, additional actions to complete the work are selected and undertaken, commonly resulting in a new iteration.

If this step is skipped, it is hard to be sure whether the desired or promised outcomes were actually achieved, and any lessons from this iteration, which would support a course correction if needed, will be lost.

The ITIL story: Did we get there?

 Craig: *After a few months we managed to hit our target of having 90 per cent of our products being biodegradable.*

 Su: *The electric cars are being introduced, but for logistical reasons it is proving more difficult to replace the petrol and diesel cars than we had anticipated. We will need to do this at a faster pace if we want to hit our five-year target. We may now have to reconsider our target, and decide whether we should do more to support it, or if it needs to be revised.*

 Radhika: *Our offices now have biodegradable cups and environmentally friendly light bulbs. Some of the old plastic cups are still being used, but we have stopped purchasing more, so once they run out they'll be gone.*

4.6.1.7 Step 7: How do we keep the momentum going?

 Key message

If the improvement has delivered the expected value, the focus of the initiative should shift to marketing these successes and reinforcing any new methods introduced. This is to ensure that the progress made will not be lost and to build support and momentum for the next improvements.

The organizational change management and **knowledge management practice**s should be used to embed the changes in the organization and ensure that the improvements and changed behaviours are not at risk of reversion. Leaders and managers should help their teams to truly integrate new work methods into their daily work and institutionalize new behaviours.

If the expected results of the improvement were not achieved, stakeholders need to be informed of the reasons for the failure of the initiative. This requires a thorough analysis of the improvement, documenting and communicating the lessons learned. This should include a description of what can be done differently in the next iteration, based on the experience gathered. Transparency is important for future efforts, regardless of the results of the current iteration.

If this step is skipped, then it is likely that improvements will remain isolated and independent initiatives, and any progress made may be lost over time. It may also be difficult to get support for future improvements, and embed continual improvement in the organization's culture.

The ITIL service value system

Chapter 4 – The ITIL service value system

> ## The ITIL story: How do we keep the momentum going?
>
> **Craig:** *Now that we have hit our target we will monitor any new products we buy to ensure that they meet our standards of being biodegradable. We will also be on the lookout for any opportunities to replace our remaining non-biodegradable products with more environmentally friendly alternatives.*
>
> **Su:** *We've made a great start on adding new electric vehicles to the Axle fleet, but haven't hit our targets yet. Now we need to analyse what has prevented us from reaching our objectives, record what lessons we have learned, and decide what can be done differently in the future to make the introduction of electric cars more effective.*
>
> **Radhika:** *We will continue to buy ceramic cups and environmentally friendly light bulbs for our offices. We will also consider further ways to make our offices greener, and run campaigns with staff members to encourage them to become more environmentally aware.*

4.6.2 Continual improvement and the guiding principles

Following the continual improvement model, an organization may significantly benefit from applying the ITIL guiding principles. All the principles are applicable and relevant at every step of an improvement initiative. However, some of the guiding principles are especially relevant to specific steps of the continual improvement model. Following these principles at every step of an improvement increases the chances for success of the steps and the overall improvement initiative. Table 4.2 outlines to which steps of the continual improvement model each of the guiding principles is particularly relevant, although all principles are applicable to all steps at some level.

Continual improvement is not only an integral part of Lean, but also Agile (retrospectives), DevOps (continual experimentation and learning, and mastery), and other frameworks. It is one of the key components of the ITIL SVS, providing, along with the guiding principles, a solid platform for successful service management.

Table 4.2 The steps of the continual improvement model linked to the most relevant ITIL guiding principles

	Focus on value	Start where you are	Progress iteratively with feedback	Collaborate and promote visibility	Think and work holistically	Keep it simple and practical	Optimize and automate
What is the vision?	✔	✔	✔	✔	✔	✔	✔
Where are we now?	✔	✔	✔	✔	✔	✔	✔
Where do we want to be?	✔	✔	✔	✔	✔	✔	✔
How do we get there?	✔	✔	✔	✔	✔	✔	✔
Take action	✔	✔	✔	✔	✔	✔	✔
Did we get there?	✔	✔	✔	✔	✔	✔	✔
How do we keep the momentum going?	✔	✔	✔	✔	✔	✔	✔

73

Continual improvement and the theory of constraints

In an increasingly dynamic business environment, an enterprise's ability to change quickly, whether in response to external factors or to disrupt the market, can make the difference between failure and success.

When planning improvements, it is crucial to focus on the work that is the highest priority. According to the theory of constraints (ToC), the weakest link in the value chain determines the flow and **throughput** of the system. The weakest link must be elevated as much as possible (sometimes revealing a new weakest link), and all the other steps in the value chain must be organized around it.

The weakest link of a value stream can be determined with value stream mapping. This is a Lean practice that examines the stream, quantifies its waste (for example, a delay), and in so doing, identifies its weakest link. If the weakest link is the development of information systems, then the application of Agile principles and practices can improve the quality of, and the speed with which, functionality is developed. This includes the critical interaction between business and IT in which the required functionality is defined alongside the non-functional requirements. The ITIL 4 practices that help with this include, among others, software development and management, business analysis, and relationship management.

If the weakest link is the speed and reliability of deployment, then using DevOps principles, technical practices and tools can make a significant difference. The ITIL 4 practices that are relevant to this include deployment management, release management, and organizational change management.

Finally, if the weakest link is the delivery and support of IT services, then IT operations practices and tools can be used, such as the ITIL 4 practices of incident management, problem management, service desk, and infrastructure and platform management.

4.7 Practices

A practice is a set of organizational resources designed for performing work or accomplishing an objective. These resources are grouped into the four dimensions of service management (see Chapter 3). The ITIL SVS includes general management, service management, and technical management practices, as described in Chapter 5.

4.8 Summary

The ITIL SVS describes how all the components and activities of the organization work together as a system to enable value creation. Each organization's SVS has interfaces with other organizations, forming an ecosystem that facilitates value creation for the organizations, their customers, and other stakeholders.

The ITIL SVS is a powerful holistic construct for the governance and management of modern products and services that enables organizations to co-create value with consumers. The SVS includes the service value chain activities supported by universal and holistic practices that allow the organization to manage demands of all types. These range from strategic demands that enable the organization to thrive in a competitive landscape, to operational requests for information, services, or support. Every organization participates in some form of the value chain activities described here, even when many of them are performed by suppliers and partners. ITIL 4 guidance can be adapted and adopted to facilitate value, feedback, and continual improvement across the SVS.

CHAPTER 5

ITIL MANAGEMENT PRACTICES

5 ITIL management practices

The ITIL SVS includes 14 general management practices, 17 service management practices, and three technical management practices, all of which are subject to the four dimensions of service management (see Chapter 3).

Key message

In ITIL, a management practice is a set of organizational resources designed for performing work or accomplishing an objective. The origins of the practices are as follows:

● General management practices have been adopted and adapted for service management from general business management domains.

● Service management practices have been developed in service management and ITSM industries.

● Technical management practices have been adapted from technology management domains for service management purposes by expanding or shifting their focus from technology solutions to IT services.

The 34 ITIL management practices are listed in Table 5.1.

Table 5.1 The ITIL management practices

General management practices	Service management practices	Technical management practices
Architecture management	Availability management	Deployment management
Continual improvement	Business analysis	Infrastructure and platform management
Information security management	Capacity and performance management	Software development and management
Knowledge management	Change control	
Measurement and reporting	Incident management	
Organizational change management	IT asset management	
Portfolio management	Monitoring and event management	
Project management	Problem management	
Relationship management	Release management	
Risk management	Service catalogue management	
Service financial management	Service configuration management	
Strategy management	Service continuity management	
Supplier management	Service design	
Workforce and talent management	Service desk	
	Service level management	
	Service request management	
	Service validation and testing	

ITSM in the modern world: high-velocity service delivery

In business innovation and differentiation, speed to market is a key success factor. If an organization takes too long to implement a new business idea, it is likely to be done faster by someone else. Because of this, organizations have started demanding shorter time to market from their IT service providers.

For service providers that have always used modern technology, this has not been a big challenge. They have adopted modern ways of scaling their resources and established appropriate practices for project and product management, testing, integration, deployment, release, delivery, and support of IT services. These practices have been documented and have triggered the development of new IT management movements and practices, such as DevOps. However, for organizations bearing a legacy of old IT architectures and IT management practices focused on control and cost efficiency, the new business demand has introduced a greater challenge.

The high-velocity service delivery paradigm includes:

- focus on fast delivery of new and changed IT services to users
- continual analysis of feedback provided for IT services at every stage of their lifecycle
- agility in processing the feedback, giving rise to continual and fast improvement of IT services
- an end-to-end approach to the service lifecycle, from ideation, through creation and delivery, to consumption of services
- integration of product and service management practices
- digitalization of IT infrastructure and adoption of cloud computing
- extensive automation of the service delivery chain.

High-velocity service delivery influences all the practices of a service provider, including general management practices, service management practices, and technical management practices. For example, an organization aiming to deliver and improve its services faster than others needs to consider:

- Agile project management
- Agile financial management
- product-based organizational structure
- adaptive risk management, and audit and compliance management
- flexible architecture management
- specific architecture technology solutions, such as microservices
- complex partner and supplier environments
- continual monitoring of technology innovations and experimenting
- human-centred design
- infrastructure management focused on cloud computing.

Even if only some of the services in a provider's portfolio need high-velocity delivery, organizational changes of a significant scale are required to enable this, especially if the organization has a legacy of low-velocity services, practices, and habits. Moreover, bi-modal IT, where high-velocity service management is combined with traditional practices, introduces even more complexity and greater challenges. However, for many modern organizations, high-velocity service delivery is no longer an option but a necessity, and they must improve their service management practices to respond to this challenge.

5.1 General management practices

5.1.1 Architecture management

 Key message

The purpose of the **architecture management practice** is to provide an understanding of all the different elements that make up an organization and how those elements interrelate, enabling the organization to effectively achieve its current and future objectives. It provides the principles, standards, and tools that enable an organization to manage complex change in a structured and Agile way.

Just as the modern organization's environment and ecosystem have become more complex, so have its challenges. These include not only how to increase efficiency and automation, but also how to better manage the complexity of the environment and how to achieve organizational agility and resilience. Without the visibility and coordination made possible by a proper architecture management practice, an organization can become a labyrinth of third-party contracts, variant processes across different organizational silos, various products and services that have been needlessly customized for different customers, and a legacy infrastructure. The result is a complex landscape where any change becomes far more difficult to implement and introduces a much higher risk.

A complete architecture management practice should address all architecture domains: business, service, information, technology, and environment. For a smaller and less complex organization, the architect can develop a single integrated architecture.

Architecture types

Business architecture

The business architecture allows the organization to look at its capabilities in terms of how they align with all the detailed activities required to create value for the organization and its customers. These are then compared with the organization's strategy and a gap analysis of the target state against current capabilities is performed. Identified gaps between the baseline and target state are prioritized and these capability gaps are addressed incrementally. A 'roadmap' describes the transformation from current to future state to achieve the organization's strategy.

Service architecture

Service architecture gives the organization a view of all the services it provides, including interactions between the services and service models that describe the structure (how the service components fit together) and the dynamics (activities, flow of resources, and interactions) of each service. A service model can be used as a template or blueprint for multiple services.

Information systems architecture, including data and applications architectures

The information architecture describes the logical and physical data assets of the organization and the data management resources. It shows how the information resources are managed and shared for the benefit of the organization.

Information is a valuable asset for the organization, with actual and measurable value. Information is the basis for decision-making, so it must always be complete, accurate, and accessible to those who are authorized to access it. Information systems must therefore be designed and managed with these concepts in mind.

Technology architecture

The technology architecture defines the software and hardware infrastructure needed to support the portfolio of products and services.

Environmental architecture

The environmental architecture describes the external factors impacting the organization and the drivers for change, as well as all aspects, types, and levels of environmental control and their management. The environment includes developmental, technological, business, operational, organizational, political, economic, legal, regulatory, ecological, and social influences.

Figure 5.1 shows the contribution of architecture management to the service value chain, with the practice being involved in all value chain activities; however, it is most instrumental in the plan, improve, and design and transition value chain activities:

- **Plan** The architecture management practice is responsible for developing and maintaining a reference architecture that describes the current and target architectures for the business, information, data, application, technology, and environment perspectives. This is used as a basis for all the plan value chain activity.

- **Improve** Many opportunities for improvement are identified through review of the business, service, information, technical, and environment architectures.

- **Engage** The architecture management practice facilitates the ability to understand the organization's readiness to address new or under-served markets and a wider variety of products and services, and more quickly respond to changing circumstances. The architecture management practice is responsible for assessing the organization's capabilities in terms of how they align with all the detailed activities required to co-create value for the organization and its customers.

- **Design and transition** Once a new or changed product or service is approved to be developed, the architecture, design, and build teams will continually evaluate whether the product/service meets the investment objectives. The architecture management practice is responsible for the service architecture, which describes the structure (how the service components fit together) and the dynamics (activities, flow of resources, and interactions) of the service. A service model can be used as a template or blueprint for multiple services and is essential to the design and transition activity.

- **Obtain/build** The reference architectures (business, service, information, technical, and environmental) facilitate identification of what products, services, or service components need to be obtained or built.

- **Deliver and support** The reference architectures are used continually as part of the operation, restoration, and maintenance of products and services.

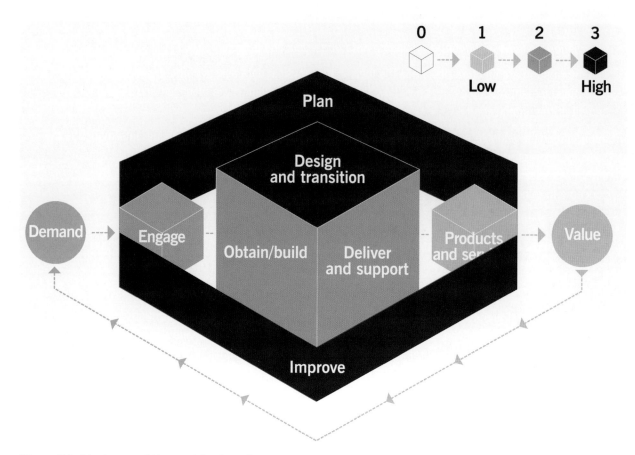

Figure 5.1 Heat map of the contribution of architecture management to value chain activities

5.1.2 Continual improvement

 ## Key message

The purpose of the continual improvement practice is to align the organization's practices and services with changing business needs through the ongoing improvement of products, services, and practices, or any element involved in the management of products and services.

Included in the scope of the continual improvement practice is the development of improvement-related methods and techniques and the propagation of a continual improvement culture across the organization, in alignment with the organization's overall strategy. The commitment to and practice of continual improvement must be embedded into every fibre of the organization. If it is not, there is a real risk that daily operational concerns and major project work will eclipse continual improvement efforts.

Key activities that are part of continual improvement practices include:

- encouraging continual improvement across the organization
- securing time and budget for continual improvement
- identifying and logging improvement opportunities

- assessing and prioritizing improvement opportunities
- making **business case**s for improvement action
- planning and implementing improvements
- measuring and evaluating improvement results
- coordinating improvement activities across the organization.

There are many methods, models, and techniques that can be employed for making improvements. Different types of improvement may call for different improvement methods. For example, some improvements may be best organized into a multi-phase project, while others may be more appropriate as a single quick effort.

The ITIL SVS includes the continual improvement model (see Figure 4.3), which can be applied to any type of improvement, from high-level organizational changes to individual services and **configuration item**s (CIs). The model is described in section 4.6.

When assessing the current state, there are many techniques that can be employed, such as a strength, weakness, opportunity, and threat (SWOT) analysis, a balanced scorecard review, internal and external assessments and audits, or perhaps even a combination of several techniques. Organizations should develop competencies in methodologies and techniques that will meet their needs.

Approaches to continual improvement can be found in many places. Lean methods provide perspectives on the elimination of waste. Agile methods focus on making improvements incrementally at a cadence. DevOps methods work holistically and ensure that improvements are not only designed well, but applied effectively. Although there are a number of methods available, organizations should not try to formally commit to too many different approaches. It is a good idea to select a few key methods that are appropriate to the types of improvement the organization typically handles and to cultivate those methods. In this way, teams will have a shared understanding of how to work together on improvements to facilitate a greater amount of change at a quicker rate.

This does not mean, however, that the organization should not try new approaches or allow for innovation. Those in the organization with skills in alternative methods should be encouraged to apply them when it makes sense, and if this effort is successful, the alternative method may be added to the organization's repertoire. Older methods may gradually be **retire**d in favour of new ones if better results are achieved.

Continual improvement is everyone's responsibility. Although there may be a group of staff members who focus on this work full-time, it is critical that everyone in the organization understands that active participation in continual improvement activities is a core part of their job. To ensure that this is more than a good intention, it is wise to include contribution to continual improvement in all job descriptions and every employee's objectives, as well as in contracts with external suppliers and contractors.

The highest levels of the organization need to take responsibility for embedding continual improvement into the way that people think and work. Without their leadership and visible commitment to continual improvement, attitudes, behaviour, and culture will not evolve to a point where improvements are considered in everything that is done, at all levels.

Training and other enablement assistance should be provided to staff members to help them feel prepared to contribute to continual improvement. Although everyone should contribute in some way, there should at least be a small team dedicated full-time to leading continual improvement efforts and advocating the practice across the organization. This team can serve as coordinators, guides, and mentors, helping others in the organization to develop the skills they need and navigating any difficulties that may be encountered.

When third-party suppliers form part of the service landscape, they should also be part of the improvement effort. When contracting for a supplier's service, the contract should include details of how they will measure, report on, and improve their services over the life of the contract. If data will be required from suppliers to operate internal improvements, that should be specified in the contract as well. Accurate data, carefully analysed and understood, is the foundation of fact-based decision-making for improvement. The continual improvement practice should be supported by relevant data sources and data analysis to ensure that each potential improvement is sufficiently understood and prioritized.

To track and manage improvement ideas from identification through to final action, organizations use a database or structured document called a continual improvement register (CIR). There can be more than one CIR in an organization, as multiple CIRs can be maintained on individual, team, departmental, business unit, and organizational levels. Some organizations maintain a single master CIR, but segment how it is used and by whom at a more granular level.

Improvement ideas can also initially be captured in other places and through other practices, such as during project execution or software development activities. In this case, it is important to document for attention the improvement ideas that come up as part of ongoing continual improvement. As new ideas are documented, CIRs are used to constantly reprioritize improvement opportunities. The use of CIRs provides additional value because they help to make things visible. This is not limited to what is currently being done, but also to what is already complete and what has been set aside for further consideration at a later date.

It does not matter exactly how the information in a CIR is structured, or what the collections of improvement ideas are called in any given organization. What is important is that improvement ideas are captured, documented, assessed, prioritized, and appropriately acted upon to ensure that the organization and its services are always being improved.

The continual improvement practice is integral to the development and maintenance of every other practice as well as to the complete lifecycle of all services and indeed the SVS itself. That said, there are some practices that make a special contribution to continual improvement. For example, the organization's **problem management practice** can uncover issues that will be managed through continual improvement. The changes initiated

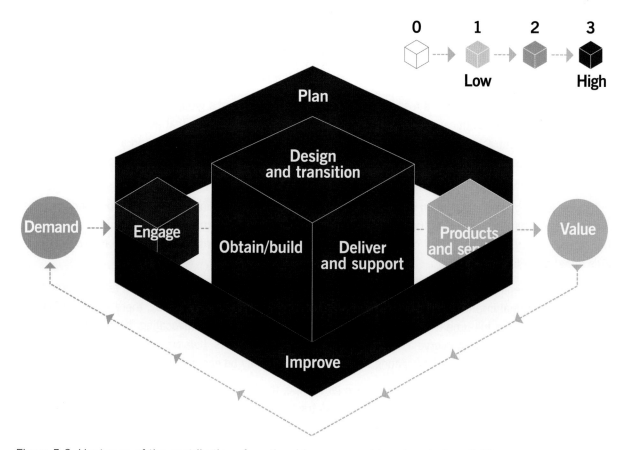

Figure 5.2 Heat map of the contribution of continual improvement to value chain activities

through continual improvement may fail without the critical contributions of organizational change management. And many improvement initiatives will use project management practices to organize and manage their execution.

Figure 5.2 shows the contribution of continual improvement to the service value chain, with the practice being involved in all value chain activities:

● **Plan** The continual improvement practice is applied to planning activities, methods, and techniques to make sure they are relevant to the organization's current objectives and context.

● **Improve** The continual improvement practice is key to this value chain activity. It structures resources and activities, enabling improvement at all levels of the organization and the SVS.

● **Engage, design and transition, obtain/build, and deliver and support** Each of these value chain activities is subject to continual improvement, and the continual improvement practice is applied to all of them.

5.1.3 Information security management

 Key message

The purpose of the **information security management practice** is to protect the information needed by the organization to conduct its business. This includes understanding and managing risks to the **confidentiality, integrity**, and availability of information, as well as other aspects of information security such as authentication (ensuring someone is who they claim to be) and non-repudiation (ensuring that someone can't deny that they took an action).

The required security is established by means of policies, processes, behaviours, risk management, and controls, which must maintain a balance between:

● **Prevention** Ensuring that security incidents don't occur

● **Detection** Rapidly and reliably detecting incidents that can't be prevented

● **Correction** Recovering from incidents after they are detected.

It is also important to achieve a balance between protecting the organization from harm and allowing it to innovate. Information security controls that are too restrictive may do more harm than good, or may be circumvented by people trying to do work more easily. Information security controls should consider all aspects of the organization and align with its risk appetite.

Information security management interacts with every other practice. It creates controls that each practice must consider when planning how work will be done. It also depends on other practices to help protect information.

Information security management must be driven from the most senior level in the organization, based on clearly understood governance requirements and organizational policies. Most organizations have a dedicated information security team, which carries out **risk assessment**s and defines policies, procedures, and controls. In high-velocity environments, information security is integrated as much as possible into the daily work of development and operations, shifting the reliance on control of process towards verification of preconditions such as expertise and integrity.

Information security is critically dependent on the behaviour of people throughout the organization. Staff who have been trained well and pay attention to information security policies and other controls can help to detect, prevent, and correct information security incidents. Poorly trained or insufficiently motivated staff can be a major vulnerability.

Many processes and procedures are required to support information security management. These include:

● an information security incident management process

● a risk management process

● a control review and audit process

● an **identity** and access management process

● event management

● procedures for penetration testing, vulnerability scanning, etc.

● procedures for managing information security related changes, such as firewall configuration changes.

Figure 5.3 shows the contribution of information security management to the service value chain, with the practice being involved in all value chain activities:

● **Plan** Information security must be considered in all planning activity and must be built into every practice and service.

● **Improve** Information security must be considered in all improvement value chain activity to ensure that vulnerabilities are not introduced when making improvements.

● **Engage** Information security requirements for new and changed services must be understood and captured. All levels of engagement, from operational to strategic, must support information security and encourage the

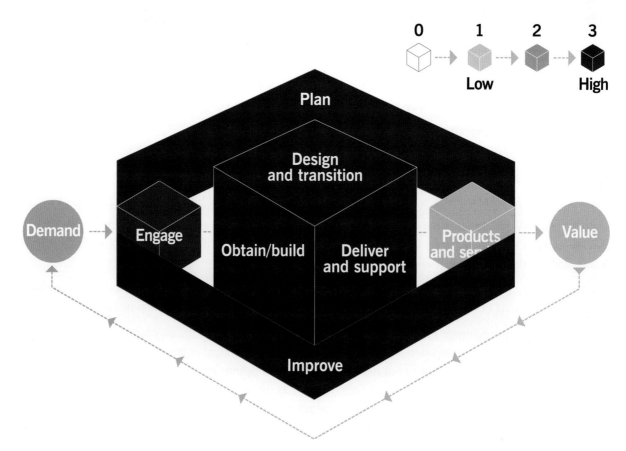

Figure 5.3 Heat map of the contribution of information security management to value chain activities

behaviours needed. All stakeholders must contribute to information security, including customers, users, suppliers, etc.

● **Design and transition** Information security must be considered throughout this value chain activity, with effective controls being designed and transitioned into operation. The design and transition of all services must consider information security aspects as well as all other utility and **warranty requirements**.

● **Obtain/build** Information security must be built into all components, based on the risk analysis, policies, procedures, and controls defined by information security management. This applies whether the components are built internally or procured from suppliers.

● **Deliver and support** Detection and correction of information security incidents must be an integral part of this value chain activity.

The ITIL story: Axle's information security management

 Su: *Our travel app stores a lot of sensitive data, including customer and credit card details. Our role is to make sure this data is secure.*

 Marco: *Some of the data is also stored and processed by our partners, who helped us to develop the app and continue to support the app on our behalf.*

 Radhika: *We use the data to analyse customer demand and the use of our fleet, track the conditions of our cars, and analyse our customers' preferences to create tailored offerings.*

 Su: *Our consumers need to know that their data is safe and will not be misused. We regularly undergo external audits to provide assurance for our stakeholders and to confirm compliance with national and international regulations.*

 Henri: *As CIO, I make sure everyone who works in and with Axle is aware of the importance of information security, and follows Axle policies and procedures concerning information security management.*

5.1.4 Knowledge management

 Key message

The purpose of the knowledge management practice is to maintain and improve the effective, efficient, and convenient use of information and knowledge across the organization.

Knowledge is one of the most valuable assets of an organization. The knowledge management practice provides a structured approach to defining, building, re-using, and sharing knowledge (i.e. information, skills, practices, solutions, and problems) in various forms. As methods of capturing and sharing knowledge move more towards digital solutions, the practice of knowledge management becomes even more valuable.

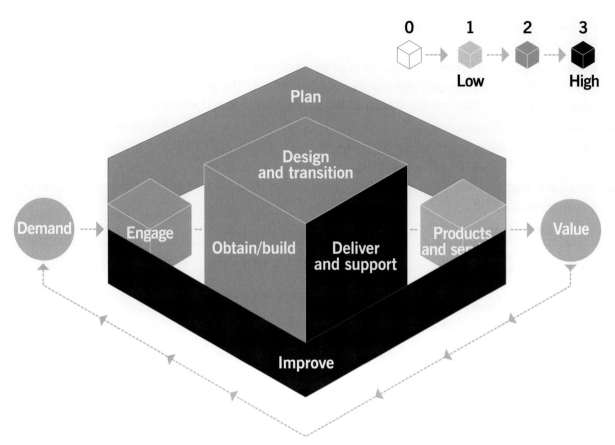

Figure 5.4 Heat map of the contribution of knowledge management to value chain activities

It is important to understand that 'knowledge' is not simply information. Knowledge is the use of information in a particular context. This needs to be understood with both the user of the knowledge and the relevant situation in mind. For example, information presented in the form of a 300-page manual is not useful for a service desk analyst who needs to find a fast solution. A better example of knowledge that is fit for purpose might be a simplified set of instructions or reference points that allow the analyst to find the relevant content quickly.

Knowledge management aims to ensure that stakeholders get the right information, in the proper format, at the right level, and at the correct time, according to their access level and other relevant policies. This requires a procedure for the acquisition of knowledge, including the development, capturing, and harvesting of unstructured knowledge, whether it is formal and documented or informal and tacit knowledge.

Figure 5.4 shows the contribution of knowledge management to the service value chain, with the practice being involved in all value chain activities:

● **Plan** Knowledge management helps the organization to make sound portfolio decisions and to define its strategy and other plans, and supports financial management.

● **Improve** This value chain activity is based on an understanding of the current situation and trends, supported by historical information. Knowledge management provides context for the assessment of achievements and improvement planning.

● **Engage** Relationships at all levels, from strategic to operational, are based on an understanding of the context and history of those relationships. Knowledge management helps to better understand stakeholders.

● **Design and transition** As with the obtain/build value chain activity, knowledge of the solutions and technologies available, and the re-use of information, can make this value chain activity more effective.

- **Obtain/build** The efficiency of this value chain activity can be significantly improved with sufficient knowledge of the solutions and technologies available, and through the re-use of information.

- **Deliver and support** Ongoing value chain activity in this area benefits from knowledge management through re-use of solutions in standard situations and a better understanding of the context of non-standard situations that require analysis.

The ITIL story: Axle's knowledge management

Radhika: *Because we're using an Agile deployment for our app development, we need to make sure our staff have up-to-date knowledge on new features. Just as importantly, knowledge needs to be retired when it's out of date. For example, we recently discovered the printing feature of our app was not being used by our customers. We removed printing and replaced it with a new function to send information from the app by email instead. As part of release management, we've already provided updated knowledge articles to our service desk to reflect the change.*

Su: *Knowledge management is more than just data collection. At Axle, we focus on open communication and the sharing of knowledge. To promote collaboration and visibility, we make sure that information, problems, and concerns are openly shared between our teams and branches.*

Henri: *But we also need to follow information security policies and make sure that openness does not mean carelessness.*

Marco: *We're testing new systems based on AI to improve our forecasting and decision-making at all levels, from strategic planning to user support.*

5.1.5 Measurement and reporting

 Key message

The purpose of the measurement and reporting practice is to support good decision-making and continual improvement by decreasing the levels of uncertainty. This is achieved through the collection of relevant data on various managed objects and the valid assessment of this data in an appropriate context. Managed objects include, but are not limited to, products and services, practices and value chain activities, teams and individuals, suppliers and partners, and the organization as a whole.

Many of these managed objects are connected, and so are their respective metrics and indicators. For example, to set clear objectives for measurement and reporting, there is a need to understand organizational goals. These can be based on a number of areas: profit, growth, competitive advantage, customer retention, operational/public service, etc. (see the focus on value guiding principle in section 4.3.1). In such cases, it is important to establish a clear relationship between high-level and subordinate goals and the objectives that relate to them.

For the set goals, operational critical success factors (CSFs) can be defined. Based on these CSFs, a set of related key performance indicators (KPIs) can then be agreed upon, against which success can be measured.

Definitions

- **Critical success factor (CSF)** A necessary precondition for the achievement of intended results.
- **Key performance indicator (KPI)** An important metric used to evaluate the success in meeting an objective.

5.1.5.1 KPIs and behaviour

KPIs for individuals can work as a competitive motivator, and this will drive positive results if the KPIs are set to meet clear business goals. However, target-setting for individuals can also have a negative side, driving inappropriate or unsuitable behaviours. This typically happens if there is too much focus placed on individual KPIs. For example, service desk staff might be heavily driven to keep calls short, but this can negatively impact on customer satisfaction, and even resolution times, if issues are not properly dealt with.

Operational KPIs should ideally be set for teams rather than focusing too closely on individuals. This means that there can be some flexibility in the targets and behaviours allowed by the team as a whole. Individuals will, of course, still need some specific guidelines for their performance, but this should be clearly within the goals of the team and organization, and all targets should be set in the context of providing value for the organization.

5.1.5.2 Reporting

Data collected as metrics is usually presented in the form of reports or **dashboard**s. It is important to remember that reports are intended to support good decision-making, so their content should be relevant to the recipients of the information and related to the required topic. Reports and dashboards should make it easy for the recipient to see what needs to be done and then take action. As such, a good report or dashboard should answer two main questions: how far are we from our targets and what bottlenecks prevent us from achieving better results?

Figure 5.5 shows the contribution of measurement and reporting to the service value chain, with the practice being involved in all value chain activities:

- **Plan** Measurement and reporting enables strategy and service portfolio decisions by providing details on current performance of products and services.
- **Improve** Performance is constantly monitored and evaluated to support continual improvement, alignment, and value creation.
- **Engage** Engagement with stakeholders is based on correct, up-to-date, and sufficient information provided in the form of dashboards and reports.
- **Design and transition** Measurement and reporting provides information for management decisions at every stage before going live.
- **Obtain/build** The practice ensures transparency of all development and procurement activities, enabling effective management and integration with all other value chain activities.
- **Deliver and support** Ongoing management of products and services is based on correct, up-to-date, and sufficient performance information.

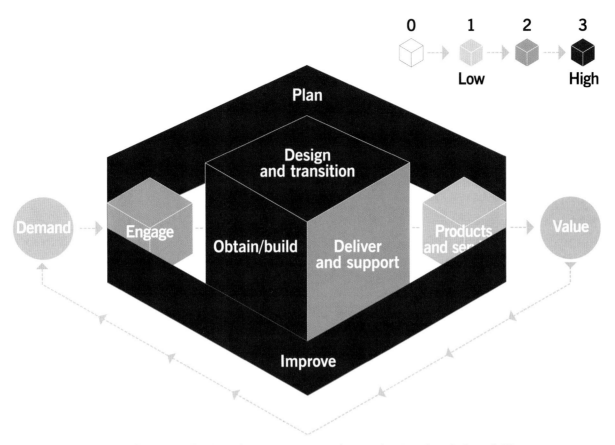

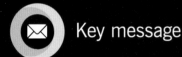

Figure 5.5 Heat map of the contribution of measurement and reporting to value chain activities

5.1.6 Organizational change management

Key message

The purpose of the **organizational change management practice** is to ensure that changes in an organization are smoothly and successfully implemented, and that lasting benefits are achieved by managing the human aspects of the changes.

Improvements invariably require people to change the way they work, their behaviour, and sometimes their role. Regardless of whether the change is to a practice, the structure of the organization, related to technology, or is the introduction of a new or changed service, people are essential to the success of the change. The organizational change management practice aims to ensure that everyone affected by the change accepts and supports it. This is achieved by removing or reducing resistance to the change, eliminating or addressing adverse impacts, and providing training, awareness, and other means of ensuring a successful transition to the changed state.

Organizational change management contributes to every part of the SVS, wherever the cooperation, participation, and enthusiasm of the people involved are required. For an improvement initiative to be successful, no matter what the level or scope of the change is, there are certain elements that are essential to addressing the human factor. Organizational change management must ensure that the following are established and maintained throughout the change:

- **Clear and relevant objectives** To gain support, the objectives of the change must be clear and make sense to the stakeholders, based on the context of the organization. The change must be seen to be of real value.

- **Strong and committed leadership** It is critical that the change has the active support of sponsors and day-to-day leaders within the organization. A sponsor is a manager or business leader who will advocate, and can authorize, the change. Leaders should visibly support and consistently communicate their commitment to the change.

- **Willing and prepared participants** To be successful, a change needs to be made by willing participants. In part, this willingness will come from the participants being convinced of the importance of the change. In addition, the more prepared participants feel they are to make the changes asked of them through relevant training, awareness, and regular communications, the keener they will be to go forward.

- **Sustained improvement** Many changes fail because, after some time has passed, people revert to old ways of working. Organizational change management seeks to continually reinforce the value of the change through regular communication, addressing any impacts and consequences of the change, and the support of sponsors and leaders. The communication of value will be stronger when metrics are used to validate the message.

5.1.6.1 Activities of organizational change management

The key activities of effective organizational change management are outlined in Table 5.2.

Table 5.2 Organizational change management activities

Activity	Helps to deliver
Creation of a sense of urgency	Clear and relevant objectives, willing participants
Stakeholder management	Strong and committed participants
Sponsor management	Strong and committed leadership
Communication	Willing and prepared participants
Empowerment	Prepared participants
Resistance management	Willing participants
Reinforcement	Sustained improvement

The activities of organizational change management interact with those of many other practices, particularly continual improvement and project management. Other practices with important links to organizational change management include measurement and reporting, workforce and talent management, and relationship management.

The various audiences affected by the change must be identified and their characteristics defined. Not all people will respond to the same messaging or be motivated by the same drivers. It is particularly important in organizational change management to take cultural differences into consideration, whether they are based on geography, nationality, corporate history, or other factors.

Unlike other practices, accountability for organizational change management cannot be transferred to an external supplier. Someone within the organization itself must be accountable for organizational change management, even if the execution of some or most of the organizational change management activities is delegated to other people or groups including suppliers. External expertise may, however, be sought to supplement the organizational change management capabilities of an organization. Sometimes organizations struggle with the key skillsets needed for organizational change management and can benefit from the support and guidance of an external supplier. Even if external help is used, the overall leadership support must still come from the organization itself.

Figure 5.6 shows the contribution of organizational change management to the service value chain, with the practice being involved in all value chain activities:

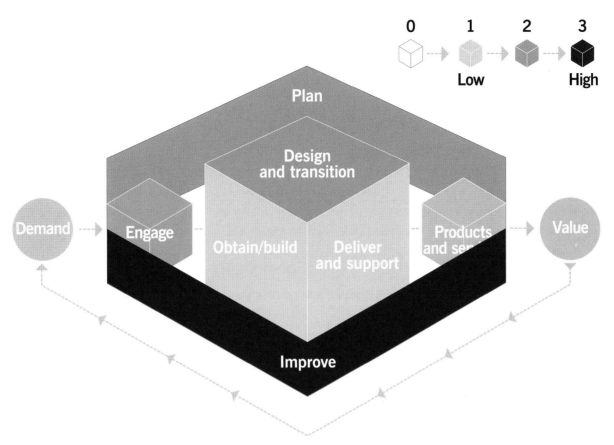

Figure 5.6 Heat map of the contribution of organizational change management to value chain activities

- **Plan** Decisions regarding change at the portfolio level cause the initiation of organizational change management to support an approved initiative.
- **Improve** Without proper organizational change management, improvement cannot be sustained.
- **Engage** The organizational change management practice actively engages with stakeholders at all stages of a change.
- **Design and transition** Organizational change management is essential for the deployment of a new service or a significant change to an existing one.
- **Obtain/build** Organizational change management ensures engagement and cooperation within and across projects.
- **Deliver and support** Organizational change management continues during live operations and support to ensure that the change has been adopted and is sustained.

5.1.7 Portfolio management

 ## Key message

The purpose of the **portfolio management practice** is to ensure that the organization has the right mix of programmes, projects, products, and services to execute the organization's strategy within its funding and resource constraints.

Portfolio management is a coordinated collection of strategic decisions that together enable the most effective balance of organizational change and business as usual. Portfolio management achieves this through the following activities:

- Developing and applying a systematic framework to define and deliver a portfolio of products, services, programmes, and projects in support of specific strategies and objectives.

- Clearly defining products and services and linking them to the achievement of agreed outcomes, thus ensuring that all activities in the service value chain are aligned with value definition and the related CSFs.

- Evaluating and prioritizing incoming product, service, or project proposals and other change initiatives, based on resource constraints, existing commitments, and the organization's strategy and objectives.

- Implementing a strategic investment appraisal and decision-making process based on an understanding of the value, costs, risks, resource constraints, inter-dependencies, and impact on existing business activities.

- Analysing and tracking investments based on the value of products, services, programmes, and projects to the organization and its customers.

- Monitoring the performance of the overall portfolio and proposing adjustments in response to any changes in organizational priorities.

- Reviewing the portfolios in terms of progress, outcomes, costs, risk, benefits, and strategic contribution.

Portfolio management plays an important role in how resources are allocated, deployed, and managed across the organization. This facilitates the alignment of resources and capabilities with customer outcomes as part of the strategy execution within the ITIL SVS.

Portfolio management encompasses a number of different portfolios, including the following:

- **Product/service portfolio** The product/service portfolio is the complete set of products and/or services that are managed by the organization, and it represents the organization's commitments and investments across all its customers and market spaces. It also represents current contractual commitments, new product and service development, and ongoing improvement plans initiated as a result of continual improvement. The portfolio may also include third-party products and services, which are an integral part of offerings to internal and external customers.

- **Project portfolio** The project portfolio is used to manage and coordinate projects that have been authorized, ensuring objectives are met within time and cost constraints and to specification. The project portfolio also ensures that projects are not duplicated, that they stay within the agreed scope, and that resources are available for each project. It is the tool used to manage single projects as well as large-scale programmes consisting of multiple projects.

- **Customer portfolio** The customer portfolio is maintained by the organization's **relationship management practice**, which provides important input to the portfolio management practice. The customer portfolio is used to record all the organization's customers and is the relationship manager's view of the internal and external customers who receive products and/or services from the organization.

  Portfolio management uses the customer portfolio to ensure that the relationship between business outcomes, customers, and services is well understood. It documents these linkages and is validated with customers through the relationship management practice.

Agile portfolio management

The success of programmes and projects has historically been gauged by the extent to which implementation has been completed on time and within budget, and has delivered the required outputs, outcomes, and benefits. In many cases, however, organizations have struggled to demonstrate a return on their investment from change, and there is an increasing recognition that true success is only possible if the programme or project was the 'right' initiative to implement in the first place. Agile portfolio management takes this further, with an increased focus on visualizing strategic themes and the ability to reprioritize the portfolio swiftly, increase workflow, reduce batch sizes of work, and control the length of longer-term development queues.

Traditional portfolio management is focused on top-down planning with work laid out over longer time periods, but Agile portfolio management takes the concept of build–measure–learn cycles used by individual Agile teams and applies it on an organization-wide basis. Teams work together, use modular design, and share findings. This results in tremendous flexibility, which shifts the focus from continuing to execute an inflexible plan to delivering value and making tangible progress according to business strategy and goals.

Organizations practising Agile portfolio management communicate as much as possible across the business. They share knowledge and break barriers between organizational silos.

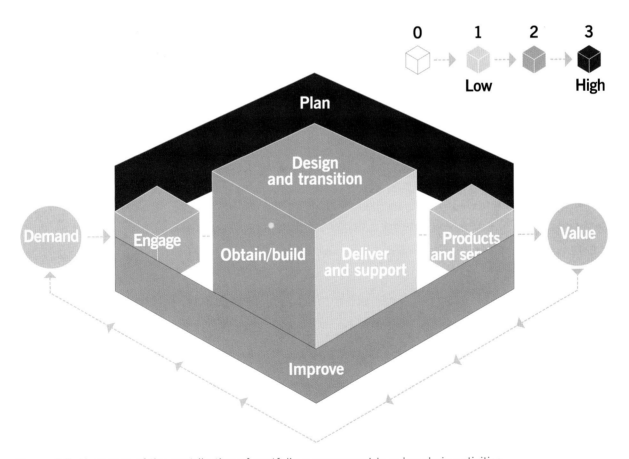

Figure 5.7 Heat map of the contribution of portfolio management to value chain activities

Figure 5.7 shows the contribution of portfolio management to the service value chain, with the practice being involved in all value chain activities:

● **Plan** Portfolio management provides important information about the status of projects, products, and services currently in the pipeline or catalogue and what strategic objectives they have been designed to meet, which is essential for planning. Portfolio management also includes reviewing the portfolios in terms of progress, value creation, costs, risk, benefits, and strategic contribution.

● **Improve** Portfolio management identifies opportunities to improve efficiency and increase collaboration, eliminate duplication between projects, and identify and mitigate risks. Improvement initiatives are prioritized and if approved may be added to the relevant portfolio.

● **Engage** When opportunities or demand are identified by the organization, the decisions on how to prioritize these are made based upon the organization's strategy plus the risk assessment and resource availability.

● **Design and transition, obtain/build, and deliver and support** Portfolio management is responsible for ensuring that products and services are clearly defined and linked to the achievement of business outcomes, so that these value chain activities are aligned with value.

5.1.8 Project management

Key message

The purpose of the **project management practice** is to ensure that all projects in the organization are successfully delivered. This is achieved by planning, delegating, monitoring, and maintaining control of all aspects of a project, and keeping the motivation of the people involved.

Projects are one of the means by which significant changes are introduced to an organization, and they can be defined as temporary structures that are created for the purpose of delivering one or more outputs (or products) according to an agreed business case. They may be a stand-alone initiative or part of a larger programme, together with other interrelated projects, for more complex pieces of transformation. However, even stand-alone projects should be considered in the context of the organization's project portfolio.

There are different approaches to the way in which projects are delivered, with the waterfall and Agile methods being the most common:

● The **waterfall method** works well in environments where the requirements are known upfront (and unlikely to significantly change), and where definition of the work is more important than the speed of delivery.

● The Agile method works best where requirements are uncertain and likely to evolve rapidly over time (for example, as business needs and priorities change), and where speed of delivery is often prioritized over the definition of precise requirements.

Successful project management is important as the organization must balance its need to:

● maintain current business operations effectively and efficiently

● transform those business operations to change, survive, and compete in the market place

● continually improve its products and services.

This balance between projects and 'business as usual' can potentially impact a number of areas, including resources (people, assets, finances), service levels, customer relationships, and productivity, and so the organization's capacity and capability must be considered as part of its project management approach.

Projects depend on the behaviour of people both within the project team and the wider organization. The best project plan amounts to very little if the right people are not involved at the right time. The relationship between the project and the organization also needs to be considered, as many project team members will be seconded from business operations on a full- or part-time basis.

Figure 5.8 shows the contribution of project management to the service value chain, with the practice being involved in all value chain activities:

- **Plan** Project management supports strategic and tactical planning with methods and tools.
- **Improve** Many improvement initiatives are large and complex, so project management is the relevant practice to manage them.
- **Engage** Stakeholder engagement is a key element in the successful delivery of any project. Project management provides the organization with stakeholder management tools and techniques.
- **Design and transition** Design of a practice or service can be managed as a project or an iteration in a larger project; the same applies to some transitions.
- **Obtain/build** Obtaining new resources as well as development and integration is usually performed as a project. Various project management techniques are applicable to this activity.
- **Deliver and support** The design, transition, and handover to internal or external service consumers for operational management needs to be well planned and executed to ensure that business as usual is not compromised. The project management practice ensures this happens.

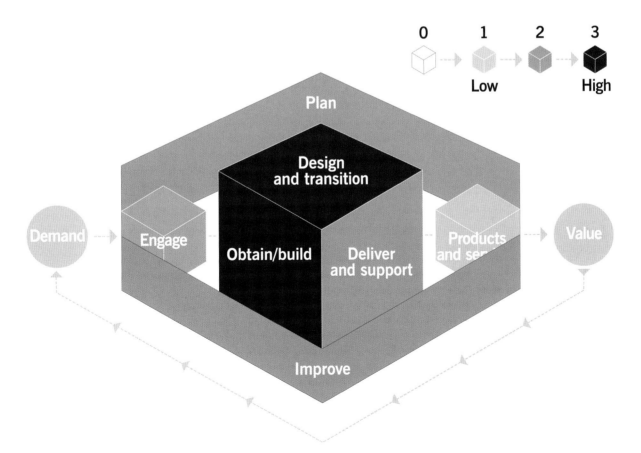

Figure 5.8 Heat map of the contribution of project management to value chain activities

5.1.9 Relationship management

 Key message

The purpose of the relationship management practice is to establish and nurture the links between the organization and its stakeholders at strategic and tactical levels. It includes the identification, analysis, monitoring, and continual improvement of relationships with and between stakeholders.

The relationship management practice ensures that:

- stakeholders' needs and drivers are understood, and products and services are prioritized appropriately
- stakeholders' satisfaction is high and a constructive relationship between the organization and stakeholders is established and maintained
- customers' priorities for new or changed products and services, in alignment with desired business outcomes, are effectively established and articulated
- any stakeholders' complaints and **escalation**s are handled well through a sympathetic (yet formal) process
- products and services facilitate value creation for the service consumers as well as for the organization
- the organization facilitates value creation for all stakeholders, in line with its strategy and priorities
- conflicting stakeholder requirements are mediated appropriately.

Service providers quite naturally focus most of their efforts on their relationships with service consumers (sponsors, customers, and users). It is a very important stakeholder group; however, organizations should ensure that they understand and manage their relationships with various stakeholders, both internal and external. The relationship management practice should apply to all relevant parties. This means that the practice contributes to all service value chain activities and multiple value streams.

Figure 5.9 shows the contribution of relationship management to the service value chain, with the practice being involved in all value chain activities:

- **Plan** Relationship management provides information on the requirements and expectations of internal and external customers. It also assists with strategic assessment and prioritization across portfolios as well as evaluating current and future market spaces, which are essential aspects of planning.
- **Improve** Relationship management seeks to harmonize and synergize different organizational relationships with internal and external customers to realize targeted benefits through continual improvement.
- **Engage** Relationship management is the practice responsible for engaging with internal and external customers to understand their requirements and priorities.
- **Design and transition** Relationship management plays a key role in coordinating feedback from internal and external customers as part of design. It also ensures that inconvenience and adverse impacts to customers during transition are prevented or minimized.
- **Obtain/build** Relationship management provides the customer requirements and priorities to help select products, services or service components to be obtained or built.
- **Deliver and support** Relationship management is responsible for ensuring that a high level of customer satisfaction and a constructive relationship between the organization and its customers are established and maintained.

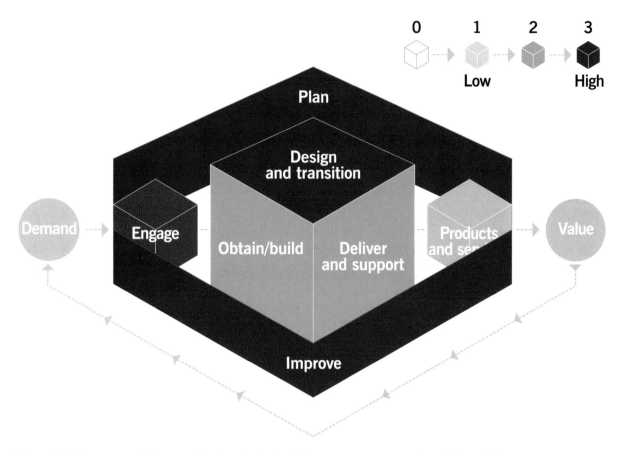

0 1 2 3
Low   High

Figure 5.9 Heat map of the contribution of relationship management to value chain activities

5.1.10 Risk management

 Key message

The purpose of the **risk management practice** is to ensure that the organization understands and effectively handles risks. Managing risk is essential to ensuring the ongoing sustainability of an organization and creating value for its customers. Risk management is an integral part of all organizational activities and therefore central to the organization's SVS (see section 2.5.3 for a definition of risk).

Risk is normally perceived as something to be avoided because of its association with threats, and although this is generally true, risk is also associated with opportunity. Failure to take opportunities can be a risk in itself. The opportunity costs of under-served market spaces and unfulfilled demand is a risk to be avoided.

The organization's portfolio can be mapped to an underlying portfolio of risks to be managed. When service management is effective, products and services in the **service catalogue** and pipeline represent opportunities to create and capture value for customers, the organization, and other stakeholders. Otherwise, those products and services can represent threats due to the possibility of failure associated with the demand patterns they attract, the commitments they require, and the costs they generate. Implementing strategy often requires changes to the product and service portfolio, which means managing associated risks.

Decisions about risk need to be balanced so that the potential benefits are worth more to the organization than the cost to address the risk. For example, innovation is inherently risky but could provide major benefits in improving products and services, achieving competitive advantage, and increasing agility and resilience. The ability of the organization to limit its exposure to risk will also be of relevance. The aim should be to make an accurate assessment of the risks in a given situation, and analyse the potential benefits. The risks and opportunities presented by each course of action should be defined to identify appropriate responses.

For risk management to be effective, risks need to be:

- **Identified** Uncertainties that would affect the achievement of objectives within the context of a particular organizational activity. These uncertainties must be considered and then described to ensure that there is common understanding.

- **Assessed** The probability, impact, and proximity of individual risks must be estimated so they can be prioritized and the overall level of risk (risk exposure) associated with the organizational activity understood.

- **Treated** Appropriate responses to risks must be planned, assigning owners and actionees, and then implemented, monitored, and controlled.

The following principles apply specifically to the risk management practice:

- **Risk is part of business** The organization should ensure that risks are appropriately managed. This does not mean that all risks are to be avoided. On the contrary, risk-taking is required to ensure long-term sustainability. However, risks need to be identified, understood, and assessed against the levels of risk the organization is willing to take (i.e. the risk appetite), and appropriately managed and monitored.

- **Risk management must be consistent across the organization** It is vital that the risk management practice is managed holistically to achieve consistency across the whole organization. To ensure effectiveness, there should be ongoing consultation with stakeholders and appropriate flexibility for different parts of the organization. This flexibility will allow tailored risk management procedures to be developed so that organizational units and/or customer-specific circumstances are addressed.

- **Risk management culture and behaviours are important** The appropriate culture and behaviours demonstrated by all levels of the organization's personnel are critical and must be embedded as part of the 'way we do things'. This will be demonstrated by behaviours and beliefs such as:
  - understanding that effective risk management is vital for the sustainability of the organization and supports the achievement of business goals
  - using proactive risk management behaviours
  - ensuring transparency and clarity of risk management procedures, roles, responsibilities, and accountabilities
  - actively encouraging and following up the reporting of risks, incidents, and opportunities
  - ensuring remuneration structures support desired behaviours (i.e. this should not discourage the reporting of incidents nor encourage over-reporting)
  - actively encouraging learning and growth in **maturity** from the organization's experiences and the experiences of other organizations.

ISO 31000:2018 Risk management

These guidelines provide an overall and general perspective of the purpose and principles of risk management. They are applicable at all levels in any type of organization. ISO 31000 states that 'the purpose of risk management is the creation and protection of value' and that risk management 'improves performance, encourages innovation and supports the achievement of objectives'.

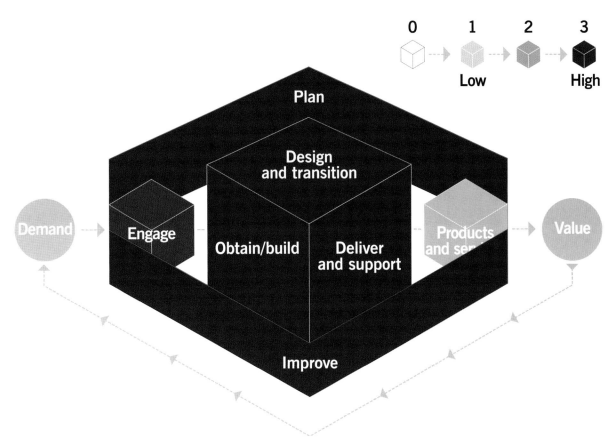

Figure 5.10 Heat map of the contribution of risk management to value chain activities

Figure 5.10 shows the contribution of risk management to the service value chain, with the practice being involved in all value chain activities:

- **Plan** Risk management provides essential inputs to the organization's strategy and planning, with a focus on risks that can drive variability of outcomes. These include:
  - shifts in customer demand and priorities
  - legal and regulatory changes
  - competitors
  - dependencies on suppliers and partners
  - technological changes
  - conflicting stakeholder requirements.
- **Improve** All improvement initiatives should be assessed and continually controlled by risk management. The practice establishes an important perspective for improvement prioritization, planning, and review.
- **Engage** The risk management practice helps to identify key stakeholders and optimize engagement based on such information as risk appetite and risk profiles.
- **Design and transition** Products and services should be designed to address prioritized risks. For example, they should be scalable to support changes in demand over time. For the organization, new or changed services carry varying levels of risk which should be identified and assessed before the change is approved. If approved, the risks should be managed as part of the change, including releases, deployments, and projects.
- **Obtain/build** Risk management should inform decisions about the obtaining or building of products, services, or service components.
- **Deliver and support** Risk management helps to ensure that the ongoing delivery of products and services is maintained at the agreed level and that all events are managed according to the risks that they introduce.

5.1.11 Service financial management

 Key message

The purpose of the **service financial management practice** is to support the organization's strategies and plans for service management by ensuring that the organization's financial resources and investments are being used effectively.

Service financial management supports decision-making by the governing body and management of the organization regarding where to best allocate financial resources. It provides visibility into the budgeting, costing, and accounting activities related to the products and services. To be effective in the context of the SVS, this practice needs to be aligned with the organization's policies and practices for portfolio management, project management, and relationship management.

Finance is the common language which allows the organization to communicate effectively with its stakeholders. Service financial management is responsible for managing the budgeting, costing, accounting, and **charging** for the activities of an organization, acting as both service provider and service consumer:

● **Budgeting/costing** This is an activity focused on predicting and controlling the income and expenditure of money within the organization. Budgeting consists of a periodic negotiation cycle to set budgets and ongoing monitoring of the current budgets. To accomplish this objective, it focuses on capturing forecasted and actual service demand. It translates this demand into anticipated operating and project costs used for setting budgets and rates to ensure adequate funding for products and services. Service-based budgeting seeks to understand the budget and establish funding models based on the full cost of providing or consuming a service.

● **Accounting** This activity enables the organization to account fully for the way its money is spent, allowing it to compare forecast vs actual costs and expenditures (particularly the ability to identify usage and costs by customer, service, and activity/**cost centre**). It usually involves accounting systems, including ledgers, charts of accounts, and journals.

● **Charging** This activity is required to formally invoice service consumers (usually external) for the services provided to them. It is important to note that while charging is an optional practice, all services require a funding model, because all costs need to be adequately funded by an agreed method.

Figure 5.11 shows the contribution of service financial management to the service value chain, with the practice being involved in all value chain activities:

● **Plan** Plans at all levels need funding based on information, including financial. Service financial management supports planning with budgets, reports, forecasts, and other relevant information.

● **Improve** All improvements should be prioritized with return on investment in mind. Service financial management provides tools and information for improvements evaluation and prioritization.

● **Engage** Financial considerations are important for establishing and maintaining service relationships with service consumers, suppliers, and partners. For some stakeholders (investors, sponsors) the financial aspect of the relationship is the most important. The practice supports this value chain activity by providing financial information.

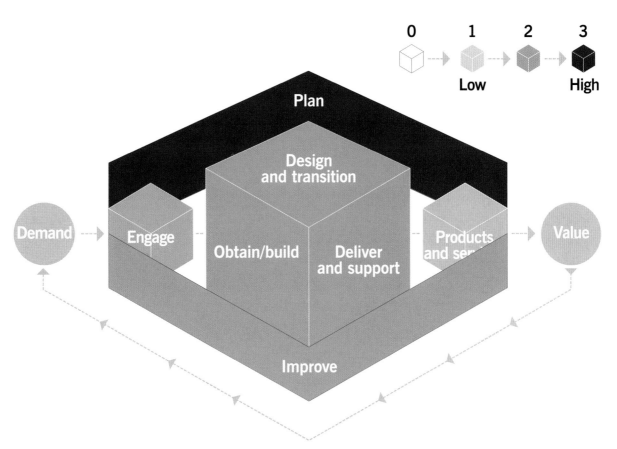

Figure 5.11 Heat map of the contribution of service financial management to value chain activities

● **Design and transition** Service financial management helps to keep this activity cost-effective by providing the means for financial planning and control. It also ensures transparency of costs for products and services for the service provider, accounting for design and transition expenditures.

● **Obtain/build** Obtaining resources of all types is supported by budgeting (to ensure sufficient funding) and accounting (to ensure transparency and evaluation).

● **Deliver and support** Ongoing operational costs are a significant part of the organization's expenditures. For commercial organizations, ongoing service delivery activities are also the source of income. Service financial management helps to ensure sufficient understanding of both. Charging (if applicable) supports the service provider and the service consumer in their relationships with billing and reporting.

Evolution of financial management with new technology

Financial management refers to the efficient and effective management of money in the most appropriate manner to accomplish the financial objectives of the organization. Since its inception, the financial management discipline has gone through various degrees of change, improvement, and innovation. A key component of this change has been the emergence of new technology. Many technological developments have impacted upon financial management, but the three key innovations are the introduction of a greater number of digital technologies, blockchain, and IT budgets and payment models.

Digital technologies

Major financial institutions are now analysing and using the latest technologies such as the cloud, **big data**, analytics, and artificial intelligence (AI) to gain, or even just to maintain, competitive advantage in the market place. However, new financial organizations are also using these technologies and starting operations without any legacy IT, **technical debt**, or bureaucratic processes, which means they tend to be more Agile.

Big data and analytics are being used by financial organizations to gain deeper insight into, and understanding of, their customers. The amount of data being captured is phenomenal and requires scalable computing power to process the data efficiently and cost-effectively. In return, this deeper customer understanding is causing financial organizations to develop new and innovative products and services. Data is now being referred to as the 'new oil', as organizations are scrambling to capture, analyse, and exploit it.

Blockchain

Another evolution in financial management is happening through a specific innovation called blockchain, again enabled only through cloud-based services. Initially blockchain was developed to enable the de-centralized management of crypto-currencies, allowing **transaction**s to be audited and verified automatically and inexpensively.

Blockchain technologies are used to manage public digital ledgers. These digital ledgers record transactions across many globally distributed computers. The distribution of **record**s ensures that each record cannot be changed without the alteration of all subsequent records (also known as blocks) and without the consensus of the entire distributed ledger (also called the network).

Global financial institutions are researching how this blockchain technology can provide them with competitive advantage by streamlining back-office functions and reducing settlement rates for banking transactions. New financial organizations are investigating blockchain to deliver alternative banking functions at a fraction of the cost and overheads of traditional banks.

IT budgets and payment models

The emergence of new technology has not just affected financial organizations, but also the way that every organization manages its IT services from a financial perspective. Much of the current wave of technological evolution has been enabled by cloud computing, and this seems likely to continue for the foreseeable future. This has led to a major change in how IT services are obtained, funded, and paid for by organizations.

Traditionally, IT resources were obtained using upfront capital expenditure (CAPEX). However, under the cloud model, the provision of IT infrastructure, platforms, and software is provided 'as a service'. This model generally uses subscription-based or pay-as-you-use charging mechanisms which are paid for out of operational expenditure (OPEX).

Another area that has seen change is the organization's approach to setting and managing IT budgets. Flexible IT budgets are required to meet the costs of scaling cloud-based services in an Agile and on-demand way. Fixed IT budgets, often forecast months in advance, struggle to account for the scaling of IT resources in this way.

Procurement rules within organizations are also having to change. There remains a place for fixed-price IT projects and services; however, cloud-based digital services are generally sold under a variable-price model, i.e. the more you use and consume, the more you pay, and vice versa. Therefore, those organizations that have not updated their procurement rules to allow them to buy variable-priced IT resources will face a large self-made barrier preventing them from using cloud-based digital services. To be as effective as possible, organizations must update their policies and educate their staff to ensure that they can purchase IT under a variable-priced model.

5.1.12 Strategy management

 Key message

The purpose of the **strategy management practice** is to formulate the goals of the organization and adopt the courses of action and allocation of resources necessary for achieving those goals. Strategy management establishes the organization's direction, focuses effort, defines or clarifies the organization's priorities, and provides consistency or guidance in response to the environment.

The starting point for strategy management is to understand the context of the organization and define the desired outcomes. The strategy of the organization establishes criteria and mechanisms that help to decide how to best prioritize resources, capabilities, and investment to achieve those outcomes, while the practice ensures that the strategy is defined, agreed, maintained, and achieved.

The objectives of strategy management are to:

- analyse the environment in which the organization exists to identify opportunities that will benefit the organization
- identify constraints that might prevent the achievement of business outcomes and define how those constraints could be removed or their effects reduced
- decide and agree the organization's perspective and direction with relevant stakeholders, including its vision, mission, and principles
- establish the perspective and position of the organization relative to its customers and competitors. This includes defining which services and products will be delivered to which market spaces and how to maintain competitive advantage
- ensure that the strategy has been translated into tactical and operational plans for each organizational unit that is expected to deliver on the strategy
- ensure the strategy is implemented through execution of the strategic plans and coordination of efforts at the strategic, tactical, and operational levels
- manage changes to the strategies and related documents, ensuring that strategies keep pace with changes to internal and external environments and other relevant factors.

Strategy management is often seen as the responsibility of the senior management and governing body of an organization. It enables them to set the objectives of the organization, to specify how the organization will meet those objectives, and to prioritize the investments that are required to meet them. However, in today's complex, fast-changing environment, traditional strategy practices, based on careful deliberation, extensive research, and scenario planning, are also evolving. Strategy is becoming more fluid and there is an increased focus on establishing the essential purpose and principles of an organization, which can serve as the guiding direction for all its actions, even as circumstances change. For example, a Lean strategy process can be used to balance the extremes of rigid planning and uncontrolled experimentation. The strategy provides the overall direction and alignment of the organization, serving as both a screen that innovative ideas must pass and a basis for evaluating the success of the SVS. It encourages employees to be creative, while ensuring that they are in harmony with the organization and pursue only valuable opportunities.

Chapter 5 – ITIL management practices

Strategy must enable value creation for the organization. A good business model describes the means of fulfilling an organization's objectives. The strategy of the organization should include some way to make its services and products uniquely valuable to its customers; it must therefore define the organization's approach for delivering better value. The need for a strategy is not limited to larger organizations; it is just as important for smaller ones, allowing them to have a clear perspective, positioning, and plans to ensure that they remain relevant to their customers.

Customers want solutions that break through performance barriers and achieve higher-quality outcomes with little or no increase in cost. Such solutions are usually made available through innovative products and services. The strategy should balance the organization's need to deliver both efficient and effective operations with innovation and future-focused activities.

The value of products and services from either the customer's or the organization's perspective may alter over time due to changing conditions, events, or other factors outside an organization's control. Strategy management ensures a carefully considered approach to the organization's relationships with customers, as well as both agility and resilience in dealing with the variations in value that define those relationships.

A high-performance strategy is one that enables an organization to consistently outperform competing alternatives over time, across business cycles, during industry disruptions, and when changes in leadership occur. It should be focused on what needs to be done across the organization to facilitate value creation.

Figure 5.12 shows the contribution of strategy management to the service value chain, with the practice being involved in all value chain activities:

● **Plan** Strategy management ensures that the organization's strategy has been translated into tactical and operational plans for each organizational unit that is expected to deliver on the strategy.

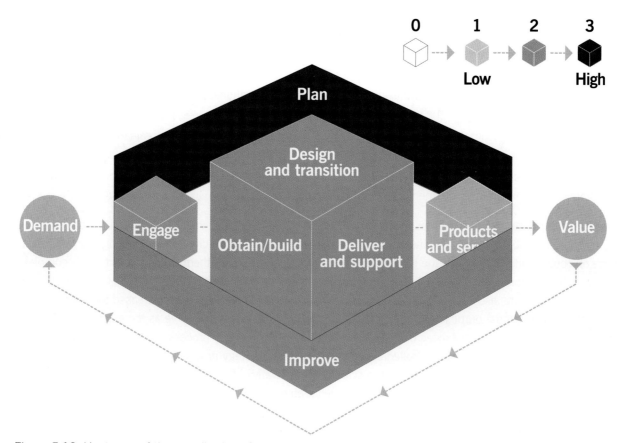

Figure 5.12 Heat map of the contribution of strategy management to value chain activities

- **Improve** Strategy management provides strategy and objectives to be used to prioritize and evaluate improvements.

- **Engage** When opportunities or demand are identified by the organization, the decisions about how to prioritize these are based upon the organization's strategy plus the risk assessment and resource availability.

- **Design and transition, obtain/build, and deliver and support** Strategy management ensures the strategy is implemented through execution of the strategic plans in coordination with these activities. It also provides feedback to enable the measurement and evaluation of products and services during design and transition.

5.1.13 Supplier management

 Key message

The purpose of the **supplier management practice** is to ensure that the organization's suppliers and their performances are managed appropriately to support the seamless provision of quality products and services. This includes creating closer, more collaborative relationships with key suppliers to uncover and realize new value and reduce the risk of failure.

Activities that are central to the practice include:

- **Creating a single point of visibility and control to ensure consistency** This should be across all products, services, service components, and procedures provided or operated by internal and external suppliers, including customers acting as suppliers.

- **Maintaining a supplier strategy, policy, and contract management information**

- **Negotiating and agreeing contracts and arrangements** Agreements need to be aligned with business needs and service targets. Contracts with external suppliers might need to be negotiated or agreed through the legal, procurement, commercial, or contracts functions of the organization. For an internal supplier there will need to be an internal agreement.

- **Managing relationships and contracts with internal and external suppliers** This should be done when planning, designing, building, orchestrating, transitioning, and operating products and services, working closely with procurement and performance management.

- **Managing supplier performance** Supplier performance should be monitored to ensure that they meet the terms, conditions, and targets of their contracts and agreements, while aiming to increase the value for money obtained from suppliers and the products/services they provide.

5.1.13.1 Sourcing, supplier strategy, and relationships

The supplier strategy, sometimes called the sourcing strategy, defines the organization's plan for how it will leverage the contribution of suppliers in the achievement of its overall service management strategy.

Some organizations may adopt a strategy that dictates the use of suppliers only in very specific and limited circumstances, while another organization may choose to make extensive use of suppliers in product and service provision. A successful sourcing strategy requires a thorough understanding of an organization's objectives, the resources required to deliver that strategy, the environmental (e.g. market) factors, and the risks associated with implementing specific approaches.

There are different types of supplier relationship between an organization and its suppliers that need to be considered as part of the organization's sourcing strategy. These include:

- **Insourcing** The products or services are developed and/or delivered internally by the organization.
- **Outsourcing** The process of having external suppliers provide products and services that were previously provided internally. Outsourcing involves substitution, i.e. the replacement of internal capability by that of the supplier.
- **Single source or partnership** Procurement of a product or service from one supplier. This can either be a single supplier who supplies all services directly or an external service integrator who manages the relationships with all suppliers and integrates their services on behalf of the organization. These close relationships (and the mutual interdependence they create) foster high quality, reliability, short lead times, and cooperative action.
- **Multi-sourcing** Procurement of a product or service from more than one independent supplier. These products and services can be combined to form new services which the organization can provide to internal and external customers. As organizations place more focus on increased specialization and compartmentalization of capabilities to increase agility, multi-sourcing is increasingly a preferred option. Traditionally organizations have managed these suppliers separately across different parts of the organization, but there is a move towards developing an internal service integration capability or selecting an external service integrator.

Individual suppliers can provide support services and products that independently have a relatively minor and fairly indirect role in value generation, but collectively make a much more direct and important contribution to this and the implementation of the organization's strategy.

5.1.13.2 Evaluation and selection of suppliers

The organization should evaluate and select suppliers based on:

- **Importance and impact** The value of the service to the business, provided by the supplier
- **Risk** The risks associated with using the service
- **Costs** The cost of the service and its provision.

Other important factors in evaluating and selecting suppliers include the willingness or feasibility of a supplier to customize its offerings or work cooperatively in a multi-supplier environment; the level of influence of the organization or service integrator on the supplier's performance; and the degree of dependence of one supplier on other suppliers.

5.1.13.3 Activities

Activities of the supplier management practice include:

- **Supplier planning** The purpose of this activity is to understand new or changed service requirements and review relevant enterprise documentation to develop a sourcing strategy and supplier management plan, working in conjunction with other practices such as business analysis, portfolio management, service design, and service level management.
- **Evaluation of suppliers and contracts** The purpose of this activity is to identify, evaluate, and select suppliers for the delivery of new or changed business services.
- **Supplier and contract negotiation** The purpose of this activity is to develop, negotiate, review, update, finalize, and award supplier contracts. The failure of negotiations will trigger a new contract, an updated contract, or a contract termination.

- **Supplier categorization** This procedure aims to categorize suppliers on a periodic basis and after the awarding of new or updated contracts. Commonly used categories include strategic, tactical, and commodity suppliers.

- **Supplier and contract management** The purpose of this activity is to ensure that the organization obtains value for money and the delivery of the agreed performance of the supplier against the contract and targets.

- **Warranty management** The purpose of this activity is to manage warranty requirements or clauses and make warranty claims when a warranty issue arises, in conjunction with performance management.

- **Performance management** This activity includes the setup and continuous tracking of operational measures that have been mutually agreed with internal and external suppliers. It focuses on the key measures, which can then be consolidated on a supplier scorecard. Monitoring will allow for the identification of systemic problems and improvement opportunities and provide a basis for reporting.

- **Contract renewal and/or termination** This procedure aims to manage contract renewals and terminations, which are triggered by either specific or periodic reviews of supplier performance.

5.1.13.4 Service integration

Service integration is responsible for coordinating or orchestrating all the suppliers involved in the development and delivery of products and services. It focuses on the end-to-end provision of service, ensuring control of all interfaces and outcomes from suppliers, and facilitating collaboration between suppliers. An organization can either perform the role of service integrator itself, or use a third-party service integrator. It is possible to develop a hybrid model, where the organization is responsible for some of the service integration function and augments that capability with that of an external service integrator. The service integration function can also be operated by a lead supplier. The service integrator is also responsible for assurance; this includes performance management and reporting, defining roles and responsibilities, maintaining relationships across all parties, and heading regular forums and steering committees to address issues, agree priorities, and make decisions.

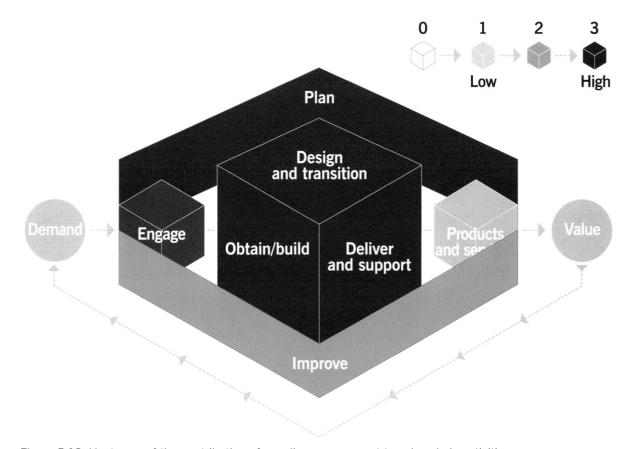

Figure 5.13 Heat map of the contribution of supplier management to value chain activities

Figure 5.13 shows the contribution of supplier management to the service value chain, with the practice being involved in all value chain activities:

● **Plan** Supplier management provides the organization's approved sourcing strategy and plan.

● **Improve** The practice identifies opportunities for improvement with existing suppliers, is involved in the selection of new suppliers, and provides ongoing supplier performance management.

● **Engage** Supplier management is responsible for engaging with all suppliers and for the evaluation and selection of suppliers; for negotiating and agreeing contracts and agreements; and for ongoing management of supplier relationships.

● **Design and transition** Supplier management is responsible for defining requirements for contracts and agreements related to new or changed products or services, in alignment with the organization's needs and service targets.

● **Obtain/build** Supplier management supports the procurement or obtaining of products, services, and service components from third parties.

● **Deliver and support** Supplier performance for live services is managed by this practice to ensure that suppliers meet the terms, conditions, and targets of their contracts and agreements.

The ITIL story: Axle's supplier management

Marco: *I've been assigned to the supplier management role at Axle. This means I'll be managing the monthly governance forums with our suppliers to track their service performance as outlined in their **service level agreement**s. I'll make sure the contractual obligations of our suppliers are in line with Axle Car Hire business outcomes.*

Radhika: *For example, we promise our customers that the cars will always be clean. We used to have our cars cleaned weekly, but to meet the new service promise, Craig's Cleaning will clean the cars each time they're returned to the lot.*

Henri: *Axle's services depend on multiple partners and suppliers. We work with car dealers and manufacturers, tyre manufacturers, cleaners, and roadside assistance providers. We also have Axle agents who promote our offerings, and partners in a loyalty programme who provide their services to our clients on special terms.*

Radhika: *We use many partners' and suppliers' services for our IT systems as well. This supports Axle's work on many levels, from internet access to software development.*

Marco: *Greater digitalization at Axle means more opportunity to build IT into our service offerings. The Axle app makes it possible to book and pay for car hire via personal devices. The Axle Aware system is installed in every car and is supported by IT and our partners. Fleet maintenance is planned based on the hire history of our vehicles, and controlled by our IT systems.*

Henri: *Because of this, Axle's business is now heavily dependent on IT and non-IT suppliers. Integrating and coordinating these services is part of supplier management. We expect our suppliers to provide a consistent level of quality for Axle and our customers.*

5.1.14 Workforce and talent management

Key message

The purpose of the **workforce and talent management practice** is to ensure that the organization has the right people with the appropriate skills and knowledge and in the correct roles to support its business objectives. The practice covers a broad set of activities focused on successfully engaging with the organization's employees and people resources, including planning, recruitment, onboarding, learning and development, performance measurement, and succession planning.

Workforce and talent management plays a critical role in establishing **organizational velocity** by helping organizations to proactively understand and forecast future demand for services. It also ensures that the right people with the necessary competencies are available at the right time to deliver the services required.

Achieving this objective reduces backlogs, improves quality, avoids rework caused by defects, and reduces wait time while also closing knowledge and skills gaps. As organizations transform their practices and automation and organizational capabilities to support the digital economy and improve speed to market, having the right talent becomes critical.

Workforce and talent management enables organizations, leaders, and managers to focus on creating an effective and actionable people strategy, and to execute that strategy at various levels within the organization. A good strategy should support the identification of roles and associated knowledge, as well as the skills and attitudes needed to keep an organization running day to day. It should also address the emerging technologies and leadership and organizational change capabilities required to position the organization for future growth.

The idea of managing and developing an organization's workforce and talent is not new. However, with the increased use of third-party suppliers and the rapid adoption of automation for repeatable work, traditional roles are changing dramatically. Because of this, workforce and talent management should be the responsibility of leaders and managers at every level throughout the organization.

Definitions

- **Organizational velocity** The speed, effectiveness, and efficiency with which an organization operates. Organizational velocity influences time to market, quality, safety, costs, and risks.
- **Competencies** The combination of observable and measurable knowledge, skills, abilities, and attitudes that contribute to enhanced employee performance and ultimately result in organizational success.
- **Skills** A developed proficiency or dexterity in thought, verbal communication, or physical action.
- **Ability** The power or aptitude to perform physical or mental activities related to a profession or trade.
- **Knowledge** The understanding of facts or information acquired by a person through experience or education; the theoretical or practical understanding of a subject.
- **Attitude** A set of emotions, beliefs, and behaviours towards a particular object, person, thing, or event.

5.1.14.1 Workforce and talent management activities

The activities of this practice cover a broad range of areas and are performed by a variety of roles for specific purposes, including:

- **Workforce planning** Translating the organization's strategy and objectives into desired organizational capabilities, and then into competencies and roles.
- **Recruitment** The acquisition of new employees and contractors to fill identified gaps related to desired capabilities.
- **Performance measurement** The delivery of regular performance measurement and assessments against established job roles based on pre-defined competencies.
- **Personal development** An employee's use of published job roles and competency frameworks to proactively plan personal growth and advancement.
- **Learning and development** Targeted education and experiential learning opportunities using various formal and non-formal methods.
- **Mentoring and succession planning** Formal mentoring, engagement, and succession planning activities provided by leadership.

Figure 5.14 presents the activities of workforce and talent management.

Figure 5.14 Workforce and talent management activities

Figure 5.15 shows the contribution of workforce and talent management to the service value chain, with the practice being involved in all value chain activities; however, it is a primary focus of plan and improve activities:

● **Plan** Workforce planning is a specific output of this value chain activity, as leadership and management evaluate their current organizational capabilities in relation to future requirements for the organization's resources, as well as the products and services defined within the service portfolio.

● **Improve** All improvements require sufficiently skilled and motivated people. The workforce and talent management practice ensures understanding and fulfilment of these requirements.

● **Engage** Workforce and talent management is closely linked to this value chain activity. It works with practices such as relationship management, service request management, and service desk to understand and forecast changing service demand requirements, and how this will impact and direct workforce planning and talent management activities.

● **Design and transition** Talent management is important to this value chain activity. Specific focus is given to knowledge, skills, and abilities related to systems and design thinking.

● **Obtain/build** Talent management focuses specifically on knowledge, skills, and abilities related to collaboration, customer focus, quality, speed, and cost management.

● **Deliver and support** Specific focus by talent management is given to knowledge, skills, and abilities related to customer service, performance management, and customer interactions and relationships.

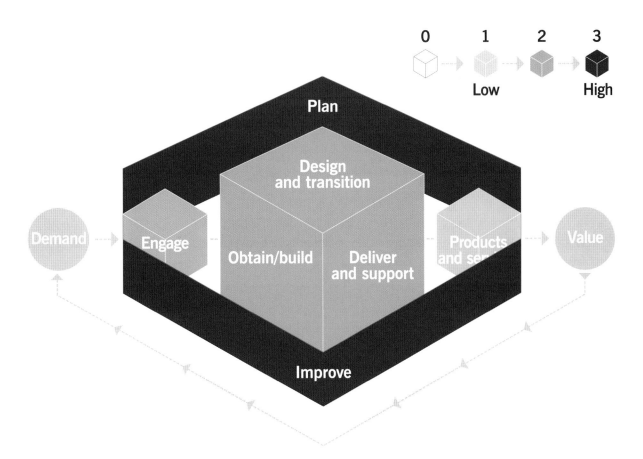

Figure 5.15 Heat map of the contribution of workforce and talent management to value chain activities

5.2 Service management practices

5.2.1 Availability management

Key message

The purpose of the **availability management practice** is to ensure that services deliver agreed levels of availability to meet the needs of customers and users.

Definition: Availability

The ability of an IT service or other configuration item to perform its agreed function when required.

Availability management activities include:

- negotiating and agreeing achievable targets for availability
- designing infrastructure and applications that can deliver required availability levels
- ensuring that services and components are able to collect the data required to measure availability
- monitoring, analysing, and reporting on availability
- planning improvements to availability.

In the simplest terms, the availability of a service depends on how frequently the service fails, and how quickly it recovers after a failure. These are often expressed as **mean time between failures (MTBF)** and **mean time to restore service (MTRS)**:

- MTBF measures how frequently the service fails. For example, a service with a MTBF of four weeks fails, on average, 13 times each year.
- MTRS measures how quickly service is restored after a failure. For example, a service with a MTRS of four hours will, on average, fully recover from failure in four hours. This does not mean that service will always be restored in four hours, as MTRS is an average over many incidents.

Older services were often designed with very high MTBF, so that they would fail infrequently. More recently there has been a shift towards optimizing service design to minimize MTRS, so that services can be recovered very quickly. The most effective way to do this is to design anti-fragile solutions, which recover automatically and very quickly, with virtually no business impact. For some services, even a very short failure can be catastrophic, and for these it is more important to focus on increasing MTBF.

The way that availability is defined must be appropriate for each service. It is important to understand users' and customers' views on availability and to define appropriate metrics, reports, and dashboards. Many organizations

Chapter 5 – ITIL management practices

calculate percentage availability based on MTBF and MTRS, but these percentage figures rarely match customers' experience, and are not appropriate for most services. Other things that should be considered include:

● which vital business functions are affected by different application failures

● at what point is slow performance so bad that the service is effectively unusable

● when does the service need to be available, and when can the service provider carry out maintenance activities.

Measurements that work well for some services include:

● **User outage minutes** Calculated by multiplying incident duration by the number of users impacted, or by adding up the number of minutes each user is affected. This works well for services that directly support user productivity; for example, an email service.

● **Number of lost transactions** Calculated by subtracting the number of transactions from the number expected to have happened during the time period. This works well for services that support transaction-based business processes, such as manufacturing support.

● **Lost business value** Calculated by measuring how business productivity was impacted by the failures of supporting services. This is easily understood by customers and can be useful for planning investment in improved availability. However, it can be difficult to identify which lost business value was caused by IT service failures and which had other causes.

● **User satisfaction** Service availability is one of the most important and visible characteristics of services, and has a great influence on user satisfaction. It is important to make sure that users are satisfied with service availability in addition to meeting formally agreed availability targets.

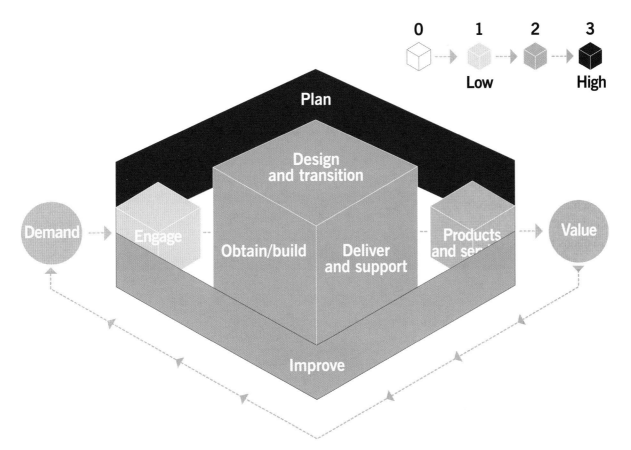

Figure 5.16 Heat map of the contribution of availability management to value chain activities

Most organizations do not have dedicated availability management staff. The activities needed are often distributed around the organization. Some organizations include availability management activities as part of risk management, while others combine it with service continuity management or with capacity and performance management. Some organizations have site reliability engineers (SREs) who manage and improve the availability of specific products or services.

A process is needed for the regular testing of failover and recovery mechanisms. Many organizations also have a process for calculating and reporting availability metrics; however, availability management is driven as much by culture, experience, and knowledge as by following procedures.

Figure 5.16 shows the contribution of availability management to the service value chain, with the practice being involved in all value chain activities:

- **Plan** Availability management must be considered in service portfolio decisions and when setting goals and direction for services and practices.
- **Improve** When planning and making improvements, availability management ensures that services are not degraded.
- **Engage** Availability requirements for new and changed services must be understood and captured.
- **Design and transition** New and changed services must be designed to meet availability targets and testing of availability controls is needed during transition.
- **Obtain/build** Availability is a consideration when building components or obtaining them from third parties.
- **Deliver and support** This activity includes measurement of availability and reacting to events which might affect the ability to meet availability targets.

5.2.2 Business analysis

 Key message

The purpose of the **business analysis practice** is to analyse a business or some element of it, define its associated needs, and recommend solutions to address these needs and/or solve a business problem, which must facilitate value creation for stakeholders. Business analysis enables an organization to communicate its needs in a meaningful way, express the rationale for change, and design and describe solutions that enable value creation in alignment with the organization's objectives.

Analysis and solutions should be approached in a holistic way that includes consideration of processes, organizational change, technology, information, policies, and strategic planning. The work of business analysis is performed primarily by business analysts (BAs), although others may contribute.

In IT, business analysis practices are frequently applied in software development projects, but they are also appropriate to higher-level architectures, services, and the organization's service value system (SVS) in general. To restrict the application of business analysis to software development alone is to run the risk of developing incomplete solutions.

The key activities associated with business analysis are:

- analysing business **system**s, business processes, services, or architectures in the changing internal and external context

- identifying and prioritizing parts of the SVS, and products and services that require improvement, as well as opportunities for innovation
- evaluating and proposing actions that can be taken to create the desired improvement. Actions may include not only IT system changes, but also process changes, alterations to organizational structure, and staff development
- documenting the business requirements for the supporting services to enable the desired improvements
- recommending solutions following analysis of the gathered requirements and validating these with stakeholders.

Business requirements can be utility-focused or warranty-focused.

Definitions

- **Warranty requirements** Typically non-functional requirements captured as inputs from key stakeholders and other practices. Organizations should aim to manage a library of pre-defined warranty **acceptance criteria** for use in practices such as project management and software development and management.
- **Utility requirements** Functional requirements which have been defined by the customer and are unique to a specific product.

Business analysis should ensure the most efficient and comprehensive achievement of these activities, but not make the error of analysis without intent of subsequent action. An organization should not attempt to analyse an issue so deeply or for so long that a timely solution cannot be achieved, or try to solve every problem with a single, massive initiative that fails to facilitate value creation in enough time to be of practical use. The processes associated with this practice should guard against these mistakes.

The scope of work for the business analysis practice includes using and evaluating information from operations and support to build knowledge of how the services and practices are performing in the live environment. This knowledge will not only help to identify areas for improvement in the current service design, but also reveal lessons learned that will improve future designs.

The role of business analysis may be defined differently from organization to organization, but it is a recognized discipline with a specific set of skills. Business analysis requires not only critical thinking and evaluation, but also listening, communication, and facilitation skills, the ability to analyse and document business processes and **use case**s, and perform data analysis and **modelling**.

When the system or service being analysed crosses many organizational boundaries, it is important that the various business units involved adopt a partner relationship to ensure a holistic analysis and comprehensive solution proposal. If compromises are needed from one or more of these units, a collaborative, partner-like relationship will facilitate a solution that will provide value for all the parties.

Without the right information, business analysis cannot be successful, and to be effective, it needs access to all information related to the area under analysis. For business processes, for example, business analysts will need access to all process documentation, including process flows, procedures and work instructions, policies, and process metrics. They may need to interview not only the person responsible for the business process, but also those who participate in each part of the process to compile a clear view of the process and the related issues.

The technologies deployed usually include whatever system the organization uses to gather and document requirements, as well as project management systems and reporting tools for gathering and processing data and information for analysis. Other technologies that can be of assistance when presenting the results of analysis are visual modelling and mapping tools and features of many of the typical office productivity suites such as spreadsheets, presentation software, and word processing.

As with all practices, business analysis cannot ensure successful solutions in isolation. For example, strategy management practices provide high-level guidance to business analysis, which then directs analysis and solution recommendations. In turn, the recommendations from business analysis can influence technical and other strategies. To ensure the participation of the right parties, business analysis relies on relationship management. Furthermore, the natural progression through the service value chain requires interaction between business analysis activities and those from service design, software development and management, measurement and reporting, and many others.

Figure 5.17 shows the contribution of business analysis to the service value chain, with the practice being involved in all value chain activities:

● **Plan** Business analysis contributes to strategic decision-making on what will be done and how.

● **Improve** All levels of evaluation and improvement benefit from business analysis, which is particularly applicable at strategic and tactical levels.

● **Engage** Business analysis is key to the gathering of requirements during this value chain activity.

● **Design and transition** Gathering, prioritization, and analysis of accurate requirements can help ensure that a high-quality solution is designed and progressed to operation.

● **Obtain/build** Business analysis skills are integral to the definition of an agreed solution.

● **Deliver and support** Data from the ongoing delivery of a service can be part of business analysis activities when designing changes to the service, as well as when looking for opportunities for continual improvement.

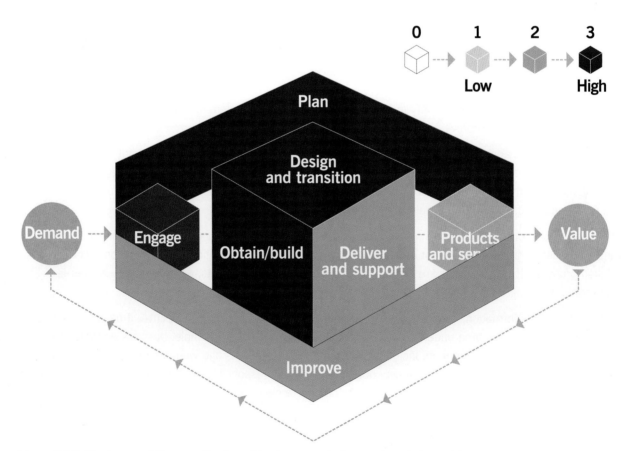

Figure 5.17 Heat map of the contribution of business analysis to value chain activities

5.2.3 Capacity and performance management

 Key message

The purpose of the **capacity and performance management practice** is to ensure that services achieve agreed and expected performance, satisfying current and future demand in a cost-effective way.

 Definition: Performance

A measure of what is achieved or delivered by a system, person, team, practice, or service.

Service performance is usually associated with the number of service actions performed in a timeframe and the time required to fulfil a service action at a given level of demand. Service performance depends on service capacity, which is defined as the maximum throughput that a CI or service can deliver. Specific metrics for capacity and performance depend on the technology and business nature of the service or CI.

The capacity and performance management practice usually deals with service performance and the performance of the supporting resources on which it depends, such as infrastructure, applications, and third-party services. In many organizations, the capacity and performance management practice also covers the capacity and performance of the personnel.

The capacity and performance management practice includes the following activities:

- service performance and capacity analysis:
    - research and monitoring of the current service performance
    - capacity and performance modelling
- service performance and **capacity planning**:
    - capacity requirements analysis
    - demand forecasting and resource planning
    - performance improvement planning.

Service performance is an important aspect of the expectations and requirements of customers and users, and therefore significantly contributes to their satisfaction with the services they use and the value they perceive. Capacity and performance analysis and planning contributes to service planning and building, as well as to ongoing service delivery, evaluation, and improvement. An understanding of capacity and performance models and patterns helps to forecast demand and to deal with incidents and defects.

Figure 5.18 shows the contribution of capacity and performance management to the service value chain, with the practice being involved in all service value chain activities:

- **Plan** Capacity and performance management supports tactical and operational planning with information about actual demand and performance, and with modelling and forecasting tools and methods.

- **Improve** Improvements are identified and driven by performance information provided by this practice.
- **Engage** Customers' and users' expectations are managed and supported by information about performance and capacity constraints and capabilities.
- **Design and transition** Capacity and performance management is essential for product and service design: it helps to ensure that new and changed services are designed for optimum performance, capacity, and scalability.
- **Obtain/build** Capacity and performance management helps to ensure that components and services being obtained or built meet performance needs of the organization.
- **Deliver and support** Services and service components are supported and tested by performance and capacity targets, metrics and measurement, and reporting targets and tools.

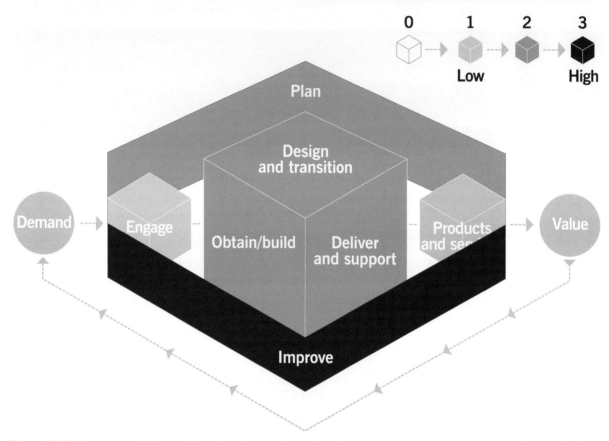

Figure 5.18 Heat map of the contribution of capacity and performance management to value chain activities

5.2.4 Change control

 Key message

The purpose of the **change control practice** is to maximize the number of successful service and product changes by ensuring that risks have been properly assessed, authorizing changes to proceed, and managing the **change schedule**.

Definition: Change

The addition, modification, or removal of anything that could have a direct or indirect effect on services.

The scope of change control is defined by each organization. It will typically include all IT infrastructure, applications, documentation, processes, supplier relationships, and anything else that might directly or indirectly impact a product or service.

It is important to distinguish change control from organizational change management. Organizational change management manages the people aspects of changes to ensure that improvements and organizational transformation initiatives are implemented successfully. Change control is usually focused on changes in products and services.

Change control must balance the need to make beneficial changes that will deliver additional value with the need to protect customers and users from the adverse effect of changes. All changes should be assessed by people who are able to understand the risks and the expected benefits; the changes must then be authorized before they are deployed. This assessment, however, should not introduce unnecessary delay.

The person or group who authorizes a change is known as a **change authority**. It is essential that the correct change authority is assigned to each type of change to ensure that change control is both efficient and effective. In high-velocity organizations, it is a common practice to decentralize change approval, making the peer review a top predictor of high performance.

There are three types of change that are each managed in different ways:

- **Standard changes** These are low-risk, pre-authorized changes that are well understood and fully documented, and can be implemented without needing additional authorization. They are often initiated as service requests, but may also be operational changes. When the procedure for a **standard change** is created or modified, there should be a full risk assessment and authorization as for any other change. This risk assessment does not need to be repeated each time the standard change is implemented; it only needs to be done if there is a modification to the way it is carried out.

- **Normal changes** These are changes that need to be scheduled, assessed, and authorized following a process. **Change model**s based on the type of change determine the roles for assessment and authorization. Some normal changes are low risk, and the change authority for these is usually someone who can make rapid decisions, often using automation to speed up the change. Other normal changes are very major and the change authority could be as high as the management board (or equivalent). Initiation of a normal change is triggered by the creation of a change request. This may be created manually, but organizations that have an automated pipeline for **continuous integration** and continuous deployment often automate most steps of the change control process.

- **Emergency changes** These are changes that must be implemented as soon as possible; for example, to resolve an incident or implement a security patch. **Emergency change**s are not typically included in a change schedule, and the process for assessment and authorization is expedited to ensure they can be implemented quickly. As far as possible, emergency changes should be subject to the same testing, assessment, and authorization as normal changes, but it may be acceptable to defer some documentation until after the change has been implemented, and sometimes it will be necessary to implement the change with less testing due to time constraints. There may also be a separate change authority for emergency changes, typically including a small number of senior managers who understand the business risks involved.

The change schedule is used to help plan changes, assist in communication, avoid conflicts, and assign resources. It can also be used after changes have been deployed to provide information needed for incident management, problem management, and improvement planning. Regardless of who the change authority is, they may need to communicate widely across the organization. Risk assessment, for instance, may require them to gather input from many people with specialist knowledge. Additionally, there is usually a need to communicate information about the change to ensure people are fully prepared before the change is deployed.

Figure 5.19 shows the contribution of change control to the service value chain, with the practice being involved in all value chain activities:

● **Plan** Changes to product and service portfolios, policies, and practices all require a certain level of control, and the change control practice is used to provide it.

● **Improve** Many improvements will require changes to be made, and these should be assessed and authorized in the same way as all other changes.

● **Engage** Customers and users may need to be consulted or informed about changes, depending on the nature of the change.

● **Design and transition** Many changes are initiated as a result of new or changed services. Change control activity is a major contributor to transition.

● **Obtain/build** Changes to components are subject to change control, whether they are built in house or obtained from suppliers.

● **Deliver and support** Changes may have an impact on delivery and support, and information about changes must be communicated to personnel who carry out this value chain activity. These people may also play a part in assessing and authorizing changes.

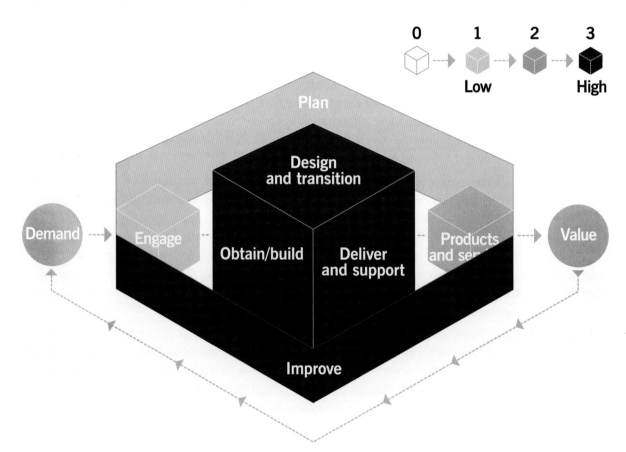

Figure 5.19 Heat map of the contribution of change control to value chain activities

The ITIL story: Change control

 Henri: *The car hire market is developing faster than ever. To make sure that Axle meets customer demands and capitalizes on opportunities, we need to have speed-to-market and to experiment with new ideas. Our new service offerings will see a lot of change at Axle. Some teams will need to double, while others may reduce. We need to bring everyone at Axle on board.*

 Radhika: *The change control practice at Axle makes sure that our services achieve the right balance of flexibility and reliability.*

 Marco: *Some of our processes are highly automated and designed for the fast deployment of changes. These are perfect for changes to our booking app and some of our IT systems.*

 Su: *In other cases, such as when we update our vehicles, we use a mix of manual and automated testing. For example, the Axle Aware road monitoring and safety system requires consultation and approval before we can update it.*

 Marco: *Systems such as Axle Aware can't be altered like the booking app. The priority for those changes is that we act safely and comply with appropriate regulations. That's more important than time to market.*

5.2.5 Incident management

Key message

The purpose of the incident management practice is to minimize the negative impact of incidents by restoring normal service operation as quickly as possible.

Definition: Incident

An unplanned interruption to a service or reduction in the quality of a service.

Incident management can have an enormous impact on customer and user satisfaction, and on how customers and users perceive the service provider. Every incident should be logged and managed to ensure that it is resolved in a time that meets the expectations of the customer and user. Target resolution times are agreed, documented, and communicated to ensure that expectations are realistic. Incidents are prioritized based on an agreed classification to ensure that incidents with the highest business impact are resolved first.

Organizations should design their incident management practice to provide appropriate management and resource allocation to different types of incident. Incidents with a low impact must be managed efficiently to ensure that they do not consume too many resources. Incidents with a larger impact may require more resources and more complex management. There are usually separate processes for managing **major incident**s, and for managing information security incidents.

Information about incidents should be stored in incident records in a suitable tool. Ideally, this tool should also provide links to related CIs, changes, problems, **known error**s, and other knowledge to enable quick and efficient diagnosis and **recovery**. Modern IT service management tools can provide automated matching of incidents to other incidents, problems, or known errors, and can even provide intelligent analysis of incident data to generate recommendations for helping with future incidents.

It is important that people working on an incident provide good-quality updates in a timely fashion. These updates should include information about symptoms, business impact, CIs affected, actions completed, and actions planned. Each of these should have a timestamp and information about the people involved, so that the people involved or interested can be kept informed. There may also be a need for good collaboration tools so that people working on an incident can collaborate effectively.

Incidents may be diagnosed and resolved by people in many different groups, depending on the complexity of the issue or the incident type. All of these groups need to understand the incident management process, and how their contribution to this helps to manage the value, outcomes, costs, and risks of the services provided:

● Some incidents will be resolved by the users themselves, using self-help. Use of specific self-help records should be captured for use in measurement and improvement activities.

● Some incidents will be resolved by the service desk.

● More complex incidents will usually be escalated to a **support team** for **resolution**. Typically, the routing is based on the incident category, which should help to identify the correct team.

● Incidents can be escalated to suppliers or partners, who offer support for their products and services.

● The most complex incidents, and all major incidents, often require a temporary team to work together to identify the resolution. This team may include representatives of many stakeholders, including the service provider, suppliers, users, etc.

● In some extreme cases, **disaster recovery plans** may be invoked to resolve an incident. Disaster recovery is described in the **service continuity management practice** (section 5.2.12).

Effective incident management often requires a high level of collaboration within and between teams. These teams may include the service desk, technical support, application support, and vendors. Collaboration can facilitate information-sharing and learning, as well as helping to solve the incident more efficiently and effectively.

 Tip

Some organizations use a technique called swarming to help manage incidents. This involves many different stakeholders working together initially, until it becomes clear which of them is best placed to continue and which can move on to other tasks.

Third-party products and services that are used as components of a service require support agreements which align the obligations of the supplier with the commitments made by the service provider to customers. Incident management may require frequent interaction with these suppliers, and routine management of this aspect of supplier contracts is often part of the incident management practice. A supplier can also act as a service desk, logging and managing all incidents and escalating them to subject matter experts or other parties as required.

There should be a formal process for logging and managing incidents. This process does not usually include detailed procedures for how to diagnose, investigate, and resolve incidents, but can provide techniques for making investigation and diagnosis more efficient. There may be scripts for collecting information from users during initial contact, and this may lead directly to diagnosis and resolution of simple incidents. Investigation of more complicated incidents often requires knowledge and expertise, rather than procedural steps.

Dealing with incidents is possible in every value chain activity, though the most visible (due to effect on users) are incidents in an operational environment.

Figure 5.20 shows the contribution of incident management to the service value chain, with the practice being applied mainly to the engage, and deliver and support value chain activities. Except for plan, other activities may use information about incidents to help set priorities:

● **Improve** Incident records are a key input to improvement activities, and are prioritized both in terms of incident frequency and severity.

● **Engage** Incidents are visible to users, and significant incidents are also visible to customers. Good incident management requires regular communication to understand the issues, set expectations, provide status updates, and agree that the issue has been resolved so the incident can be closed.

● **Design and transition** Incidents may occur in **test environment**s, as well as during service release and deployment. The practice ensures these incidents are resolved in a timely and controlled manner.

● **Obtain/build** Incidents may occur in **development environment**s. Incident management practice ensures these incidents are resolved in a timely and controlled manner.

● **Deliver and support** Incident management makes a significant contribution to support. This value chain activity includes resolving incidents and problems.

Chapter 5 – ITIL management practices

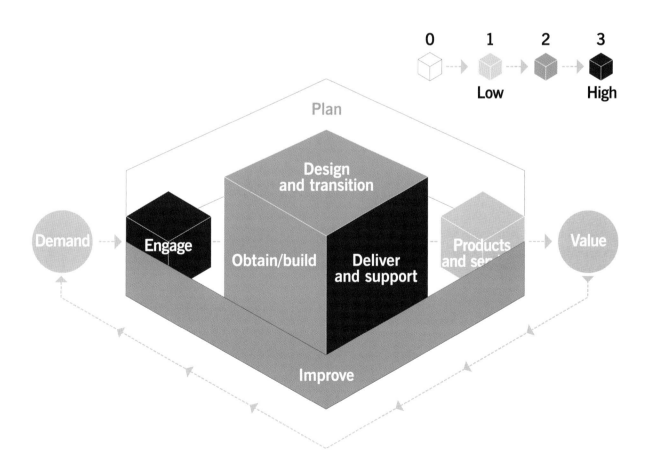

Figure 5.20 Heat map of the contribution of incident management to value chain activities

The ITIL story: Axle's incident management

 Radhika: *Axle faces many potential IT and non-IT incidents. Cars can break down, road accidents might occur, or our customers might face challenges with unfamiliar road rules.*

 Marco: *A car booking can be affected by an error in our app, or by a user getting lost due to a navigation error with our software. When incidents occur, we have to be ready to restore normal services as soon as possible. We also have to make sure our team knows how and when to switch from pre-defined recovery procedures to swarming and collective analysis.*

 Radhika: *We also make sure that such cases are followed by investigation and improvements.*

 Henri: *Axle has developed clear processes for all types of incidents, with workarounds available for cases that happen frequently, such as a tyre puncture or loss of internet connectivity.*

 Radhika: *Our teams work together with our suppliers and partners to ensure fast and effective incident response. We develop and test recovery procedures together with the partners involved in any incidents we experience.*

5.2.6 IT asset management

Key message

The purpose of the **IT asset management practice** is to plan and manage the full lifecycle of all **IT asset**s, to help the organization:

- maximize value
- control costs
- manage risks
- support decision-making about purchase, re-use, retirement, and disposal of assets
- meet regulatory and contractual requirements.

Definition: IT asset

Any financially valuable component that can contribute to the delivery of an IT product or service.

The scope of IT asset management typically includes all software, hardware, networking, cloud services, and client devices. In some cases, it may also include non-IT assets such as buildings or information where these have a financial value and are required to deliver an IT service. IT asset management can include **operational technology** (OT), including devices that are part of the Internet of Things. These are typically devices that were not traditionally thought of as IT assets, but that now include embedded computing capability and network connectivity.

Types of asset management

Asset management is a well-established practice that includes the acquisition, operation, care, and disposal of organizational assets, particularly critical infrastructure.

IT asset management (ITAM) is a sub-practice of asset management that is specifically aimed at managing the lifecycles and total costs of IT equipment and infrastructure.

Software asset management (SAM) is an aspect of IT asset management that is specifically aimed at managing the acquisition, development, release, deployment, maintenance, and eventual retirement of software assets. SAM procedures provide effective management, control, and protection of software assets.

Understanding the cost and value of assets is essential to also comprehending the cost and value of products and services, and is therefore an important underpinning factor in everything the service provider does. IT asset management contributes to the visibility of assets and their value, which is a key element to successful service management as well as being useful to other practices.

IT asset management requires accurate inventory information, which it keeps in an **asset register**. This information can be gathered in an audit, but it is much better to capture it as part of the processes that change the status of assets, for example, when new hardware is delivered, or when a new instance of a cloud service is requested. If IT asset management has good interfaces with other practices, including service configuration management, incident management, change control, and deployment management, then the asset status information can be maintained with less effort. Audits are still needed, but these can be less frequent, and are easier to do when there is already an accurate asset register.

IT asset management helps to optimize the use of valuable resources. For example, the number of spare computers an organization requires can be calculated based on service level agreement commitments, the measured performance of service requests, and demand predictions from capacity and performance management.

Some organizations discover a need for IT asset management after a software vendor requests an audit of licence use. This can be very stressful if the required information has not been maintained, and can lead to significant costs, both in carrying out the audit and then paying any additional licence costs that are identified. It is much cheaper and easier to simply maintain information about software licence use as part of normal IT asset management activity, and to provide this in response to any vendor requests. Software runs on hardware, so the management of software and hardware assets should be combined to ensure that all licences are properly managed. For the same reason, the management of cloud-based assets should also be included.

The cost of cloud services can easily get out of control if the organization does not manage these in the same way as other IT assets. Each individual use of a cloud service may be relatively cheap, but by spending in small amounts it is easy to consume much more resource than was planned, leaving the organization with a correspondingly large bill. Again, good IT asset management can help to control this.

The activities and requirements of IT asset management will vary for different types of asset:

- Hardware assets must be labelled for clear identification. It is important to know where they are and to help protect them from theft, damage, and data leakage. They may need special handling when they are re-used or decommissioned; for example, erasure or shredding of disk drives depends on information security requirements. Hardware assets may also be subject to regulatory requirements, such as the EU Waste Electrical and Electronic Equipment Directive.

- Software assets must be protected from unlawful copying, which could result in unlicensed use. The organization must ensure that licence terms are adhered to and that licences are only re-used in ways that are allowed under the contract. It is important to retain verified proof of purchase and entitlement to run the software. It is very easy to lose software licences when equipment is decommissioned, so it is important that the IT asset management process recovers these licences and makes them available for re-use where appropriate.

- Cloud-based assets must be assigned to specific products or groups so that costs can be managed. Funding must be managed so that the organization has the flexibility to invoke new instances of cloud use when needed, and to remove instances that are not needed, without the risk of uncontrolled costs. Contractual arrangements must be understood and adhered to, in the same way as for software licences.

- Client assets must be assigned to individuals who take responsibility for their care. Processes are needed to manage lost or stolen devices, and tools may be needed to erase sensitive data from them or otherwise ensure that this data is not lost or stolen with the device.

In all cases, the organization needs to ensure that the full lifecycle of each asset is managed. This includes managing asset provisioning; receiving, decommissioning, and return; hardware disposal; software re-use; leasing management; and potentially many other activities.

IT asset management maintains information about the assets, their costs, and related contracts. Therefore, the IT asset register is often combined (or federated) with the information stored in a **configuration management system (CMS)**. If the two are separate then it is important that assets can be mapped between them, usually by use of a standard naming convention. It may also be necessary to combine (or federate) the IT asset register with systems used to manage other financial assets, or with systems used to manage suppliers.

In some organizations there is a centralized team responsible for IT asset management. This team may also be responsible for configuration management. In other organizations, each technical team may be responsible for management of the IT assets they support; for example, the storage team could manage storage assets while the networking team manages network assets. Each organization must consider its own context and culture to choose the appropriate level of centralization. However, having some central roles helps to ensure asset data quality and the development of expertise on specific aspects such as software licensing and inventory systems.

IT asset management typically includes the following activities:

- Define, populate, and maintain the asset register in terms of structure and content, and the storage facilities for assets and related media

- Control the asset lifecycle in collaboration with other practices (for example, upgrading obsolete software or onboarding new staff members with a laptop and mobile phone) and record all changes to assets (status, location, characteristics, assignment, etc.)

- Provide current and historical data, reports, and support to other practices about IT assets

- Audit assets, related media, and conformity (particularly with regulations, and licence terms and conditions) and drive corrective and preventive improvements to deal with detected issues.

Figure 5.21 shows the contribution of IT asset management to the service value chain, with the practice being applied mainly to the design and transition, and obtain/build value chain activities:

- **Plan** Most policies and guidance for IT asset management comes from the service financial management practice. Some asset management policies are driven by governance and some are driven by other practices, such as information security management. IT asset management can be considered a strategic practice that helps the organization to understand and manage cost and value.

- **Improve** This value chain activity must consider the impact on IT assets, and some improvements will directly involve IT asset management in helping to understand and manage costs.

- **Engage** There may be some demand for IT asset management from stakeholders. For example, a user may report a lost or stolen mobile phone, or a customer may require reports on the value of IT assets.

- **Design and transition** This value chain activity changes the status of IT assets, and so drives most IT asset management activity.

- **Obtain/build** IT asset management supports asset procurement to ensure that assets are traceable from the beginning of their lifecycle.

- **Deliver and support** IT asset management helps to locate IT assets, trace their movements, and control their status in the organization.

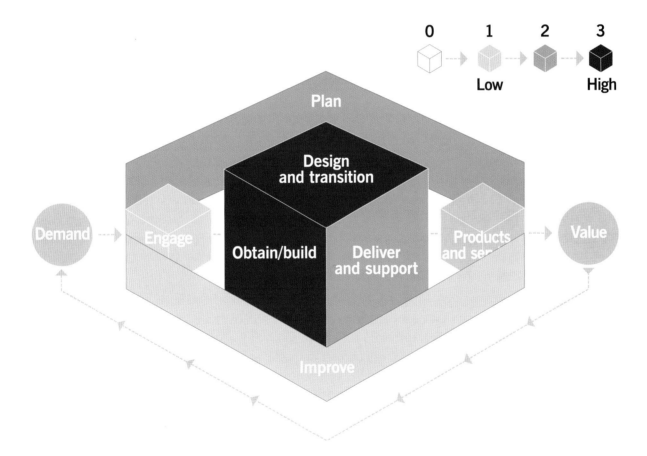

Figure 5.21 Heat map of the contribution of IT asset management to value chain activities

5.2.7 Monitoring and event management

Key message

The purpose of the **monitoring and event management practice** is to systematically observe services and service components, and record and report selected changes of state identified as events. This practice identifies and prioritizes infrastructure, services, business processes, and information security events, and establishes the appropriate response to those events, including responding to conditions that could lead to potential faults or incidents.

Definition: Event

Any change of state that has significance for the management of a service or other configuration item (CI). Events are typically recognized through notifications created by an IT service, CI, or monitoring tool.

The monitoring and event management practice manages events throughout their lifecycle to prevent, minimize, or eliminate their negative impact on the business.

The monitoring part of the practice focuses on the systematic observation of services and the CIs that underpin services to detect conditions of potential significance. Monitoring should be performed in a highly automated manner, and can be done actively or passively. The event management part focuses on recording and managing those monitored changes of state that are defined by the organization as an event, determining their significance, and identifying and initiating the correct control action to manage them. Frequently the correct control action will be to initiate another practice, but sometimes it will be to take no action other than to continue monitoring the situation. Monitoring is necessary for event management to take place, but not all monitoring results in the detection of an event.

Not all events have the same significance or require the same response. Events are often classified as informational, warning, and exceptions. Informational events do not require action at the time they are identified, but analysing the data gathered from them at a later date may uncover desirable, proactive steps that can be beneficial to the service. Warning events allow action to be taken before any negative impact is actually experienced by the business, whereas exception events indicate that a breach to an established norm has been identified (for example, to a service level agreement). Exception events require action, even though business impact may not yet have been experienced.

The processes and procedures needed in the monitoring and event management practice must address these key activities and more:

- identifying what services, systems, CIs, or other service components should be monitored, and establishing the monitoring strategy
- implementing and maintaining monitoring, leveraging both the native monitoring features of the elements being observed as well as the use of designed-for-purpose monitoring tools

- establishing and maintaining thresholds and other criteria for determining which changes of state will be treated as events, and choosing criteria to define each type of event (informational, warning, or exception)
- establishing and maintaining policies for how each type of detected event should be handled to ensure proper management
- implementing processes and automations required to operationalize the defined thresholds, criteria, and policies.

This practice is highly interactive with other practices participating in the service value chain. For example, some events will indicate a current issue that qualifies as an incident. In this case, the correct control action will be to initiate activity in the incident management practice. Repeated events showing performance outside of desired levels may be evidence of a potential problem, which would initiate activity in the problem management practice. For some events, the correct response is to initiate a change, engaging the change control practice.

Although the work of this practice, once put in place, is highly automated, human intervention is still required, and is in fact essential. For the definition of monitoring strategies and specific thresholds and assessment criteria, it can help to bring in a broad range of perspectives, including infrastructure, applications, **service owner**s, service level management, and representation from the warranty-related practices. Remember that the starting point for this practice is likely to be simple, setting the stage for a later increase in complexity, so it is important that the expectations of participants are managed.

Organizations and people are also critical to providing an appropriate response to monitored data and events, in alignment with policies and organizational priorities. Roles and responsibilities must be clearly defined, and each person or group must have easy, timely access to the information needed to perform their role.

Automation is key to successful monitoring and event management. Some service components come equipped with built-in monitoring and reporting capabilities that can be configured to meet the needs of the practice, but sometimes it is necessary to implement and configure purpose-built monitoring tools. The monitoring itself can be either active or passive. In active monitoring, tools will poll key CIs, looking at their status to generate alerts when an exception condition is identified. In passive monitoring, the CI itself generates the operational alerts.

Automated tools should also be used for the correlation of events. These features may be provided by monitoring tools or other tools such as ITSM workflow systems. There can be a huge volume of data generated by this practice, but without clear policies and strategies on how to limit, filter, and use this data, it will be of no value.

If third parties are providing products or services in the overall service architecture, they should also supply expertise in the monitoring and reporting capabilities of their offerings. Leveraging this expertise can save time when trying to operationalize monitoring and event management strategies and workflows. If some IT functions, such as infrastructure management, are partially or wholly outsourced to a supplier, they may be reluctant to expose monitoring or event data related to the elements they manage. Don't ask for data that is not truly needed, but if data is required, make sure that the provision of that data is explicitly part of the contract for the supplier's services.

Figure 5.22 shows the contribution of monitoring and event management to the service value chain, with the practice being involved in all value chain activities except plan:

- **Improve** The monitoring and event management practice is essential to the close observation of the environment to evaluate and proactively improve its health and stability.
- **Engage** Monitoring and event management may be the source of internal engagement for action.
- **Design and transition** Monitoring data informs design decisions. Monitoring is an essential component of transition: it provides information about the transition success in all environments.
- **Obtain/build** Monitoring and event management supports development environments, ensuring their transparency and manageability.
- **Deliver and support** The practice guides how the organization manages internal support of identified events, initiating other practices as appropriate.

129

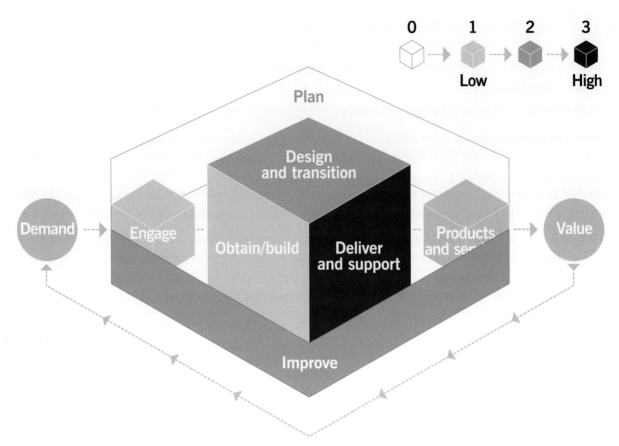

Figure 5.22 Heat map of the contribution of monitoring and event management to value chain activities

5.2.8 Problem management

Key message

The purpose of the problem management practice is to reduce the likelihood and impact of incidents by identifying actual and potential causes of incidents, and managing workarounds and known errors.

Definitions

- **Problem** A cause, or potential cause, of one or more incidents.
- **Known error** A problem that has been analysed but has not been resolved.

Figure 5.23 The phases of problem management

Every service has errors, flaws, or vulnerabilities that may cause incidents. They may include errors in any of the four dimensions of service management. Many errors are identified and resolved before a service goes live. However, some remain unidentified or unresolved, and may be a risk to live services. In ITIL, these errors are called problems and they are addressed by the problem management practice.

Problems are related to incidents, but should be distinguished as they are managed in different ways:

● Incidents have an impact on users or business processes, and must be resolved so that normal business activity can take place.

● Problems are the causes of incidents. They require investigation and analysis to identify the causes, develop workarounds, and recommend longer-term resolution. This reduces the number and impact of future incidents.

Problem management involves three distinct phases, as shown in Figure 5.23.

Problem identification activities identify and log problems. These include:

● performing trend analysis of incident records

● detection of duplicate and recurring issues by users, service desk, and technical support staff

● during major incident management, identifying a risk that an incident could recur

● analysing information received from suppliers and partners

● analysing information received from internal software developers, test teams, and project teams.

Other sources of information can also lead to problems being identified.

Problem control activities include problem analysis, and documenting workarounds and known errors.

Problems are prioritized for analysis based on the risk that they pose, and are managed as risks based on their potential impact and probability. It is not essential to analyse every problem; it is more valuable to make significant progress on the highest-priority problems than to investigate every minor problem that the organization is aware of.

Incidents typically have many interrelated causes, and the relationships between them can be complex. Problem control should consider all contributory causes, including causes that contributed to the duration and impact of incidents, as well as those that led to the incidents happening. It is important to analyse problems from the perspective of all four dimensions of service management. For example, an incident that was caused by inaccurate documentation may require not only a correction to that documentation but also training and awareness for support personnel, suppliers, and users.

When a problem cannot be resolved quickly, it is often useful to find and document a workaround for future incidents, based on an understanding of the problem. Workarounds are documented in problem records. This can be done at any stage; it doesn't need to wait for analysis to be complete. If a workaround has been documented early in problem control, then this should be reviewed and improved after problem analysis has been completed.

Definition: Workaround

A solution that reduces or eliminates the impact of an incident or problem for which a full resolution is not yet available. Some workarounds reduce the likelihood of incidents.

An effective incident workaround can become a permanent way of dealing with some problems when resolving the problem is not viable or cost-effective. In this case, the problem remains in the known error status, and the documented workaround is applied should related incidents occur. Every documented workaround should include a clear definition of the symptoms to which it applies. In some cases, workaround application can be automated.

For other problems, a way to fix the error should be found. This is a part of **error control**. Error control activities manage known errors, which are problems where initial analysis has been completed; it usually means that faulty components have been identified. Error control also includes identification of potential permanent solutions which may result in a change request for implementation of a solution, but only if this can be justified in terms of cost, risks, and benefits.

Error control regularly re-assesses the status of known errors that have not been resolved, including overall impact on customers, availability and cost of permanent resolutions, and effectiveness of workarounds. The effectiveness of workarounds should be evaluated each time a workaround is used, as the workaround may be improved based on the assessment.

Problem management activities are very closely related to incident management. The practices need to be designed to work together within the value chain. Activities from these two practices may complement each other (for example, identifying the causes of an incident is a problem management activity that may lead to incident resolution), but they may also conflict (for example, investigating the cause of an incident may delay actions needed to restore service).

Examples of interfaces between problem management, risk management, change control, knowledge management, and continual improvement are as follows:

- Problem management activities can be organized as a specific case of risk management: they aim to identify, assess, and control risks in any of the four dimensions of service management. It is useful to adopt risk management tools and techniques for problem management.

- Implementation of problem resolution is often outside the scope of problem management. Problem management typically initiates resolution via change control and participates in the **post-implementation review**; however, approving and implementing changes is out of scope for the problem management practice.

- Output from the problem management practice includes information and documentation concerning workarounds and known errors. In addition, problem management may utilize information in a knowledge management system to investigate, diagnose, and resolve problems.

- Problem management activities can identify improvement opportunities in all four dimensions of service management. Solutions can in some cases be treated as improvement opportunities, so they are included in a continual improvement register (CIR), and continual improvement techniques are used to prioritize and manage them, sometimes as part of a product backlog.

Many problem management activities rely on the knowledge and experience of staff, rather than on following detailed procedures. People responsible for diagnosing problems often need the ability to understand complex systems, and to think about how different failures might have occurred. Developing this combination of analytical and creative ability requires mentoring and time, as well as suitable training.

The ITIL story: Axle's problem management

Henri: *Axle participates in feedback programmes with all our car manufacturers. We share maintenance and repair data with them to help them to continually improve their services. In return, they alert us to any potential problems in our vehicles.*

Radhika: *Recently, we were alerted to a potential problem in our fleet. A car manufacturer had recalled a popular model in our fleet to fix an error found in the airbag activation system.*

Su: *Fortunately it was found before Axle experienced any incidents, but there was still the potential for issues to occur, which meant it was a problem we had to deal with.*

Marco: *We follow a similar practice for our other systems and services, including all of the IT components we use.*

Radhika: *Axle's incident management practice is one of our most important sources of information on errors in our systems. Any major incident we experience is followed by an investigation into the possible causes. Sometimes this will lead us to find and fix errors in the systems, and we often identify ways to decrease the number of incidents Axle will have in the future.*

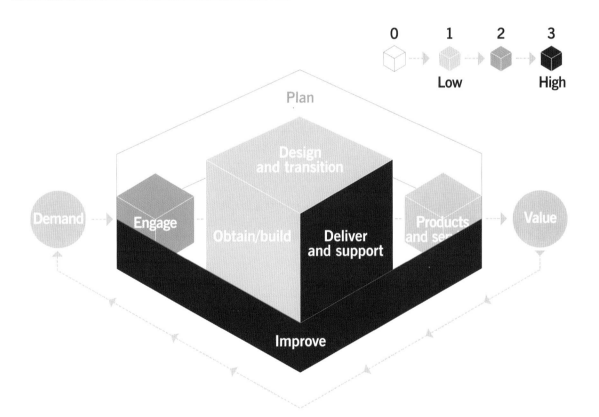

Figure 5.24 Heat map of the contribution of problem management to value chain activities

Problem management is usually focused on errors in operational environments. Figure 5.24 shows the contribution of problem management to the service value chain, with the practice being applied mainly to the improve, and deliver and support value chain activities:

- **Improve** This is the main focus area for problem management. Effective problem management provides the understanding needed to reduce the number of incidents and the impact of incidents that can't be prevented.
- **Engage** Problems that have a significant impact on services will be visible to customers and users. In some cases, customers may wish to be involved in problem prioritization, and the status and plans for managing problems should be communicated. Workarounds are often presented to users via a service portal.
- **Design and transition** Problem management provides information that helps to improve testing and knowledge transfer.
- **Obtain/build** Product defects may be identified by problem management; these are then managed as part of this value chain activity.
- **Deliver and support** Problem management makes a significant contribution by preventing incident repetition and supporting timely incident resolution.

5.2.9 Release management

Key message

The purpose of the **release management practice** is to make new and changed services and features available for use.

Definition: Release

A version of a service or other configuration item, or a collection of configuration items, that is made available for use.

A release may comprise many different infrastructure and application components that work together to deliver new or changed functionality. It may also include documentation, training (for users or IT staff), updated processes or tools, and any other components that are required. Each component of a release may be developed by the service provider or procured from a third party and integrated by the service provider.

Releases can range in size from the very small, involving just one minor changed feature, to the very large, involving many components that deliver a completely new service. In either case, a release plan will specify the exact combination of new and changed components to be made available, and the timing for their release.

A release schedule is used to document the timing for releases. This schedule should be negotiated and agreed with customers and other stakeholders. A release post-implementation review enables learning and improvement, and helps to ensure that customers are satisfied.

In some environments, almost all of the release management work takes place before deployment, with plans in place as to exactly which components will be deployed in a particular release. The deployment then makes the new functionality available.

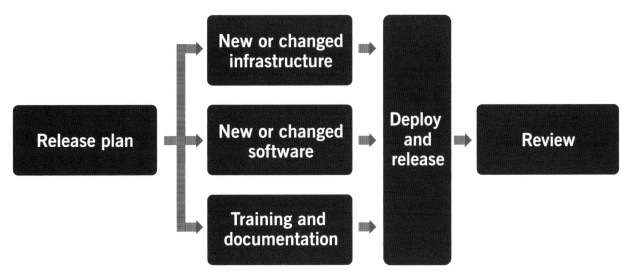

Figure 5.25 Release management in a traditional/waterfall environment

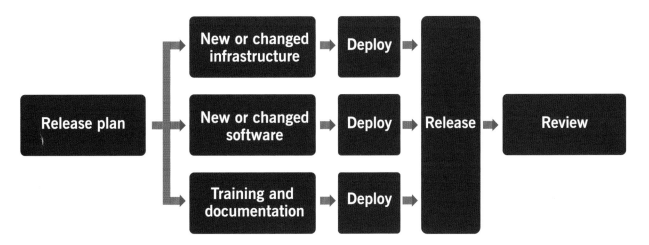

Figure 5.26 Release management in an Agile/DevOps environment

Figure 5.25 shows how release management is handled in a traditional/waterfall environment. In these environments release management and deployment may be combined and executed as a single process.

In an Agile/DevOps environment there can be significant release management activity after deployment. In these cases, software and infrastructure are typically deployed in many small increments, and release management activity enables the new functionality at a later point. This may be done as a very small change. Figure 5.26 shows how release management is handled in such an environment.

Release management is often staged, with pilot releases being made available to a small number of users to ensure that everything is working correctly before the release is given to additional groups. This staged approach can work with either of the two sequences shown in Figures 5.25 and 5.26. Sometimes a release must be made available to all users at the same time, as when a major restructuring of the underlying shared data is required.

Staging of a release is often achieved using blue/green releases or feature flags:

● Blue/green releases use two mirrored **production environment**s. Users can be switched to an environment that has been updated with the new functionality by use of network tools that connect them to the correct environment.

135

● Feature flags enable specific features to be released to individual users or groups in a controlled way. The new functionality is deployed to the production environment without being released. A user configuration setting then releases the new functionality to individual users (or groups of users) as needed.

In a DevOps environment, release management is often integrated with the continuous integration and continuous delivery toolchain. The tools of release management may be the responsibility of a dedicated person, but decisions about the release can be made by the development team. In a more traditional environment, releases are enabled by the deployment of the components. Each release is described by a release record on an ITSM tool. Release records are linked to CIs and change records to maintain information about the release.

Components of a release are often provided by third parties. Examples of third-party components include cloud infrastructure, software as a service components, and third-party support. It is also common to include third-party software, or open-source software, as part of application development. Release management needs to work across organizational boundaries to ensure that all components are compatible and to provide a seamless experience for users. It also needs to consider the impact of changes to third-party components, and to plan for how these will be released.

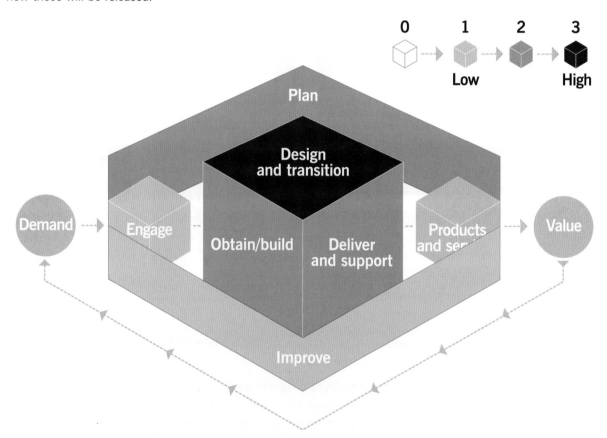

Figure 5.27 Heat map of the contribution of release management to value chain activities

Figure 5.27 shows the contribution of release management to the service value chain, with the practice being involved in all value chain activities:

● **Plan** Policies, guidance, and timelines for releases are driven by the organizational strategy and service portfolio. The size, scope, and content of each release should be planned and managed.

● **Improve** New or changed releases may be required to deliver improvements, and these should be planned and managed in the same way as any other release.

● **Engage** The content and cadence of releases must be designed to match the needs and expectations of customers and users.

- **Design and transition** Release management ensures that new or changed services are made available to customers in a controlled way.
- **Obtain/build** Changes to components are normally included in a release, delivered in a controlled way.
- **Deliver and support** Releases may impact on delivery and support. Training, documentation, release notes, known errors, user guides, support scripts, etc. are provided by this practice to facilitate service restoration.

The ITIL story: Axle's release management

 Marco: *When we release updates to our booking app, we make sure they're accompanied by user awareness and marketing campaigns for our users, customers, and teams. We provide specific training for the service desk and support teams that are internal and external.*

 Radhika: *Some changes may need extra support or the introduction of new components. For example, Axle Aware was released with a new user manual to explain the system. We also made sure the Aware system could sync with the Axle booking app before we released it.*

 Henri: *The support given to the new app and Axle Aware has really helped the release of both of these new offerings, leading to great first impressions and a strong level of adoption amongst our users and customers, as well as our own teams.*

5.2.10 Service catalogue management

 Key message

The purpose of the **service catalogue management practice** is to provide a single source of consistent information on all services and service offerings, and to ensure that it is available to the relevant audience.

The list of services within the service catalogue represents those which are currently available and is a subset of the total list of services tracked in the service provider's service portfolio. Service catalogue management ensures that service and product descriptions are expressed clearly for the target audience to support stakeholder engagement and service delivery. The service catalogue may take many forms such as a document, online portal, or a tool that enables the current list of services to be communicated to the audience.

5.2.10.1 Service catalogue management activities

The service catalogue management practice includes an ongoing set of activities related to publishing, editing, and maintaining service and product descriptions and their related offerings. It provides a view on the scope of what services are available, and on what terms. The service catalogue management practice is supported by roles such as the service owner and others responsible for managing, editing, and keeping up to date the list of available services as they are introduced, changed, or retired.

Tailored views

As described above, the service catalogue enables the creation of value and is used by many different practices within the service value chain. Because of this, it needs to be flexible regarding what service details and attributes it presents, based on its intended purpose. As such, organizations may wish to consider providing different views of the catalogue for different audiences.

The full list of services within a service catalogue may not be applicable to all customers and/or users. Likewise, the various attributes of services such as technical specifications, offerings, agreements, and costs are not applicable to all service consumer types. This means that the service catalogue should be able to provide different views and levels of detail to different stakeholders. Examples of views include:

● **User views** Provide information on service offerings that can be requested, and on provisioning details.

● **Customer views** Provide service level, financial, and service performance data.

● **IT to IT customer views** Provide technical, security, and process information for use in service delivery.

While multiple views of the service catalogue are possible, the creation of separate or isolated service catalogues within different technology systems should be avoided if possible as this will promote segregation, variability, and complexity.

For the service catalogue to be perceived as useful by the customer organization it must do more than provide a static platform for publishing information about IT services. Unless the service catalogue enables customer engagement by supporting discussions related to standard and non-standard service offerings and/or automates request and order fulfilment processes, the chances of its ongoing adoption as a useful and meaningful resource are minimal. For this reason, the views of many organizations on the service catalogue are focused on the consumable or orderable elements of service offerings. These are often called **request catalogue**s.

Definition: Request catalogue

A view of the service catalogue, providing details on service requests for existing and new services, which is made available for the user.

Figure 5.28 shows the contribution of service catalogue management to the service value chain, with the practice being involved in all value chain activities:

● **Plan** The service catalogue enables strategy and service portfolio investment decisions by providing details on current service scope and offerings.

● **Improve** Service catalogue descriptions and demand patterns are constantly monitored and evaluated to support continual improvement, alignment, and value creation.

● **Engage** The service catalogue enables strategic, tactical, and operational relationships with customers and users by enabling and potentially automating various aspects of practices such as relationship management, request management, and the service desk.

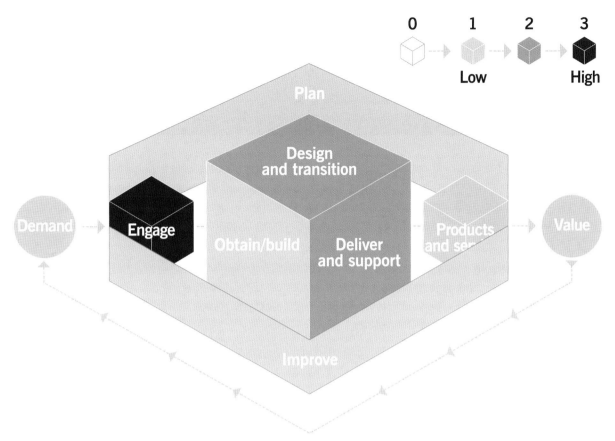

0 1 2 3

Low High

Figure 5.28 Heat map of the contribution of service catalogue management to value chain activities

- **Design and transition** The service catalogue ensures both the utility and warranty aspects of services are considered and published, including the **information security policy**, IT service continuity levels, service level agreements, and service offerings. Additional activities include the definition and creation of service descriptions, request models, and views to be published.
- **Obtain/build** Service catalogue management supports this value chain activity by providing service catalogue views for procurement of components and services.
- **Deliver and support** The service catalogue provides context for how the service will be delivered and supported, and publishes expectations related to agreements and performance.

5.2.11 Service configuration management

 Key message

The purpose of the **service configuration management practice** is to ensure that accurate and reliable information about the configuration of services, and the CIs that support them, is available when and where it is needed. This includes information on how CIs are configured and the relationships between them.

Definition: Configuration item

Any component that needs to be managed in order to deliver an IT service.

Service configuration management collects and manages information about a wide variety of CIs, typically including hardware, software, networks, buildings, people, suppliers, and documentation. Services are also treated as CIs, and configuration management helps the organization to understand how the many CIs that contribute to each service work together. Figure 5.29 is a simplified diagram showing how multiple CIs contribute to an IT service.

Configuration management provides information on the CIs that contribute to each service and their relationships: how they interact, relate, and depend on each other to create value for customers and users. This includes information about dependencies between services. This high-level view is often called a service map or service model, and forms part of the service architecture.

It is important that the effort needed to collect and maintain configuration information is balanced with the value that the information creates. Maintaining large amounts of detailed information about every component, and its relationships to other components, can be costly, and may deliver very little value. The requirements for configuration management must be based on an understanding of the organization's goals, and how configuration management contributes to value creation.

The value created by configuration management is indirect, but enables many other practices to work efficiently and effectively. As such, planning for configuration management should start by understanding who needs the configuration information, how it will be used, what is the best way for them to obtain it, and who can maintain and update this information. Sometimes it can be more efficient to simply collect the information when it is

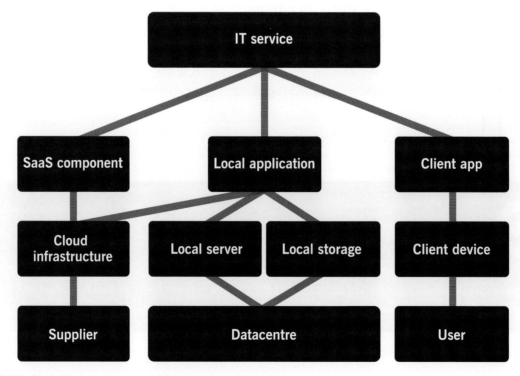

Figure 5.29 Simplified service model for a typical IT service

needed, rather than to have it collected in advance and maintained, but on other occasions it is essential to have information available in a configuration management system (CMS). The type and amount of information recorded for each type of CI should be based on the value of that information, the cost of maintaining it, and how the information will be used.

Definition: Configuration management system

A set of tools, data, and information that is used to support service configuration management.

Configuration information should be shared in a controlled way. Some information could be sensitive; for example, it could be useful to someone trying to breach security controls, or it could include personal information about users, such as phone numbers and home addresses.

Configuration information can be stored and published in a single configuration management database (CMDB) for the whole organization, but it is more common for it to be distributed across several sources. In either case it is important to maintain links between **configuration record**s, so that people can see the full set of information they need, and how the various CIs work together. Some organizations federate CMDBs to provide an integrated view. Others may maintain different types of data; for example, having separate data stores for asset management data (see section 5.2.6), configuration details, service catalogue information, and high-level service models.

Tools that are used to log incidents, problems, and changes need access to configuration records. For example, an organization trying to identify problems with a service may need to find incidents related to a specific software version, or model of disk drive. The understanding of the need for this information helps to establish what CI attributes should be stored for this organization; in this case software versions and disk drive models. To diagnose incidents, visibility of recent changes to the affected CIs may be needed, so relationships between CIs and changes must be maintained.

Many organizations use data collection tools to gather detailed configuration information from infrastructure and applications, and use this to populate a CMS. This can be effective, but can also encourage the collection of too much data without sufficient information on relationships, and how the components work together to create a service. Sometimes configuration information is used to actually create the CI, rather than just to document it. This approach is used for 'infrastructure as a code', where information on the infrastructure is managed in a data repository and used to automatically configure the environment.

A large organization may have a team that is dedicated to configuration management. In other organizations this practice can be combined with change control, or there can be a team responsible for change, configuration, and release management. Some organizations apply a distributed model where functional teams take ownership of updating and maintaining the CIs within their control and oversight.

Configuration management typically needs processes to:

● identify new CIs, and add them to the CMS

● update configuration data when changes are deployed

● verify that configuration records are correct

● audit applications and infrastructure to identify any that are not documented.

Figure 5.30 shows the contribution of configuration management to the service value chain, with the practice being involved in all value chain activities:

- **Plan** Configuration management is used for planning new or changed services.
- **Improve** Configuration management, like every other aspect of service management, should be subject to measurement and continual improvement. Since the value of configuration management typically comes from how it facilitates other practices, it is important to understand what use these practices are making of configuration information, and then identify how this can be improved.
- **Engage** Some stakeholders (partners and suppliers, consumers, regulators, etc.) may require and use configuration information, or provide their configuration information to the organization.
- **Design and transition** Configuration management documents how assets work together to create a service. This information is used to support many value chain activities, and is updated as part of the transition activity.
- **Obtain/build** Configuration records may be created during this value chain activity, describing new or changed services and components. Sometimes configuration records are used to create the code or artefact that is being built.
- **Deliver and support** Information on CIs is essential to support service restoration. Configuration information is used to support activities of the incident management and problem management practices.

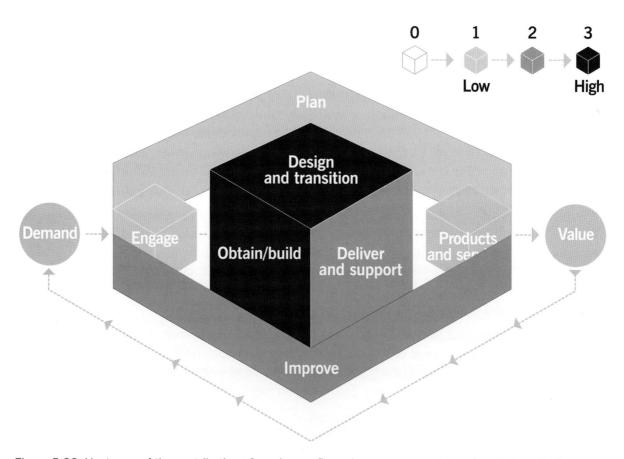

Figure 5.30 Heat map of the contribution of service configuration management to value chain activities

5.2.12 Service continuity management

Key message

The purpose of the service continuity management practice is to ensure that the availability and performance of a service are maintained at sufficient levels in case of a **disaster**. The practice provides a framework for building organizational resilience with the capability of producing an effective response that safeguards the interests of key stakeholders and the organization's reputation, brand, and value-creating activities.

Service continuity management supports an overall business continuity management (BCM) and planning capability by ensuring that IT and services can be resumed within required and agreed business timescales following a disaster or crisis. It is triggered when a service disruption or organizational risk occurs on a scale that is greater than the organization's ability to handle it with normal response and recovery practices such as incident and major incident management. An organizational event of this magnitude is typically referred to as a disaster.

Each organization needs to understand what constitutes a disaster in its own context. Establishing what is meant by a disaster must be considered and defined prior to a trigger event at both an organizational and on a per-service level using a **business impact analysis**. The Business Continuity Institute defines a disaster as:

> …a sudden unplanned event that causes great damage or serious loss to an organization. It results in an organization failing to provide critical business functions for some predetermined minimum period of time.

The sources that trigger a disaster response and recovery are varied and complex, as are the number of stakeholders and the different aspects of potential organizational impact. The complex risk management conditions related to the examples in Table 5.3 make it imperative that the service continuity management practice be thoroughly thought out, designed for flexibility, and tested on a regular basis to ensure that services can be recovered at a speed necessary for business survival.

Table 5.3 Examples of disaster sources, stakeholders involved, and organizational impact

Disaster sources	Stakeholders involved	Organizational impact
Supply chain failure	Employees	Lost income
Terrorism	Executives	Damaged reputation
Weather	Governing body	Loss of competitive advantage
Cyber attack	Suppliers	Breach of law, health and safety regulations
Health emergency	IT teams	Risk to personal safety
Political or economic event	Customers	Immediate and long-term loss of market share
Technology failure	Users	
Public crisis	Communities	

Definitions

- **Recovery time objective (RTO)** The maximum acceptable period of time following a service disruption that can elapse before the lack of business functionality severely impacts the organization. This represents the maximum agreed time within which a product or an activity must be resumed, or resources must be recovered.

- **Recovery point objective (RPO)** The point to which information used by an activity must be restored to enable the activity to operate on resumption.

- **Disaster recovery plans** A set of clearly defined plans related to how an organization will recover from a disaster as well as return to a pre-disaster condition, considering the four dimensions of service management.

- **Business impact analysis (BIA)** A key activity in the practice of service continuity management that identifies vital business functions (VBFs) and their dependencies. These dependencies may include suppliers, people, other business processes, and IT services. BIA defines the recovery requirements for IT services. These requirements include RTOs, RPOs, and minimum target service levels for each IT service.

Service continuity management versus incident management

Service continuity management focuses on those events that the business considers significant enough to be treated as a disaster. Less significant events will be dealt with as part of incident management or major incident management. The distinction between disasters, major incidents, and incidents needs to be pre-defined, agreed, and documented with clear thresholds and triggers for calling the next tier of response and recovery into action without unnecessary delay and risk.

As organizations have become increasingly dependent on technology-enabled services, the need for high-availability solutions has become critical to organizational resilience and competitiveness. Organizations achieve high availability through a combination of business planning, technical architecture resilience, availability planning, proactive risk, and information security management, as well as through incident management and problem management.

Figure 5.31 shows the contribution of service continuity management to the service value chain, with the practice being involved in all value chain activities:

- **Plan** The organization's leadership and governing body establish an initial risk appetite for the organization with defined scope, policies, supplier strategies, and investment in recovery options. Service continuity management supports this with relevant information about the current continuity status of the organization and with tools and methods for planning and forecasting.

- **Improve** Service continuity management ensures that continuity plans, measures, and mechanisms are continually monitored and improved in line with changing internal and external circumstances.

- **Engage** Engagement with various stakeholders to provide assurance with regard to an organization's readiness for disasters is supported by this practice.

- **Design and transition** Service continuity management ensures that products and services are designed and tested according to the organization's continuity requirements.

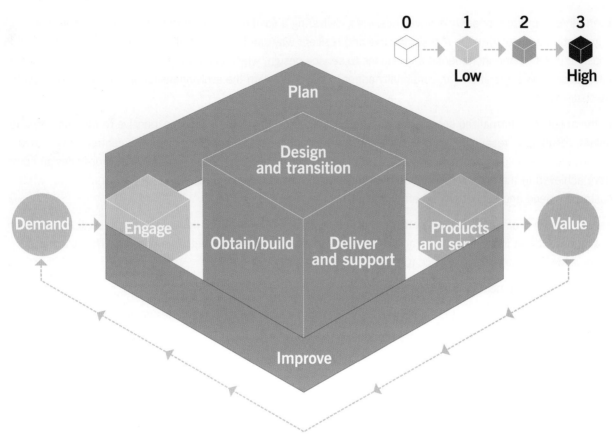

Figure 5.31 Heat map of the contribution of service continuity management to value chain activities

- **Obtain/build** Service continuity management ensures that continuity is built into the organization's services and components, and that procured components and services meet the organization's continuity requirements.

- **Deliver and support** Ongoing delivery, operations, and support are performed in accordance with continuity requirements and policies.

5.2.13 Service design

 Key message

The purpose of the **service design practice** is to design products and services that are fit for purpose, fit for use, and that can be delivered by the organization and its ecosystem. This includes planning and organizing people, partners and suppliers, information, communication, technology, and practices for new or changed products and services, and the interaction between the organization and its customers.

If products, services, or practices are not designed properly, they will not necessarily fulfil customer needs or facilitate value creation. If they evolve without proper architecture, interfaces or controls, they are less able to deliver the overall vision and needs of the organization and its internal and external customers.

Even when a product or service is well designed, delivering a solution that addresses the needs of both the organization and customer in a cost-effective and resilient way can be difficult. It is therefore important to consider iterative and incremental approaches to service design, which can ensure that products and services introduced to live operation can continually adapt in alignment with the evolving needs of the organization and its customers.

In the absence of formalized service design, products and services can be unduly expensive to run and prone to failure, resulting in resources being wasted and the product or service not being customer-centred or designed holistically. It is unlikely that any improvement programme will ever be able to achieve what proper design could have achieved in the first place. Without service design, cost-effective products and services that deliver what customers need and expect are extremely hard to achieve.

Service design practice should also ensure that the customer's journey from demand through to value realization is as pleasant and frictionless as it can be, and delivers the best customer outcome possible. This is achieved by focusing on customer experience (CX) and user experience (UX).

Adopting and implementing a service design practice focused on CX and UX will:

● result in customer-centred products and services that include stakeholders in design activities
● consider the entire environment of a product or service
● enable projects to estimate the cost, timing, resource requirement, and risks associated with service design more accurately
● result in higher volumes of successful change
● make design methods easier for people to adopt and follow
● enable service design assets to be shared and re-used across projects and services
● increase confidence that the new or changed product or service can be delivered to specification without unexpectedly affecting other products, services, or stakeholders
● ensure that new or changed products and services will be maintainable and cost-effective.

It is important that a holistic, results-driven approach to all aspects of service design is adopted, and that when changing or amending any of the individual elements of a service design, all other aspects are considered. It is for this reason that the coordination aspect of service design with the whole organization's SVS is essential. Designing and developing a new or changed product or service should not be done in isolation, but should consider the impact it will have on:

● other products and services
● all relevant parties, including customers and suppliers
● the existing architectures
● the required technology
● the service management practices
● the necessary measurements and metrics.

Consideration of these factors will not only ensure that the design addresses the functional elements of the service, but also that the management and operational requirements are regarded as a fundamental part of the design, and are not added as an afterthought.

Service design should also be used when the change being made to the product or service is its retirement. Unless the retirement of a product/service is carefully planned, it could cause unexpected negative effects on customers or the organization that might otherwise have been avoided.

Not every change to a product or service will require the same level of service design activity. Every change, no matter how small, will need some degree of design work, but the scale of the activity necessary to ensure success will vary greatly from one change type to another. Organizations must define what level of design activity is required for each category of change, and ensure that everyone within the organization is clear on these criteria.

Service design supports products and services that:

● are business- and customer-oriented, focused, and driven

● are cost-effective

● meet the information and physical security requirements of the organization and any external customers

● are flexible and adaptable, yet fit for purpose at the point of delivery

● can absorb an ever-increasing demand in the volume and speed of change

● meet increasing organizational and customer demands for continuous operation

● are managed and operated to an acceptable level of risk.

With many pressures on the organization, there can be a temptation to 'cut corners' on the coordination of practices and relevant parties for service design activities, or to ignore them completely. This should be avoided, as integration and coordination are essential to the overall quality of the products and services that are delivered.

5.2.13.1 Design thinking

Design thinking is a practical and human-centred approach that accelerates innovation. It is used by product and service designers as well as organizations to solve complex problems and find practical, creative solutions that meet the needs of the organization and its customers. It can be viewed as a complementary approach to Lean and Agile methodologies. Design thinking draws upon logic, imagination, intuition, and systems thinking to explore possibilities and to create desired outcomes that benefit customers.

Design thinking includes a series of activities:

● Inspiration and empathy, through direct observation of people and how they work or interact with products and services, as well as identifying how they might interact differently with other solutions.

● Ideation, which combines divergent and convergent thinking. Divergent thinking is the ability to offer different, unique, or variant ideas, while convergent thinking is the ability to find the preferred solution to a given problem. Divergent thinking ensures that many possible solutions are explored, and convergent thinking narrows these down to a final preferred solution.

● Prototyping, where these ideas are tested early, iterated, and refined. A prototype helps to gather feedback and improve an idea. Prototypes speed up the process of innovation by allowing service designers to better understand the strengths and weaknesses of new solutions.

● Implementation, where the concepts are brought to life. This should be coordinated with all relevant service management practices and other parties. Agile methodology can be employed to develop and implement the solution in an iterative way.

● Evaluation (in conjunction with other practices, including project management and release management) measures the actual performance of product or service implementation to ensure acceptance criteria are met, and to find any opportunities for improvement.

Design thinking is best applied by multi-disciplinary teams; because it balances the perspectives of customers, technology, the organization, partners, and suppliers, it is highly integrative, aligns well with the organization's SVS, and can be a key enabler of digital transformation.

5.2.13.2 Customer and user experience

The CX and UX aspects of service design are essential to ensuring products and services deliver the desired value for customers and the organization. CX design is focused on managing every aspect of the complete CX, including time, quality, cost, reliability, and effectiveness. UX looks specifically at the ease of use of the product or service and how the customer interacts with it.

Lean user experience

Lean user experience (Lean UX) design is a mindset, a culture, and a process that embraces Lean–Agile methods. It implements functionality in minimum viable increments, and determines success by measuring results against an outcome hypothesis. Lean UX is incredibly useful when working on projects where Agile development methods are used. The core objective is to focus on obtaining feedback as early as possible so that it can be used to make quick decisions.

Typical questions for Lean UX might include: Who are the customers of this product/service and what will it be used for? When is it used and under what circumstances? What will be the most important functionality? What are the biggest risks?

There may be more than one answer to each question, which creates a greater number of assumptions than it might be practical to handle. The team will then prioritize these assumptions by the risks they represent to the organization and its customers.

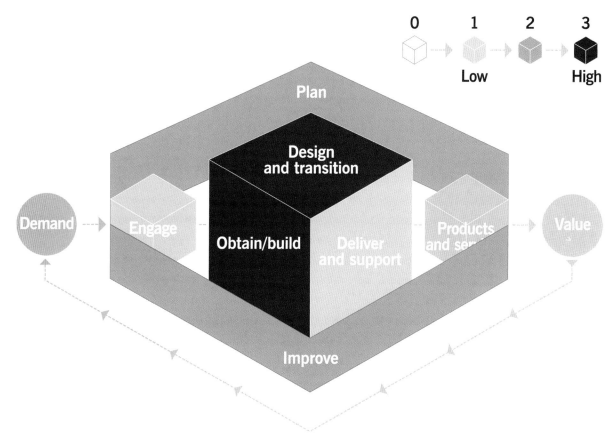

Figure 5.32 Heat map of the contribution of service design to value chain activities

Risk identification, assessment, and treatment are key requirements within all design activities; therefore risk management must be included as an integrated aspect of service design. This will ensure that the risks involved in the provision of products and services and the operation of practices, technology, and measurement methods are aligned with organizational risk and impact, because risk management is embedded within all design processes and activities.

Figure 5.32 shows the contribution of service design to the service value chain, with the practice being involved in all value chain activities:

● **Plan** The service design practice includes planning and organizing the people, partners and suppliers, information, communication, technology, and practices for new or changed products and services, and the interaction between the organization and its customers.

● **Improve** Service design can be used to improve an existing service as well as to create a new service from scratch. Services can be designed as a minimum viable service, deployed, and then iterated and improved to add further value based on feedback.

● **Engage** Service design incorporates CX and UX, which are quintessential examples of engagement.

● **Design and transition** The purpose of service design is to design products and services that are easy to use, desirable, and that can be delivered by the organization.

● **Obtain/build** Service design includes the identification of products, services, and service components that need to be obtained or built for the new or changed service.

● **Deliver and support** Service design manages the user's full journey, through operation, restoration, and maintenance of the service.

5.2.14 Service desk

Key message

The purpose of the **service desk practice** is to capture demand for incident resolution and service requests. It should also be the entry point and single point of contact for the service provider with all of its users.

Service desks provide a clear path for users to report issues, queries, and requests, and have them acknowledged, classified, owned, and actioned. How this practice is managed and delivered may vary from a physical team of people on shift work to a distributed mix of people connected virtually, or automated technology and bots. The function and value remain the same, regardless of the model.

With increased automation and the gradual removal of technical debt, the focus of the service desk is to provide support for 'people and business' rather than simply technical issues. Service desks are increasingly being used to get various matters arranged, explained, and coordinated, rather than just to get broken technology fixed, and the service desk has become a vital part of any service operation.

A key point to be understood is that, no matter how efficient the service desk and its people are, there will always be issues that need escalation and underpinning support from other teams. Support and development teams need to work in close collaboration with the service desk to present and deliver a 'joined up' approach to users and customers.

The service desk may not need to be highly technical, although some are. However, even if the service desk is fairly simple, it still plays a vital role in the delivery of services, and must be actively supported by its peer groups. It is also essential to understand that the service desk has a major influence on user experience and how the service provider is perceived by the users.

Another key aspect of a good service desk is its practical understanding of the wider business context, the business processes, and the users. Service desks add value not simply through the transactional acts of, for example, incident logging, but also by understanding and acting on the business context of this action. The service desk should be the empathetic and informed link between the service provider and its users.

With increased automation, AI, robotic process automation (RPA), and chatbots, service desks are moving to provide more self-service logging and resolution directly via online portals and mobile applications. The impact on service desks is reduced phone contact, less low-level work, and a greater ability to focus on excellent CX when personal contact is needed.

Service desks provide a variety of channels for access. These include:

● phone calls, which can include specialized technology, such as interactive voice response (IVR), conference calls, voice recognition, and others

● service portals and mobile applications, supported by service and request catalogues, and knowledge bases

● chat, through live chat and chatbots

● email for logging and updating, and for follow-up surveys and confirmations. Unstructured emails can be difficult to process, but emerging technologies based on AI and machine learning are starting to address this

● walk-in service desks are becoming more prevalent in some sectors, e.g. higher education, where there are high peaks of activity that demand physical presence

● text and social media messaging, which are useful for notifications in case of major incidents and for contacting specific stakeholder groups, but can also be used to allow users to request support

● public and corporate social media and discussion forums for contacting the service provider and for peer-to-peer support.

Some service desks have a limited support window where service cover is available (for example, 08.00–20.00, Monday–Friday). Staff are therefore expected to work in shift patterns to provide consistent support levels.

In some cases, the service desk is a tangible team, working in a single location. A centralized service desk requires supporting technologies, such as:

● intelligent telephony systems, incorporating computer-telephony integration, IVR, and automatic call distribution

● workflow systems for routing and escalation

● workforce management and resource planning systems

● a knowledge base

● call recording and quality control

● remote access tools

● dashboard and monitoring tools

● configuration management systems.

In other cases, a virtual service desk allows agents to work from multiple locations, geographically dispersed. A virtual service desk requires more sophisticated supporting technology, involving more complex routing and escalation; these solutions are often cloud-based.

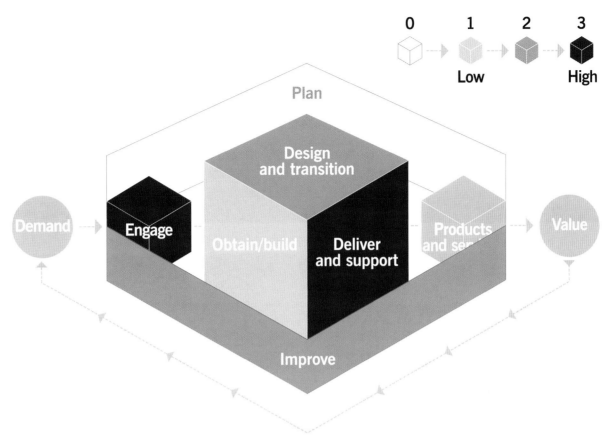

Figure 5.33 Heat map of the contribution of the service desk to value chain activities

Service desk staff require training and competency across a number of broad technical and business areas. In particular, they need to demonstrate excellent customer service skills such as empathy, incident analysis and prioritization, effective communication, and emotional intelligence. The key skill is to be able to fully understand and diagnose a specific incident in terms of business priority, and to take appropriate action to get this resolved, using available skills, knowledge, people, and processes.

Figure 5.33 shows the contribution of the service desk to the service value chain, with the practice being involved in all value chain activities except plan:

● **Improve** Service desk activities are constantly monitored and evaluated to support continual improvement, alignment, and value creation. Feedback from users is collected by the service desk to support continual improvement.

● **Engage** The service desk is the main channel for tactical and operational engagement with users.

● **Design and transition** The service desk provides a channel for communicating with users about new and changed services. Service desk staff participate in release planning, testing, and early life support.

● **Obtain/build** Service desk staff can be involved in acquiring service components used to fulfil service requests and resolve incidents.

● **Deliver and support** The service desk is the coordination point for managing incidents and service requests.

5.2.15 Service level management

Key message

The purpose of the **service level management practice** is to set clear business-based targets for service levels, and to ensure that delivery of services is properly assessed, monitored, and managed against these targets.

Definition: Service level

One or more metrics that define expected or achieved service quality.

Service level management provides the end-to-end visibility of the organization's services. To achieve this, service level management:

- establishes a shared view of the services and target service levels with customers
- ensures the organization meets the defined service levels through the collection, analysis, storage, and reporting of the relevant metrics for the identified services
- performs service reviews to ensure that the current set of services continues to meet the needs of the organization and its customers
- captures and reports on service issues, including performance against defined service levels.

The skills and competencies for service level management include relationship management, business liaison, business analysis, and commercial/supplier management. The practice requires pragmatic focus on the whole service and not simply its constituent parts; for example, simple individual metrics (such as percentage system availability) should not be taken to represent the whole service.

5.2.15.1 Service level agreements

Definition: Service level agreement

A documented agreement between a service provider and a customer that identifies both services required and the expected level of service.

Service level agreements (SLAs) have long been used as a tool to measure the performance of services from the customer's point of view, and it is important that they are agreed in the wider business context. Using SLAs may present many challenges; often they do not fully reflect the wider service performance and the user experience.

Some of the key requirements for successful SLAs include:

● They must be related to a defined 'service' in the service catalogue; otherwise they are simply individual metrics without a purpose, that do not provide adequate visibility or reflect the service perspective.

● They should relate to defined outcomes and not simply operational metrics. This can be achieved with balanced bundles of metrics, such as customer satisfaction and key business outcomes.

● They should reflect an 'agreement', i.e. engagement and discussion between the service provider and the service consumer. It is important to involve all stakeholders, including partners, sponsors, users, and customers.

● They must be simply written and easy to understand and use for all parties.

In many cases, using single-system-based metrics as targets can result in misalignment and a disconnect between service partners regarding the success of the service delivery and the user experience. For example, if an SLA is based only on the percentage of uptime of a service, it can be deemed to be successful by the provider, yet still miss out on significant business functionalities and outcomes which are important to the consumer. This is referred to as the 'watermelon SLA' effect.

The watermelon SLA effect

Traditional SLAs have been based on individual activities such as incident resolution times, system availability ('99.9'), and volume metrics (e.g. number of incidents or requests handled). Without a business context these metrics are often meaningless. For example, although a system availability of 99.6% is impressive, this still needs to align with key business requirements. The system may have an acceptable unavailability of 0.4%, but if that time falls when there is an important process happening (such as a commercial transaction, an operating theatre in use, or point-of-sale tills in use), then customer/user satisfaction will be low, regardless of whether the SLA has been met.

This can be problematic for the service provider if it thinks it is doing a great job (the reports are all green), when in fact its customers are dissatisfied with the service received and also frustrated that the provider doesn't notice this. This is known as the watermelon SLA effect, because like a watermelon, the SLA may appear green on the outside, but is actually red inside.

Service level management identifies metrics and measures that are a truthful reflection of the customer's actual experience and level of satisfaction with the whole service. These will vary across organizations and the only way to learn what these are is to find out directly from customers.

Service level management requires focus and effort to engage and listen to the requirements, issues, concerns, and daily needs of customers:

● Engagement is needed to understand and confirm the actual ongoing needs and requirements of customers, not simply what is interpreted by the service provider or has been agreed several years before.

● Listening is important as a relationship-building and trust-building activity, to show customers that they are valued and understood. This helps to move the provider away from always being in 'solution mode' and to build new, more constructive partnerships.

The activities of engaging and listening provide a great opportunity to build improved relationships and to focus on what really needs to be delivered. It also gives service delivery staff an experience-based understanding of the day-to-day work that is done with their technology, enabling them to deliver a more business-focused service.

Service level management involves collating and analysing information from a number of sources, including:

- **Customer engagement** This involves initial listening, discovery, and information capture on which to base metrics, measurement, and ongoing progress discussions. Consider asking customers some simple open questions such as:
  - What does your work involve?
  - How does technology help you?
  - What are your key business times, areas, people, and activities?
  - What differentiates a good day from a bad day for you?
  - Which of these activities is most important to you?
  - What are your goals, objectives, and measurements for this year?
  - What is the best measure of your success?
  - On what do you base your opinion and evaluation of a service or IT/technology?
  - How can we help you more?
- **Customer feedback** This is ideally gathered from a number of sources, both formal and informal, including:
  - **Surveys** These can be from immediate feedback such as follow-up questions to incidents, or from more reflective periodic surveys that gauge feedback on the overall service experience. Both are event-based.
  - **Key business-related measures** These are measures agreed between the service provider and its customer, based on what the customer values as important. This could be a bundle of SLA metrics or a very specific business activity such as a sales transaction, project completion, or operational function such as getting an ambulance to the site of an accident within x minutes.
- **Operational metrics** These are the low-level indicators of various operational activities and may include system availability, incident response and fix times, change and request processing times, and system response times.
- **Business metrics** These can be any business activity that is deemed useful or valuable by the customer and used as a means of gauging the success of the service. These can vary from some simple transactional binary measures such as ATM or POS terminal availability during business hours (09:00–17:00 daily) or successful completion of business activities such as passenger check-in.

Once this feedback is gathered and collated for ongoing review, it can be used as input to design suitable measurement and reporting models and practices.

Figure 5.34 shows the contribution of service level management to the service value chain, with the practice being applied mainly to the plan and engage activities:

- **Plan** Service level management supports planning of the product and service portfolio and service offerings with information about the actual service performance and trends.
- **Improve** Service feedback from users, as well as requirements from customers, can be a driving force for service improvement.
- **Engage** Service level management ensures ongoing engagement with customers and users through feedback processing and continual service review.
- **Design and transition** The design and development of new and changed services receives input from this practice, both through interaction with customers and as part of the feedback loop in transition.
- **Obtain/build** Service level management provides objectives for components and service performance, as well as for measurement and reporting capabilities of the products and services.
- **Deliver and support** Service level management communicates service performance objectives to the operations and support teams and collects their feedback as an input for service improvement.

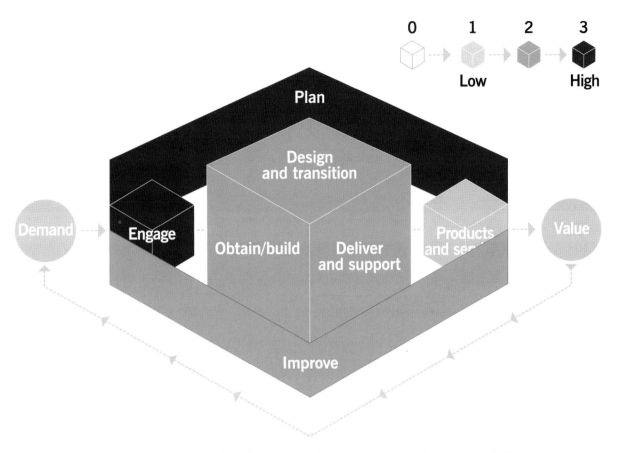

Figure 5.34 Heat map of the contribution of service level management to value chain activities

The ITIL story: Axle's service level management

Su: *We regularly gather feedback from our customers to analyse their requirements and needs, and update our service offerings to match their expectations.*

Radhika: *We can't put every single customer expectation into our rental agreements, but we care about all of them and do our best to meet them.*

Su: *We also monitor the quality of the services provided by our partners and suppliers, such as the work done for us by Craig's Cleaning. When doing this, we need to be sure that the quality of every part of our services meets or exceeds the expectations of our users.*

5.2.16 Service request management

Key message

The purpose of the **service request management practice** is to support the agreed quality of a service by handling all pre-defined, user-initiated service requests in an effective and user-friendly manner.

Definition: Service request

A request from a user or a user's authorized representative that initiates a service action which has been agreed as a normal part of service delivery.

Each service request may include one or more of the following:

- a request for a service delivery action (for example, providing a report or replacing a toner cartridge)
- a request for information (for example, how to create a document or what the hours of the office are)
- a request for provision of a resource or service (for example, providing a phone or laptop to a user, or providing a virtual server for a development team)
- a request for access to a resource or service (for example, providing access to a file or folder)
- feedback, compliments, and complaints (for example, complaints about a new interface or compliments to a support team).

Fulfilment of service requests may include changes to services or their components; usually these are standard changes. Service requests are a normal part of service delivery and are not a failure or degradation of service, which are handled as incidents. Since service requests are pre-defined and pre-agreed as a normal part of service delivery, they can usually be formalized, with a clear, standard procedure for initiation, approval, fulfilment, and management. Some service requests have very simple workflows, such as a request for information. Others, such as the setup of a new employee, may be quite complex and require contributions from many teams and systems for fulfilment. Regardless of the complexity, the steps to fulfil the request should be well-known and proven. This allows the service provider to agree times for fulfilment and to provide clear communication of the status of the request to users.

Some service requests require authorization according to financial, information security, or other policies, while others may not need any. To be handled successfully, service request management should follow these guidelines:

- Service requests and their fulfilment should be standardized and automated to the greatest degree possible.
- Policies should be established regarding what service requests will be fulfilled with limited or even no additional approvals so that fulfilment can be streamlined.
- The expectations of users regarding fulfilment times should be clearly set, based on what the organization can realistically deliver.

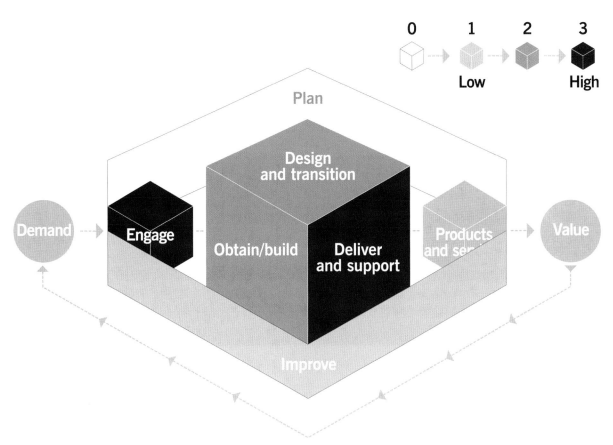

Figure 5.35 Heat map of the contribution of service request management to value chain activities

- Opportunities for improvement should be identified and implemented to produce faster fulfilment times and take advantage of automation.
- Policies and workflows should be included for the documenting and redirecting of any requests that are submitted as service requests, but which should actually be managed as incidents or changes.

Some service requests can be completely fulfilled by automation from submission to closure, allowing for a complete self-service experience. Examples include client software installation or provision of virtual servers.

Service request management is dependent upon well-designed processes and procedures, which are operationalized through tracking and automation tools to maximize the efficiency of the practice. Different types of service request will have different fulfilment workflows, but both efficiency and maintainability will be improved if a limited number of workflow models are identified. When new service requests need to be added to the service catalogue, existing workflow models should be leveraged whenever possible.

Figure 5.35 shows the contribution of service request management to the service value chain, with the practice being involved in all service value chain activities except the plan activity:

- **Improve** Service request management can provide a channel for improvement initiatives, compliments, and complaints from users. It also contributes to improvement by providing trend, quality, and feedback information about fulfilment of requests.
- **Engage** Service request management includes regular communication to collect user-specific requirements, set expectations, and to provide status updates.
- **Design and transition** Standard service components may be transitioned to the live environment through service request fulfilment.
- **Obtain/build** Acquisition of pre-approved service components may be fulfilled through service requests.

● **Deliver and support** Service request management makes a significant contribution to normal service delivery. This activity of the value chain is mostly concerned with ensuring users continue to be productive, and sometimes depends heavily on fulfilment of their requests.

5.2.17 Service validation and testing

 Key message

The purpose of the **service validation and testing practice** is to ensure that new or changed products and services meet defined requirements. The definition of service value is based on input from customers, business objectives, and regulatory requirements, and is documented as part of the value chain activity of design and transition. These inputs are used to establish measurable quality and performance indicators that support the definition of assurance criteria and testing requirements.

5.2.17.1 Service validation

Service **validation** focuses on establishing deployment and release management acceptance criteria (conditions that must be met for production readiness), which are verified through testing. Acceptance criteria can be either utility- or warranty-focused, and are defined through understanding customer, regulatory, business, risk management, and security requirements.

The service validation activities of this practice establish, verify, and document both utility- and warranty-focused service assurance criteria and form the basis for the scope and focus of testing activities.

5.2.17.2 Testing

A test strategy defines an overall approach to testing. It can apply to an environment, a platform, a set of services, or an individual service. Testing should be carried out equally on both in-house developed systems and externally developed solutions. The test strategy is based on the service acceptance criteria, and should align with the requirements of appropriate stakeholders to ensure testing matches the risk appetite and is fit for purpose.

Typical test types include:

● Utility/functional tests:
  ● **Unit test** A test of a single system component
  ● **System test** Overall testing of the system, including software and platforms
  ● **Integration test** Testing a group of dependent software modules together
  ● **Regression test** Testing whether previously working functions were impacted.
● Warranty/non-functional tests:
  ● **Performance and capacity test** Checking speed and capacity under load
  ● **Security test** Testing vulnerability, policy compliance, penetration, and denial of service risk
  ● **Compliance test** Checking that legal and regulatory requirements have been met
  ● **Operational test** Testing for backup, event monitoring, failover, recovery, and reporting

- **Warranty requirements test** Checking for verification of necessary documentation, training, support model definition, and knowledge transfer
- **User acceptance test** The test performed by users of a new or changed system to approve a release.

Figure 5.36 shows the contribution of service validation and testing to the service value chain, with the practice being involved in all value chain activities except the plan activity:

- **Improve** Metrics of service validation and testing, such as escaped defects, test coverage, and service performance against SLAs are critical success measures required to improve CX and lower risk.
- **Engage** Involvement of some stakeholders in service validation and testing activities helps to engage them and improves visibility and adoption of the services.
- **Design and transition** Service design, knowledge management, performance management, deployment management, and release management are all tightly integrated with the service validation and testing practice.
- **Obtain/build** Service validation and testing activities are closely linked to all practices related to obtaining services from external service providers, as well as to project management and software development activities in both waterfall and Agile methods.
- **Deliver and support** Known errors are captured by service validation and testing and shared with the service desk and incident management practices to enable faster service restoration timeframes. Likewise, information regarding service disruption or escaped defects are fed back into service validation and testing to increase the effectiveness and coverage of acceptance criteria and testing activities.

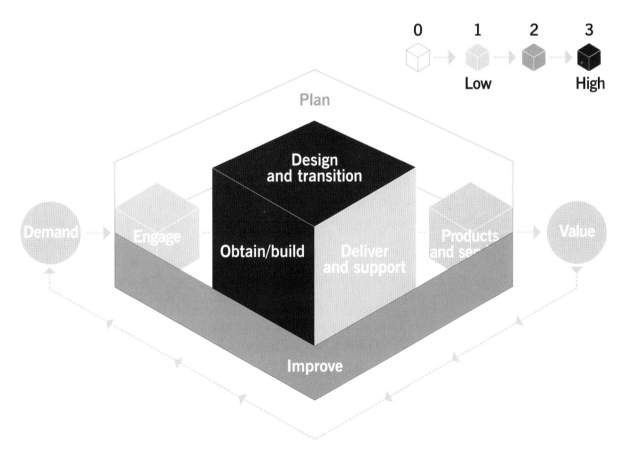

Figure 5.36 Heat map of the contribution of service validation and testing to value chain activities

5.3 Technical management practices

5.3.1 Deployment management

 Key message

The purpose of the **deployment management practice** is to move new or changed hardware, software, documentation, processes, or any other component to live environments. It may also be involved in deploying components to other environments for testing or staging.

Deployment management works closely with release management and change control, but is a separate practice. In some organizations the term 'provisioning' is used to describe the deployment of infrastructure, and deployment is only used to mean software deployment, but in this case the term deployment is used to mean both.

There are a number of distinct approaches that can be used for deployment. Many organizations use a combination of these approaches, depending on their specific services and requirements as well as the release sizes, types, and impact.

- **Phased deployment** The new or changed components are deployed to just part of the production environment at a time, for example to users in one office, or one country. This operation is repeated as many times as needed until the deployment is complete.
- **Continuous delivery** Components are integrated, tested, and deployed when they are needed, providing frequent opportunities for customer feedback loops.
- **Big bang deployment** New or changed components are deployed to all targets at the same time. This approach is sometimes needed when dependencies prevent the simultaneous use of both the old and new components. For example, there could be a database schema change that is not compatible with previous versions of some components.
- **Pull deployment** New or changed software is made available in a controlled repository, and users download the software to client devices when they choose. This allows users to control the timing of updates, and can be integrated with service request management to enable users to request software only when it is needed.

Components that are available for deployment should be maintained in one or more secure locations to ensure that they are not modified before deployment. These locations are collectively referred to as a definitive media library for software and documentation, and a definitive hardware store for hardware components.

Tools that support deployment are many and varied. They are often integrated with configuration management tools, and can provide support for audit and change management. Most organizations have tools for deploying client software, and these may be integrated with a service portal to support a request management practice.

Communication around deployments is part of release management. Individual deployments are not generally of interest to users and customers until they are released.

If infrastructure is provided as a service, then deployment of new or changed servers, storage, or networking is typically managed by the organization, often treating the infrastructure as a code, so that the organization can automate deployment. In these environments it is possible that some deployments may be under the control of

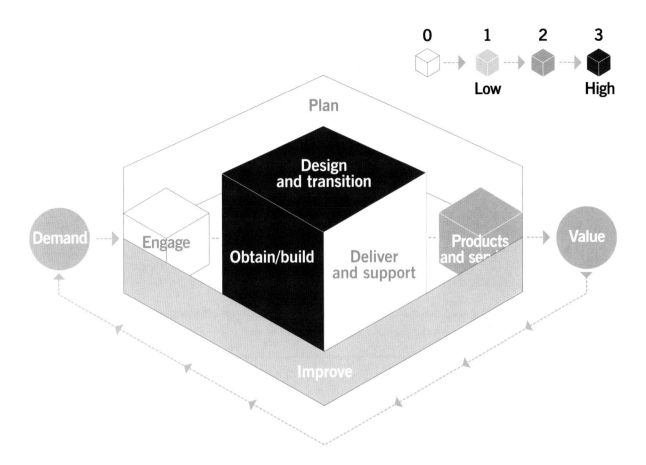

Figure 5.37 Heat map of the contribution of deployment management to value chain activities

the supplier, such as the installation of firmware updates, or if they provide the operating system as well as the infrastructure they may deploy operating system patches. The IT organization must ensure that they know what deployments are planned, and which have happened, to maintain a controlled environment.

If application development is provided as a service, then deployment may be carried out by the external application developer, by the in-house IT department, or by a service integrator. Again, it is essential that the organization is aware of all deployments so that a controlled environment can be maintained.

In an environment with multiple suppliers it is important to understand the scope and boundaries of each organization's deployment activities, and how these will interact. Most organizations have a process for deployment, and this is often supported with standard tools and detailed procedures to ensure that software is deployed in a consistent way. It is common to have different processes for different environments. For example, there may be one process for the deployment of client application software, and a completely different process for the deployment of server operating system patches.

Figure 5.37 shows the contribution of deployment management to the service value chain, with the practice being applied mainly to the design and transition, and obtain/build value chain activities, but also to the improve activity:

● **Improve** Some improvements may require components to be deployed before they can be delivered, and these should be planned and managed in the same way as any other deployment.

● **Design and transition** Deployment management moves new and changed components to live environments, so it is a vital element of this value chain activity.

● **Obtain/build** Changes can be deployed incrementally as part of this value chain activity. This is especially common in DevOps environments using a complete automated toolchain for continuous integration, delivery, and deployment.

The ITIL story: Axle's deployment management

Marco: *Before we deploy changes to our booking app, we release the changes to a test environment. After thorough testing, we make the changes available to our users and customers.*

Radhika: *We recently realized that the same logic can be applied to some of our non-digital services and components. For example, last month we introduced two brand new hybrid models for hire in some bigger cities. We created a promotional service offering for the new cars, updated our marketing materials, trained our technicians to work with the new models, and deployed everything in advance – including the vehicles. This happened before the official launch of the hybrid cars by the manufacturer. And of course, it happened with their permission.*

Su: *By the time the launch date arrived, we were ready to go. We made the cars available to hire that very day.*

Henri: *Partnering with our manufacturer meant we had a successful and well-prepared launch that created a buzz with our customers and with theirs.*

5.3.2 Infrastructure and platform management

Key message

The purpose of the **infrastructure and platform management practice** is to oversee the infrastructure and platforms used by an organization. When carried out properly, this practice enables the monitoring of technology solutions available to the organization, including the technology of external service providers.

IT infrastructure is the physical and/or virtual technology resources, such as servers, storage, networks, client hardware, middleware, and operating systems software, that provide the environments needed to deliver IT services. This includes any CI a customer uses to access the service or consume a product. IT infrastructure may be managed by the service provider or by an external supplier as dedicated, shared, or cloud services. Infrastructure and platform management may also include the buildings and facilities an organization uses to run its IT infrastructure.

The infrastructure and platform management practice includes the provision of technology needed to support activities that create value for the organization and its stakeholders. This can include being ready to adopt new technologies such as machine learning, chatbots, artificial intelligence, mobile device management, and enterprise mobility management.

It is important to consider that every single organization must develop its own strategy to achieve the intended outcome with any type of infrastructure or platform. Each organization should design its own cloud management system to orchestrate all the interrelated components of infrastructure and platform with its business goals and the intended service quality and operational efficiency.

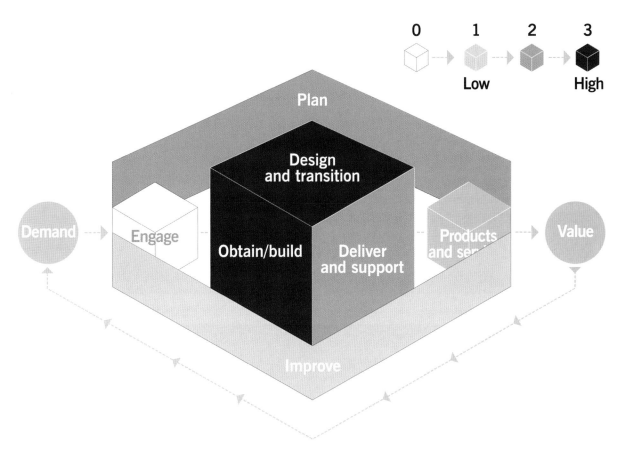

Figure 5.38 Heat map of the contribution of infrastructure and platform management to value chain activities

Figure 5.38 shows the contribution of infrastructure and platform management to the service value chain, with the practice being involved in all value chain activities except the engage activity:

● **Plan** Infrastructure and platform management provides information about technology opportunities and constraints that is used for the organization's strategic and tactical planning.

● **Improve** Information about technology opportunities that can support continual improvement, and any constraints of the technologies in use, is provided by this practice.

● **Design and transition** Product and service design benefits from the information provided about technology opportunities and constraints.

● **Obtain/build** Infrastructure and platform management is a critical contributor to this activity as it provides necessary information about the components to be obtained.

● **Deliver and support** At the operational level, infrastructure and platform management supports ongoing maintenance of the services and the infrastructure, including any executions of patch management, backups, etc.

Cloud service models

Cloud service models include:

- **Software as a service (SaaS)** The consumer can use the applications running in the cloud infrastructure without having to control or even manage the underlying cloud infrastructure.

- **Platform as a service (PaaS)** The consumer can deploy onto the cloud acquired applications created using programming languages, services, libraries, and/or tools supported by the supplier without having to control or even manage the underlying cloud infrastructure. They have control over the deployed applications and sometimes the configuration settings for the application and hosting environment.

- **Infrastructure as a service (IaaS)** The consumer can get processing, storage, and/or any other computing resources without having to control the underlying infrastructure.

Cloud service deployment models

Every service model can be deployed in several ways, either independently or using a mix of the following:

- **Private cloud** This type of cloud may be located within the organization's premises or outside of it. It is a cloud infrastructure or platform to be used exclusively by a specific organization which, at the same time, can have one or several consumers. This cloud is normally managed and owned by an organization, a provider, or a combination of both.

- **Public cloud** This type of cloud is located on the cloud provider premises. It is provisioned for open use and may be owned, managed, and operated by any type of organization interested in using it.

- **Community cloud** A community cloud may be owned, managed, and operated by one or more of the stakeholders in the community, and it may exist on or off the organization's premises. This cloud deployment model consists of several cloud services that are meant to support and share a collection of cloud service customers with the same requirements and who have a relationship with one another.

- **Hybrid cloud** This cloud infrastructure is a composition of two or more distinct cloud infrastructures (private, community, or public) that remain unique entities, but are bound together by standardized or proprietary technology that enables data and application portability.

ITIL practices and cloud computing

The advent of the cloud has been one of the greatest challenges and opportunities within the IT world for decades. The promise of rapid, elastic storage and IT services available at the touch of a button is one that many organizations struggle to deliver internally, not because the benefits are not there to be had, but rather because their own ITSM processes and controls have not been adapted to support a radically different way of working.

The management and control of IT services is a key skill of IT departments no matter where those services are physically located, and the processes and controls offered by ITIL are readily adaptable to support the management of those cloud services.

A coordinated response to the management of cloud services is essential. Organizations that attempt to address only a cloud service provision as an operational issue will suffer on the tactical front, just as an organization that attempts to control cloud services on a tactical front will suffer at the strategic level. A joined-up approach covering all three levels, strategic, tactical, and operational, is required.

Apart from the infrastructure and platform management practice, the operation and management of cloud-based services involves many other practices. It should be noted that this is not a comprehensive list:

- **Service financial management** One of the adjustments that IT departments often have to make for cloud computing is to their fiscal planning, which typically uses both traditional capital expenditure (CAPEX) and operational expenditure (OPEX). With the advent of cloud computing, OPEX is preferred over CAPEX, as cloud services are often consumed as utilities and paid out of the operational budget. If cloud services are quicker and easier to access than in-house services, the costs associated with them will grow as more parts of the business use them. The IT cost model must be adjusted, and the service financial management practice can help to determine the techniques and controls required to ensure that the organization does not run out of OPEX unexpectedly.

- **Supplier management** The focus of this practice will need to change from simply selecting suppliers and onboarding them to acting as the front end for a full-on release management process. This will ensure that areas such as IT security, data protection, and regulatory compliance are routinely assessed prior to the onboarding of a new cloud offering.

- **Capacity and performance management** Coupled with service financial management, this practice should establish and monitor budgets, with thresholds tracked and warnings published if an upswing in demand leads to an increase in the cost of cloud services.

- **Change control** The boundaries of this practice will have to be redefined, as cloud service providers often make changes with minimal customer involvement, and almost no customer approval. Products and services built on top of cloud services will need to make far greater use of standard changes to unlock the benefits that cloud platforms (and associated business models) provide.

- **Incident management** The focus of this practice will change from knowing how to fix in-house issues, to knowing which service is supported by which cloud provider, and what information they will require to resolve an issue. Greater care will be needed to support impacted customers and teams.

- **Deployment management** This practice will continue to be critical to IT departments, but the ability to safely onboard or offboard a cloud provider will become a common requirement for IT departments. Deployment management will be a key capability for successful IT organizations, to ensure new cloud capabilities are rapidly deployed and embedded within the in-house service offerings.

5.3.3 Software development and management

 Key message

The purpose of the **software development and management practice** is to ensure that applications meet internal and external stakeholder needs, in terms of functionality, reliability, maintainability, compliance, and auditability.

The term 'software' can be used to describe anything from a single program (or suite of programs) to larger constructs (such as an operating system, an operating environment, or a database) on which various smaller application programs, processes, or workflows can run. Therefore the term includes, but is not limited to, desktop applications, or mobile apps, embedded software (controlling machines and devices), and websites.

Software applications, whether developed in house or by a partner or vendor, are of critical importance in the delivery of customer value in technology-enabled business services. As a result, software development and management is a key practice in every modern IT organization, ensuring that applications are fit for purpose and use.

The software development and management practice encompasses activities such as:

- solution architecture
- solution design (user interface, CX, service design, etc.)
- software development
- software testing (which can include several components, such as unit testing, integration testing, regression testing, information security testing, and user acceptance testing)
- management of code repositories or libraries to maintain integrity of artefacts
- package creation, for the effective and efficient deployment of the application
- version control, sharing, and ongoing management of smaller blocks of code.

The two generally accepted approaches to software development are referred to as the waterfall and Agile methods (see section 5.1.8 for more information on these methods).

Software management is a wider practice, encompassing the ongoing activities of designing, testing, operating, and improving software applications so they continue to facilitate value creation. Software components can be continually evaluated using a lifecycle that tracks the component from ideation through to ongoing improvement, and eventually retirement. This lifecycle is represented in Figure 5.39.

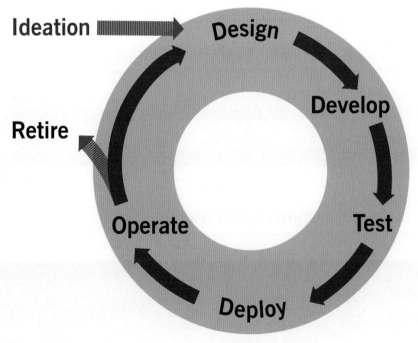

Figure 5.39 The software lifecycle

Figure 5.40 shows the contribution of software development and management to the service value chain, with the practice being involved in all value chain activities except the engage activity:

- **Plan** Software development and management provides information about opportunities and constraints related to the creation and changing of the organization's software.
- **Improve** Service improvements involving software components of the services, especially those developed in house, rely on this practice.
- **Design and transition** Software development and management allows the organization to holistically design and manage changes to products and services.
- **Obtain/build** The creation of in-house products and the configuration of products developed by partners and suppliers depend on this practice.
- **Deliver and support** Software development and management provides delivery and support teams with documentation needed to use products that facilitate the co-creation of value.

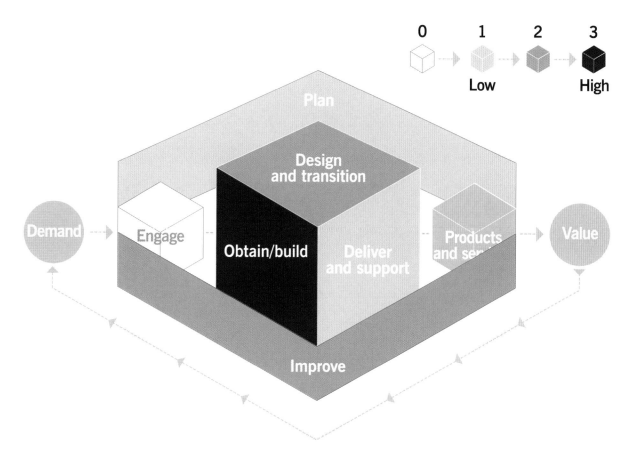

Figure 5.40 Heat map of the contribution of software development and management to value chain activities

END NOTE

THE ITIL STORY, ONE YEAR ON

End note

The ITIL story, one year on

It has been a year since Henri joined Axle Car Hire. There has been significant positive change during this period. New services, such as biometrics and the advanced driver assistance system, are being widely adopted by Axle's consumers, and the company continues to gain a reputation for fast and reliable service.

Customer loyalty has improved, with a large increase in the number of repeat bookings. Axle has also been awarded Partner of the Year by two major clients, including Food for Fuel.

The Axle Green improvement initiative is well underway, with many targets to make the company more environmentally friendly already met. Efforts to make up half of the Axle fleet with electric cars are also going well, and the company has made great progress towards hitting this target. Henri's vision to become the most recognized car-hire brand in the world, offering a full travel experience, is within reach.

Axle sees how the concepts of ITIL are helping it to fulfil its objectives. The adoption and adaptation of ITIL guidance helps Axle to deliver high-quality services and create value for itself and its customers.

APPENDIX A

EXAMPLES OF VALUE STREAMS

 Examples of value streams

This section demonstrates how the service value chain can be applied to practical situations and provides examples of value streams. These value streams show how activity might flow through the value chain. These are not models to be copied, but simply examples to give an understanding of how the value chain should be used.

The examples include some sample job roles. These are just roles that might exist in the fictional organization being described and are not recommended roles for every organization. To aid understanding, the first value stream is described in some detail; in subsequent examples only a table has been provided.

A.1 A user needs an incident to be resolved

In this first example of a value stream, the WiFi in a warehouse is not working properly because a wireless access point has failed. This has a significant impact on the business because the forklift driver cannot receive instructions quickly enough, and as such there is a risk that a business deadline will be missed. This may seem like a relatively straightforward incident; however, it can't be resolved by simply mechanically following the steps of a predetermined incident management procedure.

First, someone must notice that there is an incident and know how to report it, and it must be possible for that person to communicate the urgency of the situation accurately so that it can be prioritized correctly. The person receiving the report must have both the authority to escalate the incident and the procedures for doing so, and for monitoring the progress of the incident. Resources must be in place to allow for a sufficiently rapid escalation; someone must have the skills, knowledge, and tools required to investigate the incident; and there have to be procedures in place that allow standard changes to be implemented without a requirement to obtain additional approval. It must be possible for someone to access accurate configuration information and to log the repair once it has been completed. It must also be possible to log that a spare part has been consumed and to re-order it against future need. If the repair is to be of any value, however, the warehouse needs to be told what has happened, so that normal working can be resumed. It is also important to check how well the incident was resolved, to see if there are any lessons to be learned.

Table A.1 summarizes the different actions and resources required to resolve this apparently simple incident. The table shows how multiple practices support this work, with some practices supporting multiple value chain activities at different times.

Table A.1 Value streams for incident resolution

Value chain activity/ input/outcomes	Practices	Roles	Activities
Demand		Warehouse manager, forklift driver	It is discovered that there is no WiFi coverage in one area of the warehouse. This means that the forklift driver needs to drive across the warehouse to pick up their instructions, causing delays and risking missed business deadlines.
Engage	Service desk, incident management	Warehouse manager, service desk agent	The warehouse manager phones the service desk and describes the issue. It is agreed that this is a Priority 2 incident, and the manager is notified of the expected resolution time.
			Information about this incident is logged by the service desk agent.
Deliver and support	Service desk, incident management	Service desk agent, network support engineer	The incident is rapidly escalated to the network support team.
Deliver and support, improve	Incident management, change control, service configuration management, IT asset management, continual improvement	Network support engineer	The network support engineer identifies that the wireless access point has failed and replaces it with a spare from the store.
			This is a standard change, so the engineer needs no additional approval. Information required to configure the new access point is obtained from the CMS. IT asset information is updated to show that this spare part has been consumed.
			The network engineer updates the incident management system and marks the case as resolved.
			The network engineer thinks about what happened and whether they could have predicted this issue or resolved it more quickly.
Engage	Service desk, incident management	Service desk agent, warehouse manager	The service desk agent contacts the warehouse manager to check that everything is now working properly, then closes the incident.
Value		Warehouse manager, forklift driver	WiFi coverage is restored and the forklift driver can now work efficiently.
Engage, improve	Service desk, incident management, continual improvement	Warehouse manager, service desk manager	A brief satisfaction survey is emailed to the warehouse manager, which they complete and return. The scores are used to identify trends, and the comments are passed to the service desk manager for consideration.

A.2 An error in third-party software creates issues for a user

In this example a user discovers an issue when using an application. The vendor has a patch available and this needs to be installed to rectify the situation. Note that this incident takes a very different path through the service value chain, and is supported by a different balance of practices than the previous incident.

Table A.2 Value streams for software issues

Value chain activity/input/outcomes	Practices	Roles	Activities
Demand		Admin assistant	An admin assistant in an office is unable to enter an appointment in their calendar due to a bug in the software they are using. The software won't allow a non-standard character to be used in a room name.
Engage	Service desk, incident management	Admin assistant, service desk agent	The admin assistant phones the service desk and describes the issue. It is agreed that this is a Priority 3 incident, and the admin assistant is notified of the expected resolution time. Information about this incident is logged by the service desk agent.
Deliver and support	Incident management	Service desk agent	The service desk agent researches the vendor website and discovers that this particular issue is resolved in the latest version of the client software.
Deliver and support	Incident management, supplier management	Service desk agent, second-line support	The incident is escalated to second-line support. Second-line support checks the vendor contract, and the release notes for the client software.
Deliver and support, obtain/build, engage	Incident management, service request management, deployment management, service validation and testing	Second-line support, admin assistant	Second-line support contacts the user and arranges for them to test the new version of the client software to see if this resolves their issue. They then add this version to the service portal so that the user can install it.
Deliver and support	Incident management, service validation and testing, service request management	Admin assistant, service desk	The user installs the new version of the software using the service portal, and tests whether this resolves their issue. The service desk ensures that the user is satisfied with this solution.
Value		Admin assistant	The software now works correctly and the user can add appointments to the calendar using non-standard characters in room names.
Engage, improve	Service desk, incident management, continual improvement	Admin assistant, service desk manager	A brief satisfaction survey is emailed to the admin assistant, which they complete and return. The scores are used to identify trends, and the comments are passed to the service desk manager for consideration.
Improve	Continual improvement, service validation and testing, service request management, release management, deployment management	Second-line support	Second-line support carries out more extensive testing of the new version of the client software before making it available to all users via the service portal. The upgrade to replace the previous version is then deployed in a controlled way.

A.3 Business requirement for a significant new IT service

In this example the internal IT department of a shoe manufacturer identifies a need for a new IT service.

Table A.3 Value streams for creation of an IT service

Value chain activity/ input/outcomes	Practices	Roles	Activities
Demand		Sales director, sales managers	The sales director and managers identify the need for a new website that allows customers to design and order personalized shoes.
Engage	Relationship management	Sales director, business relationship manager (BRM)	The sales director and BRM discuss the new website and agree to investigate the value, outcomes, costs, and risks of putting it in place to see if it is feasible.
Plan	Portfolio management, architecture management	BRM, IT strategy team, enterprise architect, development manager	The creation of the new service is discussed, and the costs and risks of various approaches are identified. This opportunity is prioritized above other work that is being done to decide if the resources are available to carry it out.
Plan	Service financial management, risk management	Financial analyst, IT development manager, project management office	The potential costs and risks of various approaches are discussed and input is provided to portfolio management.
Engage	Relationship management	Sales director, BRM	The sales director and BRM discuss the expected value, outcomes, costs, and risks for the new service and agree that they want to continue.
Plan	Portfolio management	BRM, IT strategy team	The new service is added to the service portfolio and documented.
Plan, design and transition	Portfolio management, project management, service design	Project manager, development manager	The project manager and development manager start to plan the work needed to create the new service. People are assigned to do the necessary work.
Engage	Relationship management, project management, business analysis	Sales director, sales managers, business analysts, software development team	More detailed requirements for the utility and warranty of the first release of the new IT service are established.
Obtain/build	Software development and management, project management, service design	Software development team	The software development team build a backlog, identify the minimum viable product, and develop sufficient functionality that the business can review and comment on it.
Obtain/build, design and transition, improve	Software development and management, project management, service design	Software development team, BRM, sales director, sales managers	The first iteration of the service is reviewed and feedback offered. Based on this, the product backlog is re-prioritized.
Obtain/build, design and transition	Service level management, availability management, capacity and performance management, information security management, service continuity management, measurement and reporting, incident management	Software development team, service level manager, infrastructure manager, BRM, sales director	Detailed warranty requirements for the new service are negotiated and agreed. Requirements are defined for monitoring, measuring and reporting, and supporting the service.
Obtain/build, design and transition	Software development and management, service desk, incident management	Software development team, service desk manager	Training and documentation are provided to enable support of the new service.

Table continues

Table A.3 *continued*

Value chain activity/ input/outcomes	Practices	Roles	Activities
Obtain/build, design and transition, improve	Software development and management, project management, service design, organizational change management, deployment management, release management	Software development team, BRM, sales director, sales managers	Further incremental releases of the new service are created, based on close collaboration between the software development team and the users of the service.
Value	Project management, relationship management, service level management, measurement and reporting	Project manager, BRM, service level manager, sales director, sales managers	The effectiveness of the new service is evaluated to check how well it is working. This is compared with initial predictions. It is agreed how ongoing value will be measured and reported.
Engage, deliver and support, improve	Incident management, problem management, continual improvement	Service desk, software development team, infrastructure support team	Ongoing support is provided for incidents and problems on the new service.
Value, improve	Relationship management, service level management	Service level manager, sales director	Regular monthly meetings are held to discuss service performance and identify improvement opportunities.

A.4 Regulatory change requires new software development

In this example a financial organization must get ready to meet new regulatory requirements.

Table A.4 Value streams for new software development

Value chain activity/ input/outcomes	Practices	Roles	Activities
Demand		Legal director, compliance manager	A number of IT services need to be updated to meet new regulatory requirements.
Engage	Relationship management	Legal director, compliance manager, CIO	The new regulatory requirements are discussed and it is agreed that a project will be created to manage the implementation.
Plan	Portfolio management, service financial management, risk management	CIO, IT strategy team, project manager, IT development manager	The costs and risks of various approaches are identified. Timescales and resources for the work are agreed.
Plan, engage, design and transition	Project management, service design, business analysis	Project manager, IT development manager, business analyst, product manager	Planning of the work begins. People are assigned to do the work. A communication plan is created and all staff who need to be involved are notified.
Obtain/build	Software development and management, service validation and testing, service design	Software development teams	Each software team manages a backlog and develops code for the areas assigned to them. Each team also develops tests for inclusion in the automated pipeline. All code is automatically integrated and tested twice a day, ensuring that code written by different teams works together.
Design and transition, engage	Project management, service design, service validation and testing	Project manager, IT development manager, software development teams, compliance manager	Release and deployment plans are discussed and agreed. The level of testing needed and who will authorize each deployment are agreed before deployment begins.

Value chain activity/ input/outcomes	Practices	Roles	Activities
Obtain/build, design and transition	Service design, organizational change management, deployment management, service configuration management	Software development teams	The deployment of new software is triggered as soon as it is ready. Individual change requests are not required for this, as the risk assessment has been carried out earlier and the automation ensures that the code is deployed exactly as planned. Configuration data is used to drive the deployment, so no separate activity is needed to update this.
Value	Project management, relationship management	Project manager, CIO, legal director, compliance manager	The updated service is evaluated to ensure that all regulatory requirements will be met.
Engage, design and transition	Project management, release management, service desk, service catalogue management	Project manager, software development teams, product manager, service catalogue manager	The new functionality is released by setting a flag that enables new features to be visible to users. The service desk and other staff who need to know that this is now enabled are notified. The service catalogue is updated.
Value, improve	Project management, service design, relationship management, continual improvement	Project manager, IT development manager, CIO, legal director, compliance manager	The project is reviewed and closed. Improvement opportunities are identified and added to a continual improvement register.

177

Appendix A – Examples of value streams

FURTHER
RESEARCH

Further research

AXELOS publications

AXELOS (2018) *A Guide to AgileSHIFT™*. The Stationery Office, London.

AXELOS (2017) *Managing Successful Projects with PRINCE2®*. The Stationery Office, London.

AXELOS (2015) *PRINCE2 Agile®*. The Stationery Office, London.

AXELOS (2015) *RESILIA®: Cyber Resilience Best Practice*. The Stationery Office, London.

Cabinet Office (2011) *Managing Successful Programmes*. The Stationery Office, London.

Office of Government Commerce (2010) *Management of Risk: Guidance for Practitioners*. The Stationery Office, London.

Office of Government Commerce (2010) *Management of Value*. The Stationery Office, London.

Other publications

Goldratt, E. and Cox, J. (1992) *The Goal: A Process of Ongoing Improvement*. North River Press.

Hall, J. (2016). ITSM, DevOps, and why three-tier support should be replaced with Swarming. https://medium.com/@JonHall_/itsm-devops-and-why-the-three-tier-structure-must-be-replaced-with-swarming-91e76ba22304

Humble, J., Molesky, J. and O'Reilly, B. (2015) *Lean Enterprise: How High Performance Organizations Innovate at Scale*. O'Reilly Media.

Kim, G., Behr, K. and Spafford, G. (2013) *The Phoenix Project: A Novel About IT, DevOps and Helping Your Business Win*. IT Revolution Press.

Kim, G., Debois, P. and Willis, J. (2016) *The DevOps Handbook: How to Create World-Class Agility, Reliability, and Security in Technology Organizations*. IT Revolution Press.

Vargo, S. L. and Lusch, R. F. (2016) Institutions and axioms: an extension and update of service-dominant logic. *Journal of the Academy of Marketing Science* 44(4), pp. 5–23.

Vargo, S. L. and Lusch, R. F. (2011) Service-dominant logic: a necessary step. *European Journal of Marketing* 45(7), pp. 1289–1309.

Vargo, S. L. and Lusch, R. F. (2008) Service-dominant logic: continuing the evolution. *Journal of the Academy of Marketing Science* 36, pp. 1–10.

Websites

Agile Manifesto: http://www.agilemanifesto.org

COBIT® 2019: http://www.isaca.org/Cobit/pages/default.aspx

Cynefin Framework for decision making: https://cognitive-edge.com

International Organization for Standardization (ISO) 20000: https://www.iso.org/standard/70636.html

Lean IT: http://leanitassociation.com

The IT4IT™ standards: https://publications.opengroup.org/standards/it4it

The Open Group Architecture Framework (TOGAF®) standards: https://publications.opengroup.org/standards/togaf

The Standard + Case approach: applying Case management to ITSM: http://www.itskeptic.org/standard-case

Three ways of DevOps: https://itrevolution.com/?s=three+ways+of+devops

GLOSSARY

Glossary

acceptance criteria

A list of minimum requirements that a service or service component must meet for it to be acceptable to key stakeholders.

Agile

An umbrella term for a collection of frameworks and techniques that together enable teams and individuals to work in a way that is typified by collaboration, prioritization, iterative and incremental delivery, and timeboxing. There are several specific methods (or frameworks) that are classed as Agile, such as Scrum, Lean, and Kanban.

architecture management practice

The practice of providing an understanding of all the different elements that make up an organization and how those elements relate to one another.

asset register

A database or list of assets, capturing key attributes such as ownership and financial value.

availability

The ability of an IT service or other configuration item to perform its agreed function when required.

availability management practice

The practice of ensuring that services deliver agreed levels of availability to meet the needs of customers and users.

baseline

A report or metric that serves as a starting point against which progress or change can be assessed.

best practice

A way of working that has been proven to be successful by multiple organizations.

big data

The use of very large volumes of structured and unstructured data from a variety of sources to gain new insights.

business analysis practice

The practice of analysing a business or some element of a business, defining its needs and recommending solutions to address these needs and/or solve a business problem, and create value for stakeholders.

business case

A justification for expenditure of organizational resources, providing information about costs, benefits, options, risks, and issues.

business impact analysis (BIA)

A key activity in the practice of service continuity management that identifies vital business functions and their dependencies.

business relationship manager (BRM)

A role responsible for maintaining good relationships with one or more customers.

call

An interaction (e.g. a telephone call) with the service desk. A call could result in an incident or a service request being logged.

call/contact centre

An organization or business unit that handles large numbers of incoming and outgoing calls and other interactions.

capability

The ability of an organization, person, process, application, configuration item, or IT service to carry out an activity.

capacity and performance management practice

The practice of ensuring that services achieve agreed and expected performance levels, satisfying current and future demand in a cost-effective way.

capacity planning

The activity of creating a plan that manages resources to meet demand for services.

change

The addition, modification, or removal of anything that could have a direct or indirect effect on services.

change authority

A person or group responsible for authorizing a change.

change control practice

The practice of ensuring that risks are properly assessed, authorizing changes to proceed and managing a change schedule in order to maximize the number of successful service and product changes.

change model

A repeatable approach to the management of a particular type of change.

change schedule

A calendar that shows planned and historical changes.

charging

The activity that assigns a price for services.

cloud computing

A model for enabling on-demand network access to a shared pool of configurable computing resources that can be rapidly provided with minimal management effort or provider interaction.

compliance

The act of ensuring that a standard or set of guidelines is followed, or that proper, consistent accounting or other practices are being employed.

confidentiality

A security objective that ensures information is not made available or disclosed to unauthorized entities.

configuration

An arrangement of configuration items (CIs) or other resources that work together to deliver a product or service. Can also be used to describe the parameter settings for one or more CIs.

configuration item (CI)

Any component that needs to be managed in order to deliver an IT service.

configuration management database (CMDB)

A database used to store configuration records throughout their lifecycle. The CMDB also maintains the relationships between configuration records.

configuration management system (CMS)

A set of tools, data, and information that is used to support service configuration management.

configuration record

A record containing the details of a configuration item (CI). Each configuration record documents the lifecycle of a single CI. Configuration records are stored in a configuration management database.

continual improvement practice

The practice of aligning an organization's practices and services with changing business needs through the ongoing identification and improvement of all elements involved in the effective management of products and services.

continuous deployment

An integrated set of practices and tools used to deploy software changes into the production environment. These software changes have already passed pre-defined automated tests.

continuous integration/continuous delivery

An integrated set of practices and tools used to merge developers' code, build and test the resulting software, and package it so that it is ready for deployment.

control

The means of managing a risk, ensuring that a business objective is achieved, or that a process is followed.

cost

The amount of money spent on a specific activity or resource.

cost centre

A business unit or project to which costs are assigned.

critical success factor (CSF)

A necessary precondition for the achievement of intended results.

culture

A set of values that is shared by a group of people, including expectations about how people should behave, ideas, beliefs, and practices.

customer

A person who defines the requirements for a service and takes responsibility for the outcomes of service consumption.

customer experience (CX)

The sum of functional and emotional interactions with a service and service provider as perceived by a service consumer.

dashboard

A real-time graphical representation of data.

deliver and support

The value chain activity that ensures services are delivered and supported according to agreed specifications and stakeholders' expectations.

demand

Input to the service value system based on opportunities and needs from internal and external stakeholders.

deployment

The movement of any service component into any environment.

deployment management practice

The practice of moving new or changed hardware, software, documentation, processes, or any other service component to live environments.

design and transition

The value chain activity that ensures products and services continually meet stakeholder expectations for quality, costs, and time to market.

design thinking

A practical and human-centred approach used by product and service designers to solve complex problems and find practical and creative solutions that meet the needs of an organization and its customers.

development environment

An environment used to create or modify IT services or applications.

DevOps

An organizational culture that aims to improve the flow of value to customers. DevOps focuses on culture, automation, Lean, measurement, and sharing (CALMS).

digital transformation

The evolution of traditional business models to meet the needs of highly empowered customers, with technology playing an enabling role.

disaster

A sudden unplanned event that causes great damage or serious loss to an organization. A disaster results in an organization failing to provide critical business functions for some predetermined minimum period of time.

disaster recovery plans

A set of clearly defined plans related to how an organization will recover from a disaster as well as return to a pre-disaster condition, considering the four dimensions of service management.

driver

Something that influences strategy, objectives, or requirements.

effectiveness

A measure of whether the objectives of a practice, service or activity have been achieved.

efficiency

A measure of whether the right amount of resources have been used by a practice, service, or activity.

emergency change

A change that must be introduced as soon as possible.

engage

The value chain activity that provides a good understanding of stakeholder needs, transparency, continual engagement, and good relationships with all stakeholders.

environment

A subset of the IT infrastructure that is used for a particular purpose, for example a live environment or test environment. Can also mean the external conditions that influence or affect something.

error

A flaw or vulnerability that may cause incidents.

error control

Problem management activities used to manage known errors.

escalation

The act of sharing awareness or transferring ownership of an issue or work item.

event

Any change of state that has significance for the management of a service or other configuration item.

external customer

A customer who works for an organization other than the service provider.

failure

A loss of ability to operate to specification, or to deliver the required output or outcome.

feedback loop

A technique whereby the outputs of one part of a system are used as inputs to the same part of the system.

four dimensions of service management

The four perspectives that are critical to the effective and efficient facilitation of value for customers and other stakeholders in the form of products and services.

goods

Tangible resources that are transferred or available for transfer from a service provider to a service consumer, together with ownership and associated rights and responsibilities.

governance

The means by which an organization is directed and controlled.

identity

A unique name that is used to identify and grant system access rights to a user, person, or role.

improve

The value chain activity that ensures continual improvement of products, services, and practices across all value chain activities and the four dimensions of service management.

incident

An unplanned interruption to a service or reduction in the quality of a service.

incident management

The practice of minimizing the negative impact of incidents by restoring normal service operation as quickly as possible.

information and technology

One of the four dimensions of service management. It includes the information and knowledge used to deliver services, and the information and technologies used to manage all aspects of the service value system.

information security management practice

The practice of protecting an organization by understanding and managing risks to the confidentiality, integrity, and availability of information.

information security policy

The policy that governs an organization's approach to information security management.

infrastructure and platform management practice

The practice of overseeing the infrastructure and platforms used by an organization. This enables the monitoring of technology solutions available, including solutions from third parties.

integrity

A security objective that ensures information is only modified by authorized personnel and activities.

internal customer

A customer who works for the same organization as the service provider.

Internet of Things

The interconnection of devices via the internet that were not traditionally thought of as IT assets, but now include embedded computing capability and network connectivity.

IT asset

Any financially valuable component that can contribute to the delivery of an IT product or service.

IT asset management practice

The practice of planning and managing the full lifecycle of all IT assets.

IT infrastructure

All of the hardware, software, networks, and facilities that are required to develop, test, deliver, monitor, manage, and support IT services.

IT service

A service based on the use of information technology.

ITIL

Best-practice guidance for IT service management.

ITIL guiding principles

Recommendations that can guide an organization in all circumstances, regardless of changes in its goals, strategies, type of work, or management structure.

ITIL service value chain

An operating model for service providers that covers all the key activities required to effectively manage products and services.

Kanban

A method for visualizing work, identifying potential blockages and resource conflicts, and managing work in progress.

key performance indicator (KPI)

An important metric used to evaluate the success in meeting an objective.

knowledge management practice

The practice of maintaining and improving the effective, efficient, and convenient use of information and knowledge across an organization.

known error

A problem that has been analysed but has not been resolved.

Lean

An approach that focuses on improving workflows by maximizing value through the elimination of waste.

lifecycle

The full set of stages, transitions, and associated statuses in the life of a service, product, practice, or other entity.

live

Refers to a service or other configuration item operating in the live environment.

live environment

A controlled environment used in the delivery of IT services to service consumers.

maintainability

The ease with which a service or other entity can be repaired or modified.

major incident

An incident with significant business impact, requiring an immediate coordinated resolution.

management system

Interrelated or interacting elements that establish policy and objectives and enable the achievement of those objectives.

maturity

A measure of the reliability, efficiency and effectiveness of an organization, practice, or process.

mean time between failures (MTBF)

A metric of how frequently a service or other configuration item fails.

mean time to restore service (MTRS)

A metric of how quickly a service is restored after a failure.

measurement and reporting

The practice of supporting good decision-making and continual improvement by decreasing levels of uncertainty.

metric

A measurement or calculation that is monitored or reported for management and improvement.

minimum viable product (MVP)

A product with just enough features to satisfy early customers, and to provide feedback for future product development.

mission statement

A short but complete description of the overall purpose and intentions of an organization. It states what is to be achieved, but not how this should be done.

model

A representation of a system, practice, process, service, or other entity that is used to understand and predict its behaviour and relationships.

modelling

The activity of creating, maintaining, and utilizing models.

monitoring

Repeated observation of a system, practice, process, service, or other entity to detect events and to ensure that the current status is known.

monitoring and event management practice

The practice of systematically observing services and service components, and recording and reporting selected changes of state identified as events.

obtain/build

The value chain activity that ensures service components are available when and where they are needed, and that they meet agreed specifications.

operation

The routine running and management of an activity, product, service, or other configuration item.

operational technology

The hardware and software solutions that detect or cause changes in physical processes through direct monitoring and/or control of physical devices such as valves, pumps, etc.

organization

A person or a group of people that has its own functions with responsibilities, authorities, and relationships to achieve its objectives.

organizational change management practice

The practice of ensuring that changes in an organization are smoothly and successfully implemented and that lasting benefits are achieved by managing the human aspects of the changes.

organizational resilience

The ability of an organization to anticipate, prepare for, respond to, and adapt to unplanned external influences.

organizational velocity

The speed, effectiveness, and efficiency with which an organization operates. Organizational velocity influences time to market, quality, safety, costs, and risks.

organizations and people

One of the four dimensions of service management. It ensures that the way an organization is structured and managed, as well as its roles, responsibilities, and systems of authority and communication, is well defined and supports its overall strategy and operating model.

outcome

A result for a stakeholder enabled by one or more outputs.

output

A tangible or intangible deliverable of an activity.

outsourcing

The process of having external suppliers provide products and services that were previously provided internally.

partners and suppliers

One of the four dimensions of service management. It encompasses the relationships an organization has with other organizations that are involved in the design, development, deployment, delivery, support, and/or continual improvement of services.

partnership

A relationship between two organizations that involves working closely together to achieve common goals and objectives.

performance

A measure of what is achieved or delivered by a system, person, team, practice, or service.

pilot

A test implementation of a service with a limited scope in a live environment.

plan

The value chain activity that ensures a shared understanding of the vision, current status, and improvement direction for all four dimensions and all products and services across an organization.

policy

Formally documented management expectations and intentions, used to direct decisions and activities.

portfolio management practice

The practice of ensuring that an organization has the right mix of programmes, projects, products, and services to execute its strategy within its funding and resource constraints.

post-implementation review (PIR)

A review after the implementation of a change, to evaluate success and identify opportunities for improvement.

practice

A set of organizational resources designed for performing work or accomplishing an objective.

problem

A cause, or potential cause, of one or more incidents.

problem management practice

The practice of reducing the likelihood and impact of incidents by identifying actual and potential causes of incidents, and managing workarounds and known errors.

procedure

A documented way to carry out an activity or a process.

process

A set of interrelated or interacting activities that transform inputs into outputs. A process takes one or more defined inputs and turns them into defined outputs. Processes define the sequence of actions and their dependencies.

product

A configuration of an organization's resources designed to offer value for a consumer.

production environment

See live environment.

programme

A set of related projects and activities, and an organization structure created to direct and oversee them.

project

A temporary structure that is created for the purpose of delivering one or more outputs (or products) according to an agreed business case.

project management practice

The practice of ensuring that all an organization's projects are successfully delivered.

quick win

An improvement that is expected to provide a return on investment in a short period of time with relatively small cost and effort.

record

A document stating results achieved and providing evidence of activities performed.

recovery

The activity of returning a configuration item to normal operation after a failure.

recovery point objective (RPO)

The point to which information used by an activity must be restored to enable the activity to operate on resumption.

recovery time objective (RTO)

The maximum acceptable period of time following a service disruption that can elapse before the lack of business functionality severely impacts the organization.

relationship management practice

The practice of establishing and nurturing links between an organization and its stakeholders at strategic and tactical levels.

release

A version of a service or other configuration item, or a collection of configuration items, that is made available for use.

release management practice

The practice of making new and changed services and features available for use.

reliability

The ability of a product, service, or other configuration item to perform its intended function for a specified period of time or number of cycles.

request catalogue

A view of the service catalogue, providing details on service requests for existing and new services, which is made available for the user.

request for change (RFC)

A description of a proposed change used to initiate change control.

resolution

The action of solving an incident or problem.

resource

A person, or other entity, that is required for the execution of an activity or the achievement of an objective. Resources used by an organization may be owned by the organization or used according to an agreement with the resource owner.

retire

The act of permanently withdrawing a product, service, or other configuration item from use.

risk

A possible event that could cause harm or loss, or make it more difficult to achieve objectives. Can also be defined as uncertainty of outcome, and can be used in the context of measuring the probability of positive outcomes as well as negative outcomes.

risk assessment

An activity to identify, analyse, and evaluate risks.

risk management practice

The practice of ensuring that an organization understands and effectively handles risks.

service

A means of enabling value co-creation by facilitating outcomes that customers want to achieve, without the customer having to manage specific costs and risks.

service action

Any action required to deliver a service output to a user. Service actions may be performed by a service provider resource, by service users, or jointly.

service architecture

A view of all the services provided by an organization. It includes interactions between the services, and service models that describe the structure and dynamics of each service.

service catalogue

Structured information about all the services and service offerings of a service provider, relevant for a specific target audience.

service catalogue management practice

The practice of providing a single source of consistent information on all services and service offerings, and ensuring that it is available to the relevant audience.

service configuration management practice

The practice of ensuring that accurate and reliable information about the configuration of services, and the configuration items that support them, is available when and where needed.

service consumption

Activities performed by an organization to consume services. It includes the management of the consumer's resources needed to use the service, service actions performed by users, and the receiving (acquiring) of goods (if required).

service continuity management practice

The practice of ensuring that service availability and performance are maintained at a sufficient level in case of a disaster.

service design practice

The practice of designing products and services that are fit for purpose, fit for use, and that can be delivered by the organization and its ecosystem.

service desk

The point of communication between the service provider and all its users.

service desk practice

The practice of capturing demand for incident resolution and service requests.

service financial management practice

The practice of supporting an organization's strategies and plans for service management by ensuring that the organization's financial resources and investments are being used effectively.

service level

One or more metrics that define expected or achieved service quality.

service level agreement (SLA)

A documented agreement between a service provider and a customer that identifies both services required and the expected level of service.

service level management practice

The practice of setting clear business-based targets for service performance so that the delivery of a service can be properly assessed, monitored, and managed against these targets.

service management

A set of specialized organizational capabilities for enabling value for customers in the form of services.

service offering

A formal description of one or more services, designed to address the needs of a target consumer group. A service offering may include goods, access to resources, and service actions.

service owner

A role that is accountable for the delivery of a specific service.

service portfolio

A complete set of products and services that are managed throughout their lifecycles by an organization.

service provider

A role performed by an organization in a service relationship to provide services to consumers.

service provision

Activities performed by an organization to provide services. It includes management of the provider's resources, configured to deliver the service; ensuring access to these resources for users; fulfilment of the agreed service actions; service level management; and continual improvement. It may also include the supply of goods.

service relationship

A cooperation between a service provider and service consumer. Service relationships include service provision, service consumption, and service relationship management.

service relationship management

Joint activities performed by a service provider and a service consumer to ensure continual value co-creation based on agreed and available service offerings.

service request

A request from a user or a user's authorized representative that initiates a service action which has been agreed as a normal part of service delivery.

service request management practice

The practice of supporting the agreed quality of a service by handling all pre-defined, user-initiated service requests in an effective and user-friendly manner.

service validation and testing practice

The practice of ensuring that new or changed products and services meet defined requirements.

service value system (SVS)

A model representing how all the components and activities of an organization work together to facilitate value creation.

software development and management practice

The practice of ensuring that applications meet stakeholder needs in terms of functionality, reliability, maintainability, compliance, and auditability.

sourcing

The activity of planning and obtaining resources from a particular source type, which could be internal or external, centralized or distributed, and open or proprietary.

specification

A documented description of the properties of a product, service, or other configuration item.

sponsor

A person who authorizes budget for service consumption. Can also be used to describe an organization or individual that provides financial or other support for an initiative.

stakeholder

A person or organization that has an interest or involvement in an organization, product, service, practice, or other entity.

standard

A document, established by consensus and approved by a recognized body, that provides for common and repeated use, mandatory requirements, guidelines, or characteristics for its subject.

standard change

A low-risk, pre-authorized change that is well understood and fully documented, and which can be implemented without needing additional authorization.

status

A description of the specific states an entity can have at a given time.

strategy management practice

The practice of formulating the goals of an organization and adopting the courses of action and allocation of resources necessary for achieving those goals.

supplier

A stakeholder responsible for providing services that are used by an organization.

supplier management practice

The practice of ensuring that an organization's suppliers and their performance levels are managed appropriately to support the provision of seamless quality products and services.

support team

A team with the responsibility to maintain normal operations, address users' requests, and resolve incidents and problems related to specified products, services, or other configuration items.

system

A combination of interacting elements organized and maintained to achieve one or more stated purposes.

systems thinking

A holistic approach to analysis that focuses on the way that a system's constituent parts work, interrelate, and interact over time, and within the context of other systems.

technical debt

The total rework backlog accumulated by choosing workarounds instead of system solutions that would take longer.

test environment

A controlled environment established to test products, services, and other configuration items.

third party

A stakeholder external to an organization.

throughput

A measure of the amount of work performed by a product, service, or other system over a given period of time.

transaction

A unit of work consisting of an exchange between two or more participants or systems.

use case

A technique using realistic practical scenarios to define functional requirements and to design tests.

user

A person who uses services.

utility

The functionality offered by a product or service to meet a particular need. Utility can be summarized as 'what the service does' and can be used to determine whether a service is 'fit for purpose'. To have utility, a service must either support the performance of the consumer or remove constraints from the consumer. Many services do both.

utility requirements

Functional requirements which have been defined by the customer and are unique to a specific product.

validation

Confirmation that the system, product, service, or other entity meets the agreed specification.

value

The perceived benefits, usefulness, and importance of something.

value stream

A series of steps an organization undertakes to create and deliver products and services to consumers.

value streams and processes

One of the four dimensions of service management. It defines the activities, workflows, controls, and procedures needed to achieve the agreed objectives.

vision

A defined aspiration of what an organization would like to become in the future.

warranty

Assurance that a product or service will meet agreed requirements. Warranty can be summarized as 'how the service performs' and can be used to determine whether a service is 'fit for use'. Warranty often relates to service levels aligned with the needs of service consumers. This may be based on a formal agreement, or it may be a marketing message or brand image. Warranty typically addresses such areas as the availability of the service, its capacity, levels of security, and continuity. A service may be said to provide acceptable assurance, or 'warranty', if all defined and agreed conditions are met.

warranty requirements

Typically non-functional requirements captured as inputs from key stakeholders and other practices.

waterfall method

A development approach that is linear and sequential with distinct objectives for each phase of development.

work instruction

A detailed description to be followed in order to perform an activity.

workaround

A solution that reduces or eliminates the impact of an incident or problem for which a full resolution is not yet available. Some workarounds reduce the likelihood of incidents.

workforce and talent management practice

The practice of ensuring that an organization has the right people with the appropriate skills and knowledge and in the correct roles to support its business objectives.

ACKNOWLEDGEMENTS

Acknowledgements

AXELOS Ltd is grateful to everyone who has contributed to the development of this guidance and in particular would like to thank the following people.

Authoring team

Roman Jouravlev

Roman works at AXELOS as a portfolio development manager, responsible for the continual development of ITIL. He joined AXELOS in 2016 after working for more than 15 years in ITSM, mostly in Russia, as a trainer, consultant, quality manager, and (many years ago) service desk manager. Roman has authored and translated several books and many articles on IT service management.

Akshay Anand

Akshay is a product ambassador at AXELOS, working on the development of new guidance and research within the ITSM portfolio. With experience from the US, UK, and India, he previously advised Fortune 100 clients on their ITSM capabilities, implemented toolsets such as Remedy and ServiceNow, and headed up global ITSM activities at Macmillan Publishing. More recently, Akshay has focused on bringing together Agile development teams and ITSM professionals to address the challenges posed by emerging technologies. He tweets as @bloreboy.

José Carmona Orbezo

José works at AXELOS as head of product management, responsible for shaping the strategy and vision of the AXELOS product portfolio. He joined AXELOS in 2016, after completing his MBA at Manchester Business School. His background as a commercial strategist entails product management, product launch, licensing, marketing, branding, and consumer engagement.

Erin Casteel

Erin is a specialist in service management and integration, organizational governance, and cybersecurity. She is passionate about helping organizations to build, run, and improve integrated, organizational ecosystems that enable increased agility, resilience, and velocity. Erin is particularly focused on systems thinking, enterprise architecture, and organizational culture to support digital transformation. Since 2006, Erin has contributed to the development of ISO/IEC 20000, has chaired the ISO/IEC working group, and has edited and contributed to the ISO/IEC 27000 series of standards for information security management.

Mauricio Corona

Dr Corona is an experienced IT and ITSM professional, considered as one of the top 25 thought leaders in technical support and service management, and as one of the top 100 influencers in IT service management. He holds 19 ITIL certifications as well as certifications in COBIT, ISO 20000 and 27000, PRINCE2, and MCP. In addition to teaching graduate-level courses in Mexico and conducting scientific research related to digital transformation, Dr Corona is also a well-known international speaker. In 2018 he was appointed as a member of the SDI board as the global chief of transformation.

Troy DuMoulin

Troy is a leading IT governance and service management authority with more than 20 years' experience in executive IT service management training and consulting. Troy is a frequent public speaker, and is a published author and contributor to multiple ITSM and Lean IT books, such as *Defining IT Success through the Service Catalog* (2007), *ITIL V3 Planning to Implement IT Service Management* (2010) and *ITIL Continual Service Improvement* (2011). Troy was recently named as one of the top 25 industry influencers in tech support.

Philip Hearsum

Philip joined the Office of Government Commerce (later to become the Cabinet Office) in 2010. In 2013, AXELOS was born as a partnership between the Cabinet Office and Capita, and Philip moved into the role he holds today as ITSM portfolio manager. Philip is a member of the UK working group for ISO 20000. He holds the ITIL V2 Manager, V3 Expert, PRINCE2 Practitioner, RESILIA, M_O_R, ITIL Practitioner and ISO 20000 consultant certifications. He was also involved in the ITIL 2011 update, in the role of project quality assurance.

Lou Hunnebeck

An ITIL expert with more than 30 years' experience in the service industries, Lou is a principal adviser at DXC Fruition. Her passion for improving how we do what we do has led her to IT service management from a background of process consulting, training, and service management systems consulting. Devoted to advancing the art and practice of service management, Lou served as the author of *ITIL Service Design* (2011), was on the ITIL senior examination panel, served on the architect team, and was co-author for *ITIL Practitioner Guidance* (2016). Lou speaks regularly at industry meetings to spread the message of ITSM.

Margo Leach

Margo joined AXELOS in 2016, bringing diverse experience in new product delivery, product management, and digital and business transformation. Previously responsible for market-leading product portfolios and business-wide transformations, Margo has since been instrumental in the development and management of the PPM and ITSM portfolios at AXELOS. Leading the entire product function, recent successes include the release of *Managing Successful Projects with PRINCE2* (2017), the ongoing evolution of the ITIL 4 programme, and the further development with key partners of global markets for AXELOS.

Barclay Rae

Barclay is an experienced ITSM consultant, analyst, and writer. He has worked on approximately 700 ITSM projects over the last 25 years, and writes blogs and research and white papers on ITSM topics for a variety of industry organizations and vendors. Barclay is a director of EssentialSM and was CEO of *it*SMF UK from 2015 to 2018. He is also a co-author of the SDI SDC certification standards, a participant in the current ISO/IEC 20000 revision, and a co-architect of the ITIL Practitioner scheme. Barclay is an associate of SDI (as a consultant and auditor) and is a member of the SDI strategic advisory board.

Stuart Rance

Stuart is a consultant, author, and expert in ITSM and information security management. He was an author for *ITIL Practitioner* (2016), *RESILIA™: Cyber Resilience Best Practice* (2015), and *ITIL Service Transition* (2011). Stuart is an examiner for RESILIA and ITIL, and teaches these as well as CISSP and others. Stuart also provides consulting to organizations of all sizes, helping them use ideas from IT service management and information security management to increase the value they create for themselves and their customers.

Takashi Yagi

Takashi is a service management professional based in Japan, and was one of the core members of *it*SMF Japan that was established in 2003. He has been proactive in the promotion of IT service management best practice through the translation of ITIL books, including ITIL V2, ITIL V3, and the ITIL 2011 editions. Takashi is also active in the ISO world, working as the convener for the Special Committee 40 Working Group 2 in Japan, which focuses on the maintenance and development of ISO/IEC 20000. He served as the co-editor for the recently published ISO/IEC 20000-1.

The ITIL storyline

Katrina Macdermid

Katrina is an ITIL4 global ambassador, author, and creator of an innovative integrated framework, human-centred ITIL service design. She is an ITIL Master, with a solid background in designing and implementing innovative IT operating models which put the customer experience at the heart of all ITIL processes. Katrina has been responsible for the successful implementation of key strategic programmes and integrated service management in Australia's largest and iconic global organizations. She is a well-known conference speaker on human-centred ITIL service design.

Project team

David Atkins	Production manager
Rachida Chekaf	Head of translations
Clémence Court	Product and community coordinator
Adrian Crago-Graham	Head of PMO
Ricky Elizabeth	Brand and design manager
James Lord	Examinations officer
Michael Macgregor	Project manager
James Robertson	Examinations officer
Heigor Simões de Freitas	Product manager ITSM
Tom Young	Project editor

Contributors

Lief Andersson, Virginia Araújo, Craig Bennion, Joseph Caudle, Stefan Cronholm, Pavel Demin, Domitien Dijon, Marie DiRuzza, Phyllis Drucker, John Edmonds, Douglas Fidler, Alfonso Figueroa, James Gander, Ann Gerwitz, Hannes Göbel, Bob Gribben, Damian Harris, Simon Harris, Denise Heinle, Matthew Helm, Peter Hero, Jessica Hinkal, Frantz Honegger, Peter Hubbard, Dmitriy Isaychenko, Marcus Jackson, Stéphane Joret, Michael Keeling, Claudine Koers, Shirley Lacy, Anton Lykov, Celisa Manly, Caspar Miller, James Monek, David Moskowitz, Christian Nissen, Mark O'Loughlin, Tatiana Orlova, Ben Page, Mitch Pautz, Tatiana Peftieva, Donka Raytcheva, Nicola Reeves, Frances Scarff, Nikolai Schmidt-Ott, Mark Smalley, Chris Whitehead, Paul Wilkinson, Martin Wolf, Sarah Woodrow, Ulla Zeeberg

INDEX

Index

Page numbers refer to the printed book pages. In the ebook version, clicking on the link will take you to the section or paragraph where the topic starts, irrespective of the ebook page.

Index